A WALK TO THE END OF THE EARTH

A WALK TO THE END *of* THE EARTH

JEFFREY KENDALL

UNMUZZLED OX
PUBLISHING, LLC

Salem, SD
www.UnmuzzledOxPublishing.com

A Walk to the End of the Earth
Copyright © 2023 by Jeffrey Kendall

"Melissa's Prayer" used by permission.
The songs "Oh Suzanna" and "Down to the River to Pray" are in the public domain.
New American Bible: Genesis 32:29, Deuteronomy 25:4, 32:39, Psalm 41:8, 110:4, Jeremiah 1:4-5, 7a-10, 20:7, 14.
Five thousand words may be used without permission.
New International Version: Proverbs 25:2.
Five hundred verses may be used without permission.
New Jerusalem Bible: Ecclesiastes 12:5.
Five hundred words may be used without permission.
Vulgate: Deuteronomy 25:4, Psalm 109:4. The Vulgate is in the public domain.
When Mass parts are quoted in a memoir, permission from the International Committee on English in the Liturgy is not required

First Edition
Library of Congress Control Number: 2022921574

Paperback ISBN: 979-8-9873252-0-9
Hardback ISBN: 979-8-9873252-2-3
eBook ISBN: 979-8-9873252-1-6

Table of Contents

Acknowledgements

The first draft of this book had about 250,000 words. For perspective, the published version has around 87,000 words, about a third of the length of the first draft. The poor souls who read the epic version deserve special mention: Elizabeth Loeffler, Suzanne Minarcine and Margaret South.

Margaret is a professional developmental editor and made the critical suggestions that helped me limit the scope of the book. She suggested I start the book at the fountain in Le Puy-en-Velay. I took one step back and started the book at the Cathedral. I then knew the book should end at the Faro, the lighthouse at the end of the earth. She also had me cut stories that did not served the primary story, which is the God story. Some stories were minor, some not so minor, but many subplots were cut. Many people were cut, including wonderful people like Jillian and Arunya from Australia. That was not easy. Margaret also made suggestions that I transformed. She said that the book needed flashbacks, but I am responsible for the decision to place the flashbacks in (mostly) reverse chronological order. She said the flashbacks needed to be written in present tense, but after rewriting them in the present tense, I started to read the whole book in present tense in my mind and so rewrote the whole book in present tense. The book would not have gotten into a publishable form without Margaret's assistance, and her labors have been Herculean.

I then shared a 92,000-word version with several readers: Julie Davis, William R. Anderson, Fr. Paul Stenson, and Mike Weaver. Each reader brought their own perspective to the book, which illuminated different aspects of the book, but Mike, a retired Methodist minister, gave, perhaps, the most profound interpretation of the events of my walk, both the minutia and the whole. An adherent to Jungian theory, he read the book through the prism of Jungian archetypes. We spent several hours talking about my book.

I then engaged a second developmental editor: Jen Braaksma. At that point, the book was close to 85,000 words. She took a different approach than Margaret as different developmental editors might be expected to do. Jen asked a multitude of questions about various aspects of the book, and often my answers ended up being incorporated into the text of the book. Her Socratic approach was invaluable. In dialogue with her, the God story became more enfleshed, and again less important parts were minimized or cut.

Steph Spector did the copy editing on my book, and her attention to detail boggled my mind and makes my alleged attention to detail seem spurious by comparison. More than a few times I was surprised by what she found. The book became polished because of her work. Also, because of her labors, the book more closely conforms to contemporary grammatic norms. Sometimes, however, I deviate from contemporary norms, and I hope my deviations are justified by contexts.

Steph said that more issues will become apparent when the book is formatted, and she was correct. I went through the book twice more eliminating typos and rewriting sentences. I also engaged Emily Jones, who proofread my book. And again, I was surprised by what I learned and shocked by the typos. I cannot promise that all typos have been eliminated, but my cohorts and I have labored to do so.

Finally, a manuscript must become a book. Savannah Daw at Palmetto Publishing coordinated the cover and interior design, which brought the book to life. To make this happen, we conversed many times in emails and on the phone in a complex labor wherein distribution, price, aesthetics and business models were harmonized with the greater goals and purposes of this book. Danna Mathias Steele, who did the cover design and formatted the interior, made the book look wonderful. This labor is as critical as the writing, and its importance cannot be underestimated.

Melissa, my counselor for many years, deserves special mention for a multitude of reasons, but from a spiritual and literary perspective, her prayer for my Camino is one of the most beautiful prayers I have ever read and deserves to be a prayer card carried by everyone who walks the Camino. Melissa asked that her last name not be used. Please respect her privacy.

Retro-Punctuation

I have stopped pleasure reading because of the one-space-after-a-period fad. Other people I have spoken with, who used to love to read, now do not enjoy reading for the same reason. The arguments for why I think one-space is wrong and the proffering of possible compromise solutions are beyond the scope of this book. However, until a compromise is agreed upon or authors are granted a free choice in this matter, I advocate two-spaces-after-a-period as Retro-Punctuation, which makes it super cool.

To everyone searching for peace and healing.

MELISSA'S PRAYER

As you walk the Camino,
I hope the metaphor becomes real—
That you walk,
Step by step,
Both towards and into a new chapter of life,
One in which you only bring with you
That which you choose of your past.
A new creation.
A resurrection.
A return to life and living.
Fully.
Abundantly.
Joy-fully.

Melissa, Counselor

Preludes

THE DAY I LEAVE

I leave the States for my Camino on September 15, the Feast of Our Lady of Sorrows. I consider the date a bad sign.

THE NIGHT BEFORE I WALK

I open the French doors of my second-floor hotel room. In the East, lightning illuminates dark, tumultuous clouds that envelope mountain heights.

Hell of a Start

DAYS 1 – 3

I stand in shadow under the towering edifice built onto the front of La Cathédrale Notre Dame du Puy, looking West, across town and valley to mountains illuminated by the sun.

Three Roman arches in the edifice welcome the faithful to the cathedral. The central arch, tall and wide, humbles everyone who journeys to the altar and his encounter with the majesty of God in the Eucharist. From inside, the massive central arch frames homes and workplaces down in Le Puy-en-Velay, France and opens the mysteries of the Church to people who dwell below as if it is a great eye, an open font though which flows God's grace.

I ponder what I am about to undertake, a journey to a destination but more a pilgrimage into mystery. Called *Le Chemin* in French, *El Camino* in Spanish, The Way in English: the only medieval Christian pilgrimage route walked today leads to Santiago, Spain, where the body of Saint James the Apostle is said to be entombed. I do not know what God has prepared for me in Santiago but know I must walk to the end to discover the answer. I must have an answer. After seventeen miserable years as a priest, I must make sense of the insanity of my life.

The cathedral's brochure notes that the first known pilgrim to journey to Santiago was Godescale, bishop of Le Puy-en-Velay, who walked in 950 A.D. I am starting where he started and remind

3

myself that I do not believe in coincidence but providence. I want to believe the hand of providence is upon me, but that same hand wounded me. Nevertheless, as I step from the shadows into the morning's bright sunlight, I make my first steps on *Le Chemin* and hope the metaphor becomes real, that I walk from the darkness of tragedy and sorrow into the light of happiness and joy.

The line at the Charleston County jail stretches about twenty people deep and moves slowly, as visitors wait for spots to open. After an hour-long wait, I am sent to a small cubicle with a television screen and a phone. In a minute or so, the screen flicks on, and I see Anna. We pick up phones.

"You're going to have a great time," she says

"It will be an adventure, but who knows what kind of adventure."

"If I get out before you get back, I will wait for you, I promise."

Soon, a warning flashes on the screen informing us that our time is ending.

"I love you," she says.

"I love you too."

Walking through the streets of Le Puy, a town built on hills that look as if the earth heaved like the ocean in a prehistoric cataclysm and was fixed in an upheaval of peaks and troughs, I pass a sign: "St Jacques de Compostelle, 1522 km."

At my hotel, I breakfast with a French woman, who says she walks for exercise and to enjoy nature. She asks why I walk. I answer, "I have a lot to think about," a true answer, even if my answer veils the truth.

A fountain in town center marks the traditional starting point. Water pours into a circular pool from the mouths of four dolphins leaping in four directions. I bless the fountain, saying:

May all people who make this pilgrimage be re-
stored to the state of original grace and know love
here on earth and enjoy eternal life in Heaven. In
the name of the Father and of the Son and of the
Holy Spirit. Amen.

I make the sign of the cross over the font, dip my fingers into
the water and make the sign of the cross over myself.

I walk uphill on a sidewalk to an intersection and look for
a *balise,* a white rectangle over a red rectangle, which marks *Le
Chemin* in France. I see no *balise,* no sign to guide me. I wonder
if I have already lost my Way.

This is a hell of a start.

Half instinct, half guesswork, I turn right and find a brass
concha, a scallop shell, embedded in the sidewalk. The sign lay in
plain sight. I did not see it because I looked for a different sign,
the one I was told to look for.

Outside Le Puy, a *balise* painted on a fencepost sends me uphill on a dirt path across farmland. I pass small stone crosses with
rocks on their arms and cairns at their feet. I pick up a rock and
slip it into my pocket.

At an observation point, overlooking a valley and mountains,
I meet Laurant and Katrin from Paris. They speak English better
than I speak French, but none of us speak the other's language well.

"Vous êtes ici" locates our position on a map board. I mispro-
nounce it, but Katrin corrects me. When I pronounce it correctly,
she smiles, raises her hand and says, *"Voilà!"*

We come to La Roche, a hamlet named after Saint Roch and
the first named place on *Le Chemin.* Rocks form the trail and lay
scattered across it. I walk on rocks and kick rocks, and my feet
begin to throb. I ask them how to say "rocks."

"Les roches."

Jeffrey, if you were more perspicacious, you might have grasped the sign earlier.

In the village Saint-Christophe-sur-Dolaison, Laurant picks three prunes from branches hanging over a fence, hands one to Katrin and one to me. Stigmatized in my mind by their association with the work of the bowels, prunes were never on my diet, but a guest of France with new French friends, I eat the fresh prune. It tastes great.

In the village church is a statue of Saint Therese of Lisieux. Speaking broken English, Laurant and Katrin tell me about Saint Therese, a treasure of their French Catholic culture. I chuckle inwardly, smile outwardly and feel guilty about hiding my priestly identity, but I am resolved that my Way is between me and God.

Back in the countryside, they stop to picnic in a sunny field and invite me to join, but I decline. I have no food to eat or share.

After climbing through farmlands for five and a half hours and sixteen kilometers, I walk into the village Montbonnet thinking about nothing but food. In a café, I order *un sandwich au jambon et au fromage.* Ravenous, I tear a bite off with my teeth, chew once and swallow, bite after bite. Halfway through the sandwich, I notice people staring. I finish the sandwich with more civility.

I step outside, turn right and walk out of town. Before Montbonnet, I saw *balises* in one-hundred-meter intervals, but *balises* have disappeared. The bad feeling that I walked off the Way and might be lost creeps inside of me.

Trail maps in my guidebook, *The Way of St James: Le Puy to the Pyrenees (Cicerone)* show only roads, most unnamed, but an arrow indicates north. With my thirty-year-old compass and the sparse map, I determine I have walked on a road that leads north, while the Way turned east. In my myopic quest for food, I missed a turn before the café. As it happens, *Le Chemin* passes through the countryside, then comes back to the road and crosses it. I have blundered onto a shortcut.

I wonder if shortcuts violate a Camino code of honor and if I must commit Camino *seppuku*—kneel in the presence of pilgrims and beat myself with my boots—to redeem my honor. I consider turning around, but exhaustion persuades honor to take the shortcut that came out of blind appetite and in the providence of God. An hour later, I see pilgrims cross the road near the hamlet Le Cheir and return to the Way.

The day's trails have been predominantly narrow, rugged and uphill, but the worst comes at the end: a dangerous, steep descent. Several people balk at the top, some in the middle. I fall in with a group of men who walk more with machismo than wisdom. The military air of masculine peer pressure wafts on the breeze as we descend with authoritative steps and quick pace. With too much gear, too little food and too little conditioning, my body burns every reserve of energy and feels sore everywhere. The short climb into the village Saint-Privat-d'Allier wastes me.

I stop at *Accueil Randonneurs-Hébergement*, the first *gîte* I find, unable to walk another hundred meters, after walking twenty-four kilometers. The proprietor comes out and, speaking French, says he does not open until *"cinq."* He opens his hand to denote the number five.

"D'accord." It is 3:30 p.m. Too tired to stand, I sit on steps of a small patio and wait as pilgrims walk past. The proprietor soon waves me inside. Perhaps he does not want people to see a wraith haunt his stoop.

To give myself the best chance to recover, I take a private room. He places my *bâton*, my staff, in a decorative trash can and asks me to take off my boots, which he places in a rack by the front door. He then leads me up narrow stairs and down a hall with a sideways-sloping floor to a bedroom with two beds and a sink.

After a shower, I wash my sweat-soaked clothes in the sink and wring them with arms that do not want to work. With only two sets of clothes, hand-washing clothes each day portends to be a tough end-of-day task. I string paracord in my room and hang my laundry on it. The proprietor sees what I did and waves for me to follow him downstairs. On the patio, laundry lines hang in shade. I walk back up the narrow stairs, gather my wet clothes, walk back down, hang my clothes, then climb the stairs again. After a brutal day on the trail, these climbs feel like another one of God's jokes, both divine and cruel.

I close the window blind, lock the door, take off my clothes, crawl into bed naked, pull a blanket and sheet over my head, curl into a fetal position like a wounded animal hiding in a cave desperate to survive, and sleep.

I wake for dinner and go downstairs. At a long wooden table, I meet Henri and Ivonne, a French couple; Bruce and his adult son Russ from Australia; and Tim from England. The three of them travel together.

Dinner starts with Lentils de Puy, the regional specialty, which no Anglo knows how to serve. So, we invite the French couple to serve themselves first. Henri and Ivonne spoon out the green lentils with a large, shallow spoon dotted with small holes, let the broth drain into the pot, then pour the lentils on their plates. *Voilà!*

We also eat sausage and bread and drink red wine. Russ injured his wrist weeks earlier and wears a brace. I cut his sausage into bite-sized pieces. I drink too much but think too much wine will help my body.

The conversation flows between the French couple and the English speakers, as Tim, who speaks English and French, translates. French is the first language of *Le Chemin*; English the second. We balance conversation in both languages, which satisfies everyone.

The question why we walk comes up. Bruce, Russ and Tim are "on holiday."

"I have things to think about," I say. "Questions that need answers."

"Don't tell me you are trying to find yourself," Tim says. His English accent makes him sound haughty.

"It's more complicated than that," I shoot back. *I have to come up with a better answer.*

After dinner, with semi-dry clothes in my arms, I make the day's last climb up the narrow stairs.

I try to ease myself into bed but fall. I sleep the sleep of the dead.

For breakfast, the proprietor sets out coffee and one untoasted baguette per person: the normative French breakfast. How the French expect pilgrims to walk on such minimal fare baffles me. Nevertheless, staring at the bread, I realize I have to adapt to a paltry breakfast and untoasted bread. I wolf down the baguette and drink lots of coffee.

Pilgrims carry *créanciales*, pilgrim passports, to mark their progress. I bought mine at the cathedral in Le Puy. On an empty square beside the cathedral's red stamp, the proprietor presses a stamp that identifies his *gîte*.

I follow a rock-strewn, sharply undulating trail to a belvedere, where the dark grey stone Chapelle Saint Jacques stands on the mountain's stony shoulder. Two nonchalant donkeys nibble grass as pilgrims visit the chapel, then disappear down the steep side of the mountain.

The small, all-stone chapel has an arched roof and behind the altar one window open to the East. Through the window, the morning's sunlight glows like molten gold. I photograph the inside of the chapel. Looking at the photo on my camera screen, the chapel leans. Thinking I did not hold the camera level, I take a second photo based on the chapel's geometry; the chapel walls are vertical, but I feel out of balance. Then with my hands attuned with my internal sense, I take a third photo. I am balanced; the chapel tilts off-kilter.

This is a sign.

In the Gospel of John, the evangelist never used the word "miracle." Changing water into wine, the multiplication of loaves and so on are "signs," things that point to a deeper reality.

"A sign of what?" I whisper.

The past? In struggling to keep myself upright, the out-of-balance Church threw me off balance, and I fell hard. The future? Hard to know. But not the present. Unless, unbeknownst to me, I have begun to regain my balance as I walk.

Walking among people from France, Australia, Belgium and Korea, I fall in with a Canadian couple: Vincent, an American who lives in Canada, and Wan-hee, his wife, originally from South Korea. They ask why I walk.

"It's a long story. You'd have to walk to Santiago to hear it." *That's a safe deflection but not an answer.* So I add, "The real reason I'm walking is to shed the last ten pounds." *That's a deflecting bit of jocularity and accurate enough but not the truth.*

"All of us are trying to get rid of the last ten pounds," Vincent says laughing.

Together we descend a steep pitch. Roots holding dirt in place form occasional steps. Sometimes rocks provide solid places to plant a foot. Half the time, we step down sideways on rainwater-slicked clay, grabbing trees for balance.

Le Chemin winds toward Monistrol, a quaint town in a deep gorge cut by the Allier River. Pilgrims sit at tables outside restaurants by the river, and to either side, steep mountains rise in a breathtaking view that intimidates pilgrims. Some stop for the day. Others take extended lunches. Vincent and Wan-hee meet a couple they know, sit with them and converse in French. They invite me to join. Intimidated more by a conversation in French than the mountain, I start up the mountain.

I climb switchbacks that crisscross a road that climbs with switchbacks, then leave the road for a brutal ascent. I step up and down on rocks, roots and bare dirt, grab trees for balance and to pull myself along. I come out of the gorge, top the mountain, then cross a plateau with hamlets, villages, farms and pastures.

A herd of brown and white cows lumbers down the road toward me. I judge a theological exposition about creation stories in Genesis and man's dominion over the beasts of the field unwise and yield to the cows. Three men on foot, an old man in a beaten-up truck and a focused dog follow the cows.

Farther on, a balding man with a black beard sits in grass with a picnic laid out on a cloth. He is looking at his feet.

"*Todo bien?*" I ask, reflexively speaking Spanish.

He looks perplexed.

"Are you okay?"

"Yes, I am just checking my feet."

Blackberry bushes line this section of the road. Another man and I pick blackberries and leapfrog as we eat the delicacies. François from France speaks only French. Since my guidebook says knowledge of French is "essential" on *Le Chemin* and I speak almost no French, I learn new words from each French speaker

I meet. As we pass farms, François and I teach each other the names of animals. In boring fashion, I point and say, "sheep, dog, cow." With superior pedagogical acumen, François points at an animal, imitates its sounds and says its name.

"Baaaa. *Muton.*"

"Woof, woof. *Chien.*"

"Moo. *Vache.*"

Chestnut trees are in season, and nuts are dropping, sometimes three or four a minute. Chestnut trees in the United States are blighted, an environmental tragedy of epic proportion. The environmental destruction man has done to the world saddens me. I pick up a chestnut and put it in my pocket, to carry it to Santiago as an offering to God for the healing of the Earth.

Tall wooden sculptures welcome pilgrims to the town Sauges. One looks like a flower, with two leaves folded back from the stem and a bud reaching for the sun and yearning to open. At its base is a relief of pilgrim, about to take a step, with a determined, far-sighted look on his face. *That is me:* in motion, resolute, with a thousand-mile stare piercing mountains, spanning rivers, valleys and plateaus, and reaching to the end of the earth, where I hope to find the sun and bloom.

After the trauma of Monistrol, smart pilgrims stop in Sauges. I buy *deux sandwiches au jambon et au fromage,* stuff one in my backpack and eat the other as I walk. I loved the silky ham, fabulous cheese and tough bread of the first sandwich I ate in France, which I ordered because the French was easy to pronounce, but I have sickened of ham and cheese. *Jeffrey, you need to learn more French.*

The wear and tear on my body that began the day before and worsened in the *Gorges de l'Allier* becomes more pronounced. Pain accompanies every step.

I climb through farmland up into a pine forest. Thick branches sweep down to lush, dark green grass, and the trees stand in copses or alone, creating spaces of shadow and light, openness and depth, an enchanted mysteriousness that invites a man to wander among its fairy-tale beauty and become lost.

My concerns are less romantic. My legs are worn out. My feet hurt. The sun is setting. The coolness of approaching night chills my sweat-saturated clothes. I consider sleeping among the trees. I have water, an unappetizing sandwich, a sleeping pad and a woobie, a US Army poncho liner. I stare at the thick grass. Seductive, yes. Practical, no.

"I can't believe you are going to leave me where you found me," Anna *says, as I turn onto Remount Road.*

"It's not like I haven't given you a thousand chances. I set you up in a trailer, and what happened? I took you to the clinic again and again. What happened?"

"Well, I stopped doing heroin and tricking."

"Right. And then started drinking and picking up guys at bars."

"I know. I blew it. Again." She spits her words at me.

"I let you stay with me for three days and told you that you had to find a place to live, and what did you do?"

She does not answer. So, I answer for her.

"Nothing."

For the first and only time she does not throw a tantrum.

The only place Anna was ever sober was in jail. Arrested for heroin possession, she was bonded out and is required to check in regularly to avoid violating bail. I make sure she does that. Without me, I know she will break bail and have an arrest warrant issued. So, I leave her on the side of the road.

A couple weeks later, one of her girlfriends calls: "Anna's back in jail."

I reach the village La Clauze desperate for a *gîte* and find one. The weight of my backpack lightens, and my foot pain eases.

"Thank God," I say, yet I thank God warily. I want to trust God, but after my soul-crushing experiences as a priest, I doubt I can.

I open a gate and walk into a courtyard. *"Bonjour, bonsoir."*

The owner appears and says they are closed. I catch two words: *célèbre* and *anniversaire*. The next *gîte* is only *deux kilomètres* down *Le Chemin*, he continues. He guides me to another gate and points down the road.

Relief morphs into frustration, and I look down the Way of Agony. The realization that I thanked God for the end of the day's journey that has not ended fuels my angst. *God, why do you always want more suffering from me?* My backpack feels twice as heavy as before, and the asphalt road makes each exhausted step more painful. I harden my face and walk.

In the hamlet Le Falzet, I step through the open door of *Gîte d'étape, accueil à la ferme Delcros* and into a long room with a kitchen and dining table in one half, and in the other half a living room with chairs and a couch. Jean Claude from France, who speaks English, lies on the couch, book in hand. The proprietor, a short, grey-haired, always-smiling woman, settles me in a room I have to myself.

I feel sore from my shoulders to my feet. Blisters formed on several toes and popped as I walked. On the back of my heels, the skin has rubbed off. A heat rash burns the inside of my thighs. Hot water in the shower magnifies the pain.

In my generic hiker's first aid kit, I find aspirin, antiseptic wipes, safety pins and small Band-Aids. I swab raw skin with the wipes, then let it breathe until morning. The kit has nothing for a rash.

I launder my clothes in the sink and wash blood out of my socks.

Our grandmotherly host serves pea soup, a mushroom omelet, beef and potatoes, and for dessert, cheese and fruit. We drink red wine.

In the middle of dinner, a pilgrim steps in the door. He goes by Alpi, but his baptismal name is Christian, and he comes from Austria. He began in Austria, has walked about one thousand kilometers and is tall with long legs. "God, politics and cheese" are his favorite things to talk about.

So, Jean Claude recites French witticisms about cheese: "Charles de Gaulle said France is impossible to govern. There are too many cheeses," and "Bread, wine and cheese are proof that God lives in France." We howl in assent.

As the meal's final course, I take aspirin.

My body needs the recovery that comes with deep, restful sleep. In a nightmare about Anna, she tricks.

Three Band-Aids taped over each silver-dollar blister on my heels protect raw skin only a little. My thighs rub each other with each step, inflaming the rash. I walk with wider steps, but the awkward, shortened stride tires me. I return to my normal stride and endure the pain.

There has always been something abnormal about my journey as I strode through life. And too much pain.

Conversation with Christian distracts me from my suffering. We talk about hunting, gun laws, solar energy, nature, computers, language, culture and how he traveled before Le Puy-en-Velay— he stayed with host families.

We find Jean Claude sitting on a dirt embankment in a forest, and as we walk, we discuss a common pilgrim question: "Which is worse, uphill or downhill?"

Jean Claude, who had open heart surgery and blew out a knee on snow skies, says, "My knee hurts going down. My heart hurts going up."

"So, your heart is good going down, and your knee is good going up," observes Christian. We laugh.

We pass chapels dedicated to Saint Roch and another village named La Roche, appropriate since rocks pound our feet as we pound down the trail.

When Christian and I walk together, I ask, "Why are you walking?"

"I am trying to decide what to do with my life." I wonder if he is considering priesthood, since he likes to talk about God. I try nudging the conversation toward God, but Christian becomes silent and introspective. I have the impression that that part of his Way is an interior journey like mine.

"Why are you walking?" he asks.

I open a letter from Bishop David Thompson appointing me to multiple assignments in Charleston, walk over to the church and open the Liturgy of the Hours to where I stopped that morning to see what word God has for me. I read the call of Jeremiah.

The word of the LORD came to me:
"Before you were born, I dedicated you
A prophet to the nations I appointed you.
To whomever I send you, you shall go.
Whatever I command you, you shall speak.
Do not be afraid of them,
For I am with you to deliver you."

Then the LORD extended his hand and touched my mouth,
"See I place my words in your mouth.
Today I appoint you
Over nations and kingdoms,
To uproot and to tear down,
To destroy and to demolish,
To build and to plant."[1]

For answering God's call, the Jewish authorities beat Jeremiah,
put him in stocks, mocked him, rejected him, threw him into a cis-
tern and left him to die. In the desert of his soul, Jeremiah suffered
inconsolate desolation.

After two years at Saint Joseph's Church in Columbia, South
Carolina, my first assignment as a priest, I do not think being a priest
can get worse, but God's prophecy stuns me.

"God and I have a lot to talk about," I blurt out. *Voilà!* I
discover the answer.

Le Chemin climbs and descends all day, not as brutally as the
previous days, but I have walked into exhaustion the third day in
a row, exhaustion now surfeited with pain.

Jean Claude, Christian and I come back together before Saint-
Alban-sur-Limagnole and walk into town together. I pause atop
a hill which overlooks the town center. With the end in sight,
the steep downhill that separates me from rest sickens my spirit
because of how wretched my body feels. I limp downhill.

Jean Claude stops at a *gîte* where he has reservations. I find a
hotel across from the church. Christian plans to walk forty or so
kilometers. We have walked twenty-nine.

"After you walk a thousand kilometers, you'll do forty-kilo-
meter days also."

---

1 NAB, Jeremiah 1:4-5, 7a-10

"When I hit the Pyrenees, I'll roll right over them." I express confidence I do not feel.

"That's the spirit!"

Christian walks downtrail with long strides. I hobble into Hotel du Centro and get a third-floor room, mercifully accessed by an elevator.

I drop my kit on the floor and collapse on the bed. I have planned the next day, Sunday, to be a rest day to give my body an early opportunity to heal and to make sure I get to Mass. I have solved the Mass problem, but my physical condition, potentially fatal to my Camino, disheartens me.

Every time I wanted to do something when I was a child, my dad told me, "You can't do that." I heard "you can't" so many times that I came to believe "I can't," and the lie malformed me through adulthood. I now tell myself: "I cannot return home a failure. I cannot let the lie be the truth. I have to walk to the end."

Depression, which first afflicted me in my teenage years, tempts me to despair in a lethargy that sucks energy from my soul. Again, I talk to myself: "You've worked through messes before. You can do it again." I raise myself off the bed, take off my boots slowly to minimize pain, put on flip flops and start to work the problem.

Taking an outdoor table, I order *"le plat du jour,"* a featured special at restaurants in France and a great discovery. With easy French, in two minutes, I have a plate with two thick slices of pork and a pile of crunchy green beans, seasoned with coarse salt and minced garlic. As I eat, pilgrims, alone or in small groups, stop for lunch, visit the church or pass through town.

I look up "blister" and "rash" in my French phrase book. I find *"l'ampoule,"* but among eighty-two maladies in the medical section, "rash" is absent. Neither is "rash" in the dictionary. However, the helpful phrase book has the word for nudist.

Up the street, I find a pharmacy, and the pharmacist greets me with a compassionate smile and *"Bonjour."*

"Bonjour," I respond. Then, without attempting *"l'ampoule,"* I show her the silver-dollar blisters.

"C'est magnifique, si?" I say, then shake my head. *"Oui?"*

Her expression changes from pleasant to concerned. She leads me to a stand with packs of Compeed, a super band-aid worn until it falls off.

"J'ai un autre problème."

The helpful expression returns to her face. To describe the rash, without dropping my pants and becoming *un nudiste*, I say *"rouge ici et ici"* and indicate the inside of my thighs. Her facial expression again changes to concern. She hands me a cream and tells me to use it four times a day.

In my room, I swab raw skin with antiseptic, puncture new blisters with a flame-blackened needle and squeeze out fluid. From most blisters, fluid seeps out. From one blister, a thin line of fluid shoots across my backpack. I rub lotion between my thighs. I stretch my legs, and my muscles feel better.

I sleep until dinner, then dine in the hotel's café. I order *"vin rouge"* and get a whole bottle, which has happened every time I have ordered wine in France. I do not know enough French to ask for anything more specific. I first hesitated drinking a full bottle of wine. Now, to dull psychic pain, I drink the whole bottle without any qualms.

I yell into the phone. "We have been stuck in this nightmare for a year. I give you money for heroin, so you don't have to trick. I take you to the clinic so you can get off heroin. You go back to heroin and tricking. I am not giving you any more money."

Anna hangs up.

I call her the next day and the day after that and so on. She does not answer. I call her friends. They have not heard from Anna either. A couple weeks later, a prostitute girlfriend of hers calls and says, "I spoke with Anna and told her she has to call you."

Anna calls and tells me that when she hung up, she threw down the phone and said to a girlfriend whose trailer she was in, "I'm going to get really sick." She locked herself in a room for five days and withdrew from heroin. She also says that she stopped tricking. "I never want to see those eyes again."

However, she started going to bars and drinking. She met a guy who gave her a room in his condo, an arrangement I know will not last. He has anger management problems.

Anna and I go out for dinner, and when I take her back to the condo, she asks, "Can you give me $50?"

"No."

"I need it to buy wine." She is drinking two bottles a day.

"No."

She starts pulling on my arm. "Let's pull into a parking space, and I can give you a blow job for $50." She is still thinking and acting like an addict-prostitute.

"You are not going to give me a blow job."

I give her fifty dollars and decline offers for sex.

Fixed by Ruination

DAYS 4 - 7

As I sleep, my raw thighs stick together as if glued. I slip a sheet between them, but that irritates inflamed skin, so I accept the stickiness. When I roll over, my skin peels apart. I hold my breath as I endure the pain.

I wake with sore, tight muscles, but compared to the day before, they feel great. I wonder if wine has wrought a miracle. In a sober assessment, I realize my body has begun to adapt to daily punishment and nightly recovery.

The fight starts in a parking lot in Jacksonboro. Anna said she wanted to see me, but she only wants money. I say no, and she explodes. She drives off, and I drive after her. She drives fast, then slows down, like she wants me to catch her. She speeds up again, and I speed up. With each play in her game, the intensity of my emotions shoots up. She pulls into a convenience store parking lot, and I park beside her. We scream at each other.

"You don't give a fuck about me. All you want is money."

"If you loved me, you would help me."

"I have wiped out my finances helping you, and if you loved me, you would help yourself."

"Do you want to hit me?" Anna steps toward me, threatening yet inviting an assault. The urge courses through me. My muscles tighten.

She has often been assaulted by tricks and boyfriends and rationalized the assaults. After sex, one trick asked, "Are you okay?" then punched her and knocked her out. "That's just what gets him off."

When she incites me to hit her, I see it for what it is—self-abuse through assault by another prompted by her own self-hatred. Raped by her father when she was four years old, her wounds are deep and severe.

I relax my muscles. The tension leaves me.

My feet are critical. In addition to blisters and raw skin, both little toes hurt so badly that I think I have stress fractures.

I spent a lot of time and money to find good boots, and I stare at them, thinking they cannot be the problem, but the more I stare, the more intuition prods reason to see with clarity.

My wide feet have pushed the leather out to the sides of the toe boxes, but the toe boxes are unchanged. I push and pull. The leather had not been hardened as I first thought. Alico put a plastic toe box under the leather, which foot pressure cannot mold. Good leather forms to the foot, but the plastic toe box destroyed leather's magical quality. For three days and seventy-five kilometers in rugged terrain, my toes jammed against plastic. My boots have broken my feet.

The pain is so great that I wonder if I need to stop walking, and the thought of not completing my Camino plunges me into a deep depression made worse because today, September 21, 2014, is my fifty-first birthday.

I splash water on my face and put on a good face that poorly masks the sadness behind it and go to Mass. Locals and a few pilgrims fill Saint Alban, a red sandstone, Romanesque church with a slate roof. The priest says a reverent Mass with neither additions nor omissions. I feel at home even though I understand none of the French.

I have a second equipment problem, a sin of omission. I do not have an adaptor for my electronics. I intended to buy an adaptor in the Philadelphia airport, then in Charles de Gaulle. I looked for one in Lyon, in Le Puy-en-Velay and here in Saint-Alban-sur-Limagnole. I need a miracle, a pilgrim who carries two and who will give me one. *Well, God you don't work miracles for me, do you?* I look out my room's window and see an American who attended Mass at the cathedral in Le Puy. I hustle downstairs and across the square.

"Hello, we attended the same Mass in Le Puy."

"I remember. I'm Ryan."

"Jeffrey ... Say, I don't have an adaptor for my electronic stuff and can't find one to buy, and my batteries are running out. I bet you only have one."

"Only one." His GoLite pack screams minimalist.

"Yeah, no one would carry two. Can I borrow yours for ten minutes? Just to keep my camera above the red line?"

I plug in my camera, and we sit at an outdoor table. Intelligent, tall, thin, a slightly unkept black beard and from San Francisco, he has the prototypical university look. This year he is walking Le Chemin de Puy—Le Puy-en-Velay to Saint-Jean-Pied-de-Port. The year before, he walked Camino Francés—Saint-Jean-Pied-de-Port to Santiago.

He asks why I am walking.

"I have a decision to make and need space and perspective." I test one other answer.

"What kind of decision?"

"I really do not want to discuss the details. It's painful."

"I respect that," he says.

"I knew you would, and I am grateful."

"One of the good things about the Camino is that we have time to think."

"True that." I nod.

"One of the bad things about the Camino is that we have time to think."

A guffaw lifts me out of my chair. "That's even more true."

I return his adaptor, and he heads downtrail.

Back in my room, with the knife blade on my multitool, I start to cut out the plastic from the inside of my boots. As I jab, the knife slices through the leather on the outstep. Cascades of emotions and thoughts tumble though me in microsecond intervals. Disbelief, shock, anger at the stupid design, anger at myself, the laughable way I unproofed my boots' water resistance, a bout of depression, acceptance, then the possibility of a providential mistake, a happy fault. I expand the inadvertent slice, put them on and walk around. The boots still feel tight. I slice the boots on the instep where my big toes pushed against them, then whittle away leather and plastic on both sides, cutting holes on the outside and inside of each boot. When I put them on, they feel great.

I fixed my boots through ruination.

In bright, warm sunshine, I maintain a steady pace through rolling hills, open pastures and shaded woods. Yet again, endless rocks mar bucolic joy. Despite rocks' inert passivity, in the thousands of meetings between rock and boot, rocks pummel my feet.

I have met a wonderful French couple and a compatible soul from Austria, but with differing goals and paces, I walk alone. "God, I want a friend to walk with," I pray.

I walk through seemingly deserted hamlets and villages in-
habited by languid cats and industrious chickens so dismiss the
quiet emptiness of the town Aumont-Aubrac as unremarkable.
The Way leads to the church. Behind the church, chickens live
in a fenced-in yard by a house. I toss them bread, the last of my
food.

I look for a store to reprovision. Stores and restaurants are
closed. I circle through town. Everything is closed. I check my
watch: 12:30 p.m., lunch hour. Everything ought to be open.
Then a memory of something from my guidebook and a snippet
of conversation with Christian comes back to mind like a wisp
of wind that begins over the distant horizon, grows into a tem-
pest and storms into my face. Stores and restaurants in France
close on Monday. I have nothing to eat and nowhere to shop.
Dumbfounded, I wander around smiling at the irony of my predicament. I walked fifteen kilometers on bread and coffee. I need
to eat.

After a desperate half-hour, I find an open bar: *Richard Bar de
la Marie.* With no menus, the waitress and I negotiate the peril-
ous French language. She names a dish, but I do not understand
her. I ask her to write down what she said. She writes, *"Quiche
Lorraine."* A common dish in the States, I ought to have understood her instantly but did not expect her to name a familiar food.
I groped for something outside of my knowledge and deafened
myself. When I get it, I throw my head back and laugh, *"Oui,
quiche lorraine."*

I sit outside in a covered seating area. John Pierre, a French-
Canadian, arrives and sits one table away. A couple minutes later, two female pilgrims join him, then two more female pilgrims
so that all five sit together, speaking French. Manon and Josée

from Quebec introduce themselves, but sitting beside a French-language clique, loneliness feels acute.

I leave town and come upon La Chapelle de Bastide, built in 1522 with eight small benches and a statue of Mary on the altar. I once had a great relationship with Mary, but that collapsed along with my relationship with Jesus Christ and the Church. After my tormented life as a priest, I do not trust her maternal care. I ask Mary to watch over my pilgrimage with half-hearted desire.

Walking along a sunken dirt road lined with oak trees, thinking about nothing in particular, I watch my feet to avoid scattered rocks. Without rational explanation, I look up at a note written on overlapped strips of athletic tape and stuck to a small piece of wood nailed to a tree. I stop dead in my tracks and stare, shocked that I looked straight at the note, one little thing on a long trail with millions of little things.

> To
> Jeff KENDALL
> Dear Jeff
> It was really nice talking to you and enjoyed your gentle company as well as the exchange of thoughts. I am writing you because I felt that our depart was too hasty, but nonetheless I thought it necessary to get some food for the weekend. I hope you have a wonderful trip as well as a fruitful and long time to talk with "the big Boss" our God.
> Yours, Alpi from Abertilliach
> + "Happy Birthday" since it was (also) too early

My heart lifts. I have a friend on the Way! Sadly, our schedules differ.

My guidebook does not indicate a *gîte* at Les Quatre-Chemins, my day's final destination, but I have seen *gîtes* not listed in my guide. Crossroads must have a place to eat and sleep, I reason. I also pray, "God, I am putting this in your hands, to see what you provide." I find food, if cold pizza that sat out all day constitutes food in France, but there is no place to sleep. I reasoned wrong and say, "So God, I put this in your hands, and you let me down again."

I hustle to the hamlet Finieyrols, the next place with a *gîte* and six kilometers distant. I try to focus more on pace and destination than the consequence of putting something in God's hands, but the question roiling my mind is why my life always becomes more difficult when I put something in God's hands.

In one hour, I reach the solitary *Gîte et chambres d'hôtes Les Gentianes,* a farmhouse converted into a *gîte.* If there is neither bed nor food, I am in trouble.

At the front desk, I ask for a room. None are available. I ask for a bed. The woman counts and recounts in her book, looks up and says, *"Oui."* I get the last bed. I ask about dinner. She disappears into the kitchen and, after a couple minutes, returns with, *"Oui."* I arrived just in time to get food. Then, in French, she directs me to go outside, cross a small field to another building, go upstairs, turn left and walk down the hall to the last room. My bed is the top bunk in the last bunk bed.

As I cross the field, someone calls, "Jeffrey . . . Jeffrey."

Laurant and Katrin walk up, drinks in hand. I hug them. I felt like God punished me when I had to hustle six kilometers more than I wanted or needed to walk, but in his providence, I found my friends. However, my anger with and distrust of God exceeds any promptings by the Holy Spirit to thank God.

I find my room, named *Lys Martargon* after a lily, and my bed, which delights me. I understood the hospitaller's French.

I introduce myself to Suzan and Jacques from Quebec. Jacques speaks little English; Suzan is fluent. She asks about my Way, and I give her an overview—Le Puy start, Santiago finish. In an offhand manner, I mention my note.

"I didn't think anyone found notes. That's a miracle."

I admit that I forgot to buy an adaptor and ask if I might borrow one. She has two and gives me one. I almost fall over.

"That's a miracle," I say.

"Two miracles in one day. You must be blessed." She looks like she expects an affirmative answer.

I believe I am cursed by God. Nevertheless, God answered prayers for friends and an adaptor. Shoving the garbage of my life into the stuffed full-of-shit baggage room in the back of my head, I nod and say, "Amen."

Suzan tells me about a blister remedy she learned the year before when she and Jacques walked the Camino Francés. A woman drained her blisters, then injected mercurochrome into them. Suzan said it worked and brought syringes with her. She holds out her hand and offers me a syringe. I stare at it.

Anna unzips a small black pouch. On the table, she places a rubber strip, a baggie filled with a white powder, a spoon, a lighter and a syringe.

"Please, I don't want you to watch me take my medicine." Her face conveys helpless resignation even as she pleads for privacy.

My eyes fall. I look at the floor.

"Please."

I step out of the room.

I decline the syringe with the excuse: "I hate needles."

At dinner, pilgrims sit at a single long table. Since I do not speak French, I sit at the end so as not to feel out of place in the middle of a French conversation.

Aligot, the *prima dona* food dish and a regional specialty, excites the French pilgrims. Made of mashed potatoes, cream, butter and cheese, *aligot* has the consistency of gooey molten rubber. Several people spoon *aligot* out of a large bowl and slowly twirl the spoon. The more they twirl, the more the *aligot* stretches. No one who pits themselves against *aligot* twirls the spoon until the *aligot* separates. Spirits waver and arms tire before *aligot* yields. I am convinced that the *aligot* in that bowl will stretch a full kilometer.

I show my friends a photo of George, my Walker hound, and they pass the photo around the table. *"Très beau!"* several people say. Through Suzan, who translates, I tell everyone that I found George on the side of the road, he had been abused, and he patrolled my farm at night and protected my chickens from varmints. With no French equivalent, translating "varmint" requires a several-minute discussion. Someone asks who is looking after him.

"I put him down because of cancer." Groans and deflated shoulders accompany *"Je suis désolé's."*

My French becomes a topic of conversation.

"When I arrived in France, I knew almost no French, but I can eat, sleep and walk in French." Everyone laughs and teaches me how to say: *"Je peux manger, dormir et marcher en français."*

The Aubrac plateau is a geographic masterpiece of thick grasses, immense pastures, occasional woods, undulating terrain with valleys, hills, streams and boulders the size of houses. Set in thick grasses on gentle hills, the dispersal of boulders gives the impression that God walked by and dropped a handful of pebbles through his fingers. Silent, unmovable, intimating the endurance of eternity: the power of the boulders feels awesome. In a blue sky with wispy white clouds, a glorious sun crowns the land's beauty.

I photograph Laurant and Katrin with their happy smiles. Then, Suzan photographs Laurant, Katrin and me with our cameras. I smile, but with a dank, black underground lake, a wellspring of depression in the depths of my being, I force a smile, and the photograph captures my struggle, and that struggle drains energy.

Katrin searches for words to describe our relationship and tries several phrases in English. Inspired, I offer, *"Amis du Chemin."* Katrin's face lights up.

"Yes, *Amis du Chemin."* The phrase sounds more beautiful when she speaks French.

In the town Nasbinals, we buy wine, baguettes, ham, pâté and cheese at a local food store and stop at a convenience-style store that sells boots but not in wide sizes. About to give up, the sales lady's face gets that universal "I have an idea" expression, which needs no translation. I walk out with sandals on my feet.

We take coffee in the square at an outdoor table that seats four, so I sit in the awkward, fifth wheel spot. The conversation wrenches between English and French, with either Jacques or me left out. Jacques's face expresses displeasure, so I let the conversation go its French way.

The Way follows dirt, grass and gravel roads that delineate cow pastures, then turns uphill into a cow pasture. A herd of light brown cows with thin, short horns that extend outward in the *orans* position, the position of a priest's arms and hands when he prays at Mass, crowd a gate through which *Le Chemin* passes.

Walking through the herd concerns me, but the cows, either pre-occupied with their cuds or lost in prayer, ignore us.

I surge ahead, follow a cow path around the arms of a ridge, then climb to the crest where a stone cross stands. I have carried my boots tied to my backpack, since I bought the sandals. I hang the boots on the cross and shake my head at the stupidity of the design. The cow deserved better.

I stop on a hill, lie in the sun and rest my head on my backpack. Down below, with a low wooded ridge behind it and surrounded by fields and woods sits Aubrac, a small village with a church standing tall among a few dozen homes and businesses.

Everyone plans to stop here. I enjoy Laurant and Katrin's company, and Suzan is helpful, but I feel uncomfortable with Jacques. I search my intuition, which I lost years ago and need to recover. In the sun, with eyes closed and half asleep, in my mind and heart, everything says "walk." *God has something for me down the Way, something unknown and unseen, beyond the next hill, through the next valley, something, somewhere.*

I say goodbye to everyone in Aubrac, but we plan to meet in Conques. Because Conques is a prime destination where Europeans who segment-walk *Le Chemin* while on vacation stop, they insist that I need reservations if I want to stay at the monastery. Laurant promises to make reservations for me. I will arrive a day ahead, take a day off and meet them on my rest day. Reservations are an exception to my code—to plan nothing ahead as an act of faith in God's providence—based on the supposition that meeting Laurant and Katrin is God's providential plan.

Gorgeous scenery blesses my late afternoon walk, but peril accompanies every step. Treacherous rocks capable of turning an ankle dot the dirt trails. In sections where rocks have been embedded in the trail, every step meets rock. Again, my feet take a beating.

In the small town Saint-Chély-d'Aubrac, I find Tim who tells me where his group has settled. Bruce and Russ are easygoing. Tim is helpful, but his question about finding myself still rings in my ears as a small-minded insult and a pitiful reduction of the complexity of my situation.

I take a room at a hotel, and at dinner, the proprietor sits me with Suzy from London. She works in a law office and maintains a professional persona even in casual conversation but with a friendly face and a friendly smile.

Fluent in French, she teaches me *"un quart de vin rouge,"* a small carafe of red wine. There will be no more full bottles. She also teaches me *"un noisette,"* an after-dinner coffee with a touch of milk.

"Trail maps in the States rate trails as easy, moderate and strenuous," I say. "They give elevation changes in feet so that a hiker knows what he faces. My guidebook doesn't have either."

"Take a look at mine."

Michelin 161 Chemins de Compostelle, Le Puy-en-Velay to Saint-Jean-Pied-de-Port has what mine lacks. The left page has a profile with elevations, distances, estimated times and a hiker silhouetted in a green, orange or red to indicate difficulty, the right page a detailed road map. What my guidebook has are descriptions of towns, monuments, artwork and churches, along with photos. The lighter Michelin guide has the advantage in weight.

I glance at the profiles of Monistrol d'Allier and Monts d'Aubrac and mumble, "I've blundered through mountains."

Suzy nods as she sips wine.

The food is as good as the conversation: tomatoes and cucumbers with a white sauce, rabbit over bow tie pasta with mushroom gravy, two cheeses, and for dessert, bread pudding with fruit. After dinner, I take *"un noisette."*

As I lie in bed, I evaluate my choices. Twice I avoided discomfort despite the consequence that I also left friends. I followed my intuition that said that God had something for me down the Way and met Suzy, a godsend.

I think about the Catholic Church and Anna. I have a terrible decision to make. I could walk away from both.

Sockless, sandaled and in cold rain, I descend steeply to a stream, cross a bridge and pass a cemetery full of people dry, warm and at rest. I envy the dead.

I then climb through a forest on a rocky path. Occasional pebbles wedge between sandal and foot. Sometimes, a minor annoyance, I walk with them. Other times, they pain me enough to slow me. Some I shake out. When that fails, I stop and flick out the offender. To avoid the pebble problem, I walk with an awkward, unnatural, hard-to-maintain gait. Invariably, I return to my natural movement and pick up bothersome pebbles.

The climb levels out on a firm, slightly muddy pathway angling along the side of a mountain, and rain falls in a light shower. I catch a break in L'Estrade, a village where a grey-haired couple in their seventies run a *pausa café* at a communal oven built in the days of feudal lords. A wooden roof, a dry dirt floor and three grey stone walls form the building, with the oven recessed in the back wall. Benches and chairs line the walls. A round, wooden table with flowers, a coffee pot, pastries, a register and a donation box sit in the center. We communicate more with smiles than words.

When I reach the hamlet La Rozière, the rain stops, so I gobble down half *un sandwich au jambon et au fromage*. A young man, shorter than me, with short black hair and a determined mien, walks downtrail holding a red tent fly in both hands and above his head so that it flows behind him like a royal cape. We introduce ourselves and start walking together.

Yoan from Bulgaria started south of Amsterdam, where he attended university, and heads to Santiago. He camps every night and dries his tent by trailing it behind him as he walks. Before Le Puy-en-Velay, he met three pilgrims. In Le Puy, he met many pilgrims, including Christian, and they shared a bottle of wine.

We find Suzy in the small town Saint-Côme-d'Olt, and the three of us lunch together.

"What luxury item are you carrying?" Yoan asks.

Suzy chuckles and says, "Some beauty products."

"An iPad Mini," I say.

But Yoan is not forthcoming, so I ask. He hesitates and answers, "Spray to take the smell out of my boots." Laughter busts out.

Because lunch in a restaurant strains Yoan's finances, I buy his lunch, and not to make him feel self-conscious, I buy Suzy's also.

When we leave, I say hello to Russ, who enjoys a beer at a café across the square while waiting on Tim and Bruce. Russ invites me to sit. I would love his company but having just finished lunch, I am ready to walk.

Yoan and I stroll through the rolling hills of Pays d'Olt, conversing on a wide range of topics, effortlessly switching from one to another. Great company and a remarkable twenty-two-year-old, he has incipient wisdom free from the arrogance of youth.

Yoan keeps a merciful Camino code. As compensation for camping out, he samples a different pastry in every town. At a bakery in the small town Espalion, we fulfill Yoan's pledge. I also find a pilgrim shop that sells KEEN boots. The owners and I discuss what size to purchase. After the horrible experience with Alico boots, I do not trust my judgment about my own feet, which are so beaten up that it is hard to decide what size fits best. The larger the boot, the better it feels. I walk out wearing new boots.

To thank me for lunch, Yoan buys me a beer at an outdoor café. He says that of all the people he has met, his favorite conversations have been with me and Christian. I have had wonderful conversations with many pilgrims, but conversations with him and Christian have been intellectual blessings. *Amis du Chemin,* Christian, Yoan and I would make a great trio to walk together to Santiago, but our schedules differ. Yoan walks downtrail, and I take a hotel room.

Having to break in new boots on the trail, I feel like I am restarting my Camino. I try to find solace in theology. The next morning will be my eighth day. Jesus rose on Sunday, the first day of the secular week, the eighth day of the spiritual week. The eighth day celebrates resurrection, new life, new beginnings, a day of glory and hope. In me, hope comingles with despair in a murky struggle.

After one of my many diatribes about the abuses of power in the Catholic Church, Anna says, "I believe in Jesus Christ. And I am glad my parents who adopted me introduced me to the Catholic Faith. I always believe God will take care of me. Take you, for example. I think God sent you to me. I think my faith is stronger than yours."

"It is," I admit. "God doesn't give a damn about me."

Conques

DAYS 8 - 10

I follow the river Lot, then leave the river and weave through woods with gentle hills, but my worn body registers meager elevation changes I first dismissed as nothing.

In the hamlet Saint-Pierre, where *Le Chemin* climbs a steep hill, but an alterna*te circle*s the hill, Suzy calls my name. I smile when I see her. While Suzy sorts directions, I notice an unusual statue.

A genius welded hundreds of pieces of dark brown scrap metal together to form Saint James. From his skeletal left hand hangs a gourd. In his skeletal right hand, he holds a long, grey pipe as a staff. His feet look skeletal, and his legs, made of rebar, look sinuous. His cloak forms the upper two-thirds of the statue and masks an empty torso. Faint rust covers the metal except for the polished stainless-steel *concha* over his heart and his two eyes, stainless-steel nuts that shine like silvery dots in the darkness of his body. He wears a silver-aluminum, floppy hat, and his beard and hair—long, wiry and splayed—make him look like a pirate in motion. This masterpiece captures the paradox between external strength and inner emptiness and evokes resolute wildness in pursuit of a greater mission indifferent to opinions of others. The emptiness I live, the wildness I desire.

Suzy takes the alternate. I go uphill.

The path climbs with few switchbacks and little respite. Grabbing trees for balance and to pull myself along, I step from rock to rock, root to root. I walk barely fast enough to maintain balance.

I emerge from thick brush onto a flat section, with a view of the valley below. Here I meet Miza, a diminutive South Korean woman in her sixties who lives in Germany and walks alone. She is enjoying breakfast in the sunshine.

"Guten Tag," I say.

"Guten Tag." She is all smiles.

"Wie gehts?"

"Es gut. Und Sie?"

"Gut, alles gut." Not exactly true, I add, *"Müde,"* weary.

We speak a little English, and I eat nuts she offers.

Then I trudge uphill. The steepness seems never to end but gradually lessens. The trail then follows the mountain's contours with ridges on the left and gorgeous views of the Lot valley on the right.

I descend to Église de Trédou, where workmen are moving a carved rock, a cube about seventy centimeters per side. A man says something in French I interpret as a request to help and a joke. Mixing French and Spanish, I say, *"Mi rocher est ici"* and tap my backpack with my *bâton*. We all laugh.

The Way enters flat, wide corn fields. Under the roasting sun, sweat beads on my skin and runs down my face and legs. I climb back into steep hills, woods and shade, then descend to Estaing on a painfully steep path.

Nestled in a saddle where valleys and mountain arms converge, set by the river Lot, dominated by a fifteenth century château and bathed in midday sun, Estaing looks like a fairy tale setting. The downside is that the village sits across the river from *Le Chemin*. To even consider crossing the bridge to eat inspires genuine, heartfelt regret since the venture entails a mandatory backtrack, albeit short. Between walking without lunch and eating lunch with a backtrack, I choose food and five hundred extra meters.

A row of tables shaded with umbrellas line the stone wall by the river. As I stroll along, I see Suzy sitting quietly, gazing across the river, with a fashionable e-cigarette in hand.

"May I sit with you?"

"Of course. I know what you did yesterday when you bought that young man's lunch. I thought of doing it myself, but you did not have to do that for me. I insist you let me buy lunch."

We talk about the climb I took and the road she walked. We each think the other made the better choice. The catty-cornered perspectives bemuse me.

We order *"faux filet,"* said to be analogous to sirloin, but from my carnivorous perspective, it is defined more by *"faux"* than *"filet"* and inferior to sirloin in the States.

The first hour of the afternoon walk, a flat trail through woods along the river, lulls me into dreamy peacefulness until, through trees, I glimpse a looming mountain grow taller as I approach. At the toe of the foot of the mountain, the face of a steep climb disappears above treetops.

I climb a long series of switchbacks, then turn onto a road on which I crest a false top, then another false top, then another. It happens again. And again. And again. Each time, I think I have reached the top, only to be disappointed. Even when I tell myself to stop anticipating the end, I crest more false tops with dashed hopes. The excruciating, torturous psychological effect wears me down worse than the physical, like life with Anna and in the Catholic Church.

Day after day, I woke hoping Anna would go to the clinic, get a job, do something to warrant hope; night after night, I went to bed exhausted, with hope destroyed. In conversation after conversation with everyone in authority in the diocese—bishop, vicars, CFO, staff—I hoped reason, justice and charity would break the diabolical justifications for abuses of power; again and again, pharisaic self-righteousness triumphed, and I became more and more dejected.

Once the worst ends, the trail undulates steeply through farmland, until passing into a mountain forest. The last stretch follows the rim of a giant bowl, with the Gorges du Lot below and mountains beyond. Across the bowl in a sea of trees, the hamlet Golinhac sits perched on the mountain's shoulder, the end of a twenty-nine-kilometer day.

When I settle into a *gîte* and take off my new boots, new blisters do not make my feet feel significantly worse.

I share a room with a young couple from Quebec, Ben from Sweden and a couple from France, whose walk has ended. The French wife has bad knees and lies in bed, almost helpless but in good spirits. Her polite Indian husband reeks of curry.

The *gîte* makes reservations for us at the only restaurant, and the hostess seats me with Ben, the Quebec couple, and Margit and Katherine from Denmark. Everyone speaks English but seems to deliberately avoid it. The Danish women even look indignant when I ask a question. The dessert course lifts my spirits because it marks the end of the meal. I wolf down a baked apple, excuse myself and escape the lonely, linguistic predicament.

Under a cloudless sky with a golden morning sun and in temperatures close to freezing, I walk with pilgrims, if sight of another pilgrim means being with someone. No conversation is more than *"bonjour"* and *"bon Chemin."*

Except for a few sharp climbs, I walk down long, gentle descents through farms, open fields, woods and deserted hamlets to Espeyrac, a little town built on a lightly wooded hillside. Under a cart across from the church, as if watching a tennis match in slow motion, a white and brown cat moves its head slowly back and forth as pilgrims pass by. I step into Église Saint-Pierre, a simple, unadorned church with Roman and Gothic motifs. The man who sat by the wayside as François and I picked blackberries stands in the back, takes off his hat, bows his head and prays.

I climb to the Sénergues plateau, where *Le Chemin* wraps around mountains and wanders down ridges. After eighteen relatively easy kilometers, I start a roller coaster of steep climbs and maddeningly steeper, deeper descents down into Conques. Atop the last descent, I stare down an asphalt plunge and balk. I refortify my intestinal fortitude and say, "One last horror." To protect my toes, I angle my steps at forty-five degrees and, barely putting one foot in front of the other, shuffle down.

Conques' narrow streets and medieval buildings crowd the Abbey of Saint Foy. Both village and abbey sit on the side of a steep valley. A rock-filled river cuts a deep gorge far below.

I arrive before the monastery opens its rooms and its dormitory and speak with the guest master to make sure my name is on the list for a room. Then, with dozens of pilgrims, I wait in a cold, shaded courtyard. After everyone else has been escorted to a room or the dormitory, the guest master walks up, shakes his head and says, *"Je suis désolé. No chambres, no lits."*

I've walked down this road before.

Determined to get my reserved room, I point to my name on the reservation list a second time. A kind, older woman leads me to my room on stone stairs that spiral up and up. *"Madam!"* I exclaim, exasperated. She makes a huff-and-puff gesture, and we spiral higher. My cell has a bed, sink, toilet and shower.

With various things to push, pull, twist or spin, the designs of shower faucets have been diabolical in their inventiveness. I thought I had seen every imaginable design and have not seen two identical set-ups so far, and the design in this room is yet another new, different, confusing puzzle that I play with for several minutes until I get hot and cold water in the right proportions. I feel like I have earned a campaign ribbon.

On my left foot, I have a blister on my little toe, and the middle toenail is black; on my right foot, a blood blister under my big toe, a blister on my little toe and the toe beside it, and two blisters on the heel. Fear of the eighth day manifested on the ninth, a novena of days.

I go to a café across from the church and see Suzy just as she sees me.

"Do join me," she says.

After ordering wine, I confide, "I had a visceral hatred for the descent into Conques."

"That descent was a pig," she says.

"I respect pigs too much to equate them with that descent." We have a good laugh.

"What do you plan to do on your day off?"

I pause and say, "I am not going to change elevation." More laughter.

Because the next day is a rest day and Suzy intends to walk, we expect never to meet again and plan to dine together at the abbey. I spiral up to my cell and sleep off the wine.

Eighteen long tables fill the dining room, ten people to a table. Suzy and I sit with eight French. When a Frenchman learns that I am walking to Santiago, he says I have made a "mistake" and chose a "terrible" time because of bad weather in Galicia, Spain in November. I do not explain why I travel when I do but think I have come at a wonderful time, and even if not the best time in his appreciation, if I came in God's time, it is perfect. It is hard to imagine that the God-time concept informs his thought processes. Again, in the middle of a conversation with someone else, he turns to me to say what a "terrible mistake" I have made. Suzy explains his behavior, saying, "The French are precious," a word choice I do not grasp. I think him a rude, arrogant, condescending boor.

Seated by the aisle, Suzy and I have passed every course down the table and served ourselves last throughout dinner. When the cheese course comes, the table is stacked with plates and bowls, wine and water bottles, and glasses. I start to slice the tip off the Brie.

"Don't cut the cheese like that," blurts out Suzy as she reaches across the table to stop me.

The idiomatic American meaning leaps to mind.

"Etiquette dictates a particular method to slice Brie," she explains. "The center section is considered best, so a wedge of Brie is sliced along the edge so that each person gets a taste of cheese in the center."

I cut the cheese without offending the French.

After dinner, Suzy and I hug goodbye. She has been a good friend, and I am sad to think I will never see her again.

Sitting in a pew waiting for compline, I watch monks in white habits go in and out of the sacristy. I want to walk into the sacristy and tell them I am a priest. I struggle to discern why. Perhaps because priests have status in the Church. Perhaps I do not want to feel invisible. Perhaps it is authenticity.

My mother's favorite controlling phrase, spoken with forceful anger, was "you are not" completed with whatever I wanted to do.

"You are not going camping by yourself." "You are not going to your friend's house." "You are not" inherently denied my identity expressed in self-initiative and self-determination. My mother's relentless denial of me caused me to doubt my "I am."

I decide to stay in the pew because I do not want other people's knowledge of my sacramental identity to define who I am or whom they think me to be or how they interact with me. God's name is YHWH, I AM, sometimes translated I AM WHO AM. In my mind, the "I am" of human beings, made in the image and likeness of God, is found in I AM, God himself. "Who am I?" is answered by I AM WHO AM.

I sit across from Bishop Robert Baker in his office: a sixteen-foot-high ceiling, crown molding, as many square feet as a small house, winged backed chairs, a massive desk. He replaced Bishop David Thompson as bishop of Charleston soon after Bishop Thompson assigned me to work in Charleston. After years of suffering under his authority, I confront Bishop Baker with the abuses of power: not being paid, being made homeless. He sits in emotionless silence. I then tell him about the "Call of Jeremiah" prophecy, with the obvious, unspoken implication that he is the high priest who has rejected the word of God.

"You are no Jeremiah," he retorts angrily, blinded by self-righteousness to the fact that he yet again fulfilled the prophecy. His face returns to its catatonic state.

At morning Mass, a sacristan hands me an English copy of the readings. Ecclesiastes includes the ominous: "When to go uphill is an ordeal, a walk something to dread."[2] I walk to the edge of

---

2 NJB, Ecclesiastes 12:5.

Conques to look at the next day's route. *Le Chemin* climbs a wall of trees.

I take a morning coffee across from the church. The abbey's twin towers frame the church's tall façade, but a Romanesque tympanum, a stone carved relief, of the Last Judgement captivates pilgrims and tour groups.

"Stop judging me," Anna says.

"I am not judging you. Every time I talk to you about not tricking and not shooting heroin, you accuse me of judging you. There is a difference between judging someone's actions and judging a person. God judges people, people judge actions. You might be able to get away with that bullshit obfuscation with other people, but I know my theology."

"Well, I am sure you do. That must be why you, a priest, are with me, a heroin addict and a prostitute."

"I am with you because I love you, but you love heroin more than me."

"I'm an addict. What do you expect?"

"I expect you to do what you were doing the day we met. Getting off heroin."

"Well, I'm trying." She starts to cry. "To love me, you have to accept the addiction."

"No, I do not. I love you, but I hate the addiction. You are not the addiction. The addiction is not Anna, not the real Anna. It is the lie of Anna, the false Anna. I love the real Anna."

I put my arms around her. She leans her head on my shoulder.

Central sits Christ in the seat of judgment. To his left stands two angels, one holding the Book of Life and Saint Michael holding incense. To his right stands Mary wearing a starry cloak, Peter with a key in one hand and a shepherd's staff in the other, and a saint I do not know. Christ raises his right hand toward Heaven. His left hand points down toward Hell. Beneath his feet, an angel welcomes the faithful to Heaven through an open doorway, and demons feed the damned into the mouth of a beast, whose head is thrust through Hell's open door.

In Hell, Satan sits on his own throne of judgment. Around him, souls suffer punishment appropriate to their sins. Demons pull out a scandalmonger's tongue, hang a money lender by his money bag and shove a fat glutton mouth agape down into flames. Two hand-bound lovers stand beside Satan's throne awaiting his judgment.

Anna calls me every day, but I have not heard from her for a couple days, and I have not called. I wonder what she is doing but also feel a little relieved. Then she calls. "Hey, darling. I need your help." So, I drive to Charleston.

A month or so later, when she does not call for a couple days, I lie in bed worrying about what is happening to her. I call her son Brandon, several of her girlfriends, guys she knows. Nobody knows where she is. I drive to Remount Road, where she works. I do not find her. Finally, she calls, and I go to her.

"We can't seem to stay away from each other," Anna says.

We feel bound to each other. We call it love.

In contrast to the disordered chaos of Hell, saints live in their own rooms in God's house, and angels attend to them.

In the abbey's bookstore, I purchase the Michelin guidebook and realize the full extent of my blundering. On day one, from Le Puy-en-Velay to Saint-Privat-d'Allier, elevation changes were 900 meters. On day two, when I tromped in and out of the Allier gorge, elevation changes were 1,310 meters. On day six, from

Aubrac to Saint-Chély, I descended 497 meters over 8 kilometers; on day seven, from L'Estrade to La Rosière, 303 meters over 5.5 kilometers; and the descent down into Conques, 300 meters over 3 kilometers. No measurement included the countless undulations between peaks and valleys. Actual elevation changes were much greater than my simple calculations. For 215 kilometers, I blundered in profound ignorance through the Massif Central and wrecked my feet.

After midday prayer with the monks, I wander around the church. Tucked in a corner, like an unwanted present, sits a roughly chiseled statue of a pilgrim crawling up stairs hand over foot. The stairs lead to empty space, an unknown end, but the pilgrim climbs nonetheless. *Here I am:* a priest unwanted by Church authorities but a pilgrim still in the Church crawling to the edge of the abyss.

In Christian tradition, "abyss" represents both the emptiness of Hell and the depths of God's love. I wonder where I will end my Way.

Dark Night of the Soul theology also has two similar, disparate interpretations: God has abandoned the suffering servant, and God is so close that the suffering servant cannot perceive God. Discernment between the two is difficult. I wonder which Way I am walking. I hope for and want God to be with me but feel more than abandoned.

I meet Russ, Bruce and Tim in a garden by the monastery. Russ invites me to drink "one beer." He looks apprehensive. I declined their invitations twice before.

"We have to celebrate the finish of your walk," I say, with some apprehension myself.

Across from the church, we drink beer and toast our accomplishment.

"Are you carrying a rock from home?" Tim asks.

"I picked one up at the first cross I came to."

"There is a tradition in which pilgrims pick up a rock from one cross, carry it to the next cross, drop that rock, then pick up another rock."

He and I say simultaneously, "So all rocks go to Santiago." We all laugh.

"Are you carrying a *concha?*" Tim asks.

"I bought one in Le Puy-en-Velay."

"The original tradition was that pilgrims picked up a shell in Santiago to prove that they had made the Way."

I start to speak, but he interjects, "Traditions change," which is what I was about to say.

Tim works as a lawyer, which explains why I feel like he is cross-examining me. A French tour group comes through, and Tim excuses himself to listen to the guide's explanation of the tympanum. I feel relieved. Tim has interesting things to say, but conversations lack the ease that marks true friendship. Russ, Bruce and I drink more beer and laugh the afternoon away.

Bruce, who loves French cuisine, describes it as "bread for breakfast, bread for lunch and bread with something else for dinner."

In the same mocking vein, Russ decries, "Seeing one more beautiful valley and town after another."

I tell them that I learned how to slice Brie the night before. "I've probably offended half of France with my culinary ignorance."

"I didn't know that either," Russ answers. "We've probably offended the other half."

We say goodbye with handshakes and *"Bon Chemin."*

I cross the square and walk toward Laurant, Katrin, Suzan and Jacques, who just walked into Conques. *Coincidence* pops into

my head, then remind myself, *No, not coincidence. Providence.*
We make plans to meet for dinner. They settle in at the Abbey. I
spiral up to my cell and sleep off the beer.

At dinner, I end up next to the wall, with Suzan opposite me,
Jacques beside her, and to my left a Frenchmen, who speaks little
English: another awkward linguistic situation. Equally awkward
is the conversation.

Suzan, infatuated with monks, explains that priests in religious orders take vows, but diocesan priests—like me—"can do
whatever they want."

Staring at her, I cannot decide if I want to laugh or scream.

My Stick, God's Stick

DAYS 11 - 14

A monk celebrates Sunday Mass for pilgrims in a small, moldy chapel decorated with faded frescoes depicting a bird in flight holding a book, lions with wings, horses with wings, angels with wings. Lots of wings flutter about the ceiling.

After Mass Laurant, Katrin, Suzan, Jacques and I say goodbye with hugs and kisses. I even hug the standoffish Jacques. Suzan says, "By the time you arrive in Santiago, you will be changed." Fear of what change that might be brings tears to my eyes.

I descend to a stream, then as I climb out of Conques, I understand why a man might die of a heart attack in the mountains. My heart feels like it is about to explode.

Anna is dressed in a business skirt, blouse, jacket and low heels. The expression on my face communicates my quizzical reaction.

"I want to look my best," she explains. "It might not make sense to you, but I am going to feel and look horrible. At least, I want to start by feeling good about myself."

"Okay, but you are going? Yes?" The tension in my body rises.

"Yes, my bags are packed, but I have to do my makeup."

"You look great. Your makeup looks great."

She disappears into the back of the trailer, and as I wait, nerves ratchet up. Half an hour later, she reappears. "Okay. I am ready."

I pick up her bag, a carry-on.

"Oh wait, I forgot to pack something."

"The hospital has everything you need."

"If I accidentally packed paraphernalia, I'll get in trouble."

"I thought you said you forgot something."

"I have to double-check." *Her eyes flash defiance. She disappears into the back with her bag.*

After another half-hour wait, she comes out. "I just have to make one phone call."

"We need to go now." *The tension in my body has risen to the point that I feel pain in my chest.*

"I have to call Brandon."

"You are just making excuses to delay going."

"No, I am not. I am making arrangements that have to be made."

"No. You are making excuses just like you did last week when we tried to do this. He's twenty years old. If he needs help, I'll help him."

"He's my son. I need to call him." *She speaks with anger.*

She disappears into the back, and after yet another half-hour wait, she comes out and sits down on a sofa. "I am not going."

"You have to go. You have to get clean."

"You don't know what detox is like. I've been there before. They lock you in a barren room, and you sit there for days in agony. The first time I went I lasted three days. The second time I lasted one day."

"Well, you don't have a choice. Nothing we have done has worked."

"I'll go back to the clinic."

"We've tried the clinic, several times. It never worked."

Bound to her, her nightmare is my nightmare. So, to end my nightmare, she has to end her nightmare. The tension in my chest feels like a heart attack. I think, Getting Anna well is killing me.

Sitting across from a heart doctor in a white coat with a name tag and a stethoscope around his neck— all so typical and normal—I listen as he gives me the results of my stress test. I passed the physical part, walking on a treadmill while hooked up to a heart monitor. But then he starts talking about the psychological and emotional tests, which involved my filling out questionnaires. He talks around the results, and I do not grasp what he is saying.

"Doc, give it to me straight."

"You'll be dead in six months or severely handicapped for life." My eyes widen, and I nod.

"I can see it in your face," he continues. "You look extremely stressed and miserable."

Serving God in the nightmare of Saint Joseph's Church in Columbia, South Carolina under the abusive tyranny of Msgr. Charles Rowland in my first year as a priest, is killing me.

Part way up the mountain, I come to Chapelle Sainte Foy, a local pilgrimage site with a miraculous spring that cures eye problems. *What the Way needs is a spring that miraculously heals feet.* I bandaged blisters with Compeed but endure pain with each step.

Once on top of the mountain, the trail undulates sharply through woods, fields and deserted hamlets. On one section, *Le Chemin* overlays logging roads not marked with *balises*, where a compass, guesswork and an intuitive feel for the Way guide me. I do not miss a turn and feel proud. I top a short, tough ascent with low hills rolling out before me and a sunny sky above. In a field, I enjoy a picnic.

Outside the small town Prayssac, I arrive at a *pausa café* along with three attractive French women. The man who runs it looks at me, then at the women and flirts with them. I keep walking and pass through hills, farms and woodlands.

Ready to stop after nineteen rough kilometers, I enter Decazeville via another murderous asphalt descent. Poor, industrial, charmless, without a sense of peace, pervaded with a beaten down spirit, the town gives me a bad feeling. I committed to listen to my intuition. As I walk in, I know I will walk out. In a public toilet, urine covers the floor. The brutal asphalt climb out of Decazeville is worse than the descent into it.

The road flattens out, and at the church of Saint Roch in the hamlet Saint Roch, people call my name. Manon and Josée, whom I met in a bar days earlier, sit in chairs and invite me to sit. I look at the chair, down the road, then again at the chair, and sit.

"Did you stop at Jon Luc's *pausa café* in Prayssac?"

"Jon Luc was more interested in flirting with three pretty French women than talking to me."

"He makes the best coffee in France and his mother's pastries were fantastic." They go on and on about the coffee and the pastries.

We start off, and half a kilometer down the road and in a beautiful act of charity, three black children approach us and offer each of us a fig from a tree in their yard.

Manon speaks English well, Josée poorly. Sometimes Manon and I converse in English, which leaves out Josée; other times, they speak French, which excludes me: but we make it work. Josée has a pretty singing voice. She sings the French stanzas of "Ultreia," the pilgrim hymn we sang at Conques. Manon and I join on the Latin refrain. *Ultreia*, a Latin word, means "beyond, onwards, further." To me the word rings as a rally cry or a cheer to encourage pilgrims to keep walking and seeking.

In Livinhac-le-Haut, the church sits in the center of the town's main square, and rows of buildings line the sides. Opposite the church, Manon and Josée, Lonnie from Holland, and Brian from Ireland and I sit on steps to a covered walkway that leads between buildings to the *gîte municipal* around back. We tire of waiting for the *gîte municipal* to officially open and move in like we belong. After my normal end-of-hike routine—shower, laundry, first aid—my daily chores, I hang wet clothes on a line in the backyard. I pay for my bed at a nearby bar, then take a coffee and make notes in my journal. Soon everyone from the *gîte* arrives, and we wile away the afternoon with coffee, beer, pastries and conversation. Manon and Josée again talk about John Luc's coffee and pastries.

Wind heralds a coming storm, so I move my clothes onto the covered back porch.

Brian and I share a room. He assures me that he does not snore, which is welcomed news. I need a good night's sleep.

Brian does not snore, but church bells, opposite our window, ring the hours all night long. They keep me up late and wake me before sunrise.

I slip out of the room and down to the back porch. My clothes are not dry. I brought slow-drying clothes for a walk that requires fast drying clothes. Wet clothes have been a reoccurring issue. To dry my clothes, I hang them on my backpack as I walk. Rain days exacerbate this problem.

I switch on the porch light. The light illuminates a spider with inch-long legs that fell into a porcelain bathtub. He tries to crawl out but slips on the porcelain. I lower my *bâton* beside him, thinking he might crawl up the stick. He fears the stick. I move it closer. He moves away but slips back. I maneuver my *bâton* under him and lift him up. He falls off. I try again. Almost at the top, he falls off. I try again. He falls off immediately. I am not sure how long I work to rescue the spider, but it happens. The spider grabs the stick. I raise him to the top of the tub and flick him away. He lands on the floor and scuttles under the tub.

When God called me to be a priest, I thought the Catholic Church God created to be the sacrament of salvation for the world was the instrument to reorder my life, to make my life and the reason for my creation make sense. In seminary, I learned that we project our images of our father onto God and of our mother onto the Church. I was delighted to learn that I had a Father in Heaven who was not like my father on earth, a divine Father who believed I can be something, a priest. I was delighted to have a Mother who was not like my mother, a Holy Mother Church who affirmed my "I am." But abuse meted out by the Church to which God called me to be a priest disabused me of those beliefs. God called me to be a priest in the Church he created and, with his stick, beat me. God is the problem, and if God is the solution, he has not solved the problem.

> "See now that I, I alone, am he, and there is no god besides me. It is I who bring both death and life, I who inflict wounds and heal them, and from my hand no one can deliver."[3]

---

3 NAB, Deuteronomy 32:39

I am trapped in a relationship with God, not just because I am a priest, but because there is only one God, who wounded me with his Church but has not healed me.

The Way passes through fields, pastures, woods and hills with moderate climbs. Because many pilgrims finish in Conques and some have fallen by the wayside due to injury, the number of pilgrims decreases. Not as noticeable the day I left Conques, as pilgrims spread out over the trail, the decrease becomes obvious. I spend more time with no pilgrim in sight.

I come over a small rise and, down below, see Manon and Josée. With toilet paper in hand, one squats on the side of the road, while the other stands with the backpacks. They do not notice me.

I turn to cows in a pasture. *"Bonjour, Monsieur Vache. Bonjour, Madam Vache."* I glance downhill to make sure they notice me, then wait until they finish.

Manon apologizes. They did not think anyone was behind them.

"No reason to apologize. We all have to go."

We walk together for a couple kilometers, then I fall back to pee.

On a stone wall near Église de Saint-Jean-Mirabel, I enjoy an expansive view of low hills and meadows. The sun warms me as my body cools. I picnic on an apple, yogurt, bread, cheese and two squares of dark chocolate. I ration my precious dark chocolate.

Another steep, asphalt plunge welcomes me to Figeac. I step down slowly and, to take pressure off my knees and feet, plant my *bâton* on the asphalt so hard that it vibrates.

In villages like Golinac, pilgrims define the culture. In a town like Figeac, with clothes hanging from my backpack, residents' facial expressions make me feel like I belong to a subculture half a step above the homeless. However, the gracious woman at the tourist office welcomes me and gives me directions to *gîtes*. Miza, whom I met on the side of a mountain several days earlier, walks in. She walks twenty kilometers a day, day in and day out, but today is her first and only planned day off. She has a big smile, and I am happy to see a familiar, friendly face.

I step into a *gîte*, where pilgrims crowd a narrow dining room, waiting for beds: Manon and Josée, Margit and Katherine, and Dematt from Ireland and Ingrid from Brittany, who travel together. The Danish women make it clear I am last in line. I shrug.

Gale arrives to register us. She sends everyone ahead of me upstairs. I register last and get an eight-bed room to myself.

I toss my clothes into a small dryer, which sits in the kitchen and run the dryer through three cycles at the highest setting to get my clothes mostly dry. Because of the long line for the upstairs shower, Katherine comes down to use the one in my room. She walks around the dining room table wearing a T-shirt and panties, an unwelcome sight.

In a plaza with a raised, open-air platform and a roof supported by decorative, wrought iron columns, I take a table and a coffee and write in my journal. Gale comes to my table and invites me to join her and her friend for an afternoon drink. I change tables and sit with her and Alex, a local carpenter, who speaks decent English. The conversation wanders different directions, then takes a flirtatious turn.

"I have a feeling about you and me," Gale says. "If I were not married . . . *Le Chemin est Le Chemin de L'amour.*" She has a sly smile and a glint in her eyes.

"You're driving me crazy," I say as I lean across the table closer to her.

I do not like that Alex witnesses the conversation, that Gale is inebriated and married or that I am a priest and maybe have someone at home. I decide I must leave and walk away from Gale, even as my body aches and trembles.

Julian, Gale's husband, makes a wonderful dinner. The conversation, a wild mix of French and English, switches rapidly from one subject to another. What we do for a living comes up. I give my stock answer: *"Mon travail est de marcher."* Josée one-ups me. She really does walk for work. She walks a postal route. Laughter rocks the table.

Yet again, I listen to Manon and Josée brag about the coffee and pastries at John Luc's *pausa café*.

After dinner, Julian "stamps" our *créanciales*. Pilgrim stamps are often identical, with only place names changed. Some are unique, designed for a particular *gîte* or village. He draws, in outline form, the profile of the face of a man.

The Danish women drop off a multitool with a corkscrew since it cannot be carried on a plane. My multitool has no corkscrew so I grab this one, thinking a corkscrew might prove valuable.

Diffused through a veil of grey clouds, dawn's light filters down between buildings. I walk on streets darkened by shadows and brightened with soft, ambient light. Rain falls in a light shower, and the temperature has dropped.

By the time I top the climb out of Figeac, I am sweating. I open my jacket's vents and unzip it halfway, which lets my body breathe but also lets in rain. A steady shower falls, often light but sometimes hard. Soon besodden with rain and sweat from my boots to my hat, I encourage myself with the thought that once soaking wet, I cannot become more wet. Soaking has a finite limit, and I have reached it. Therefore, there is no reason to stop, and every reason to walk.

I turn up a small hill, and in front of me walks Miza. I walk so much faster than her that she must have started at 6 a.m. Four foot and eleven inches tall, in her sixties, with an uphill pace half mine, in pouring rain, an umbrella in her left hand, and alone, Miza walks through the misery with resolve and determination. On that unmarked hill, by a nameless hamlet and in the rain, I christen her the Indomitable Miza.

The rain becomes a steady, heavy shower, the meridian passes, and the temperature barely climbs above the morning low. The trail flattens, which decreases physical exertion and reduces body-generated heat. Soaking wet and cold, I too walk in misery.

Another phenomenon plagues the Way. I noticed it when I departed Conques and when I left Livenhac-le-Haut. Now I see it again. Signs listing distances and estimated walking times do not correspond with times and distances on other signs or with my empirical four-kilometer-per-hour pace.

A sign says the distance to Gréalou is 20.5 kilometers; one hour later, a sign says the distance is 20.5 kilometers. A sign says the distance to Gréalou is 9 kilometers; half an hour later, a sign says the distance is 9 kilometers. A sign says the distance to Cajarc is 17.3 kilometers: an hour later, a sign says the distance is 17.0 kilometers. A sign says walking time to Cajarc is two hours; an hour later, a sign says walking time is three hours. I rename the small town Cajarc "Retreating Cajarc."

I muse on the phenomenon of the signs, and musings morph into theories.

The Circle Theory: I wonder if I walked in circles, but I reached locations identified in my guidebook according to my four-kilometer-per-hour average.

The Personal Insanity Theory: Crazy people do not perceive reality yet think they are sane, which is why they are crazy. Sane people can perceive that they are detached from reality, but if sane people know they are crazy, then they are not sane. This theory circles on itself and can never be dismissed.

The Insane Balisage Theory: *Balisages* mark the Way with *balises*. If a schizophrenic, incapable of discerning reality or a sadistic psychopath who rejoiced in the misery of pilgrims marked the Way, that would explain the insanity of the signs.

The Camino Zone Theory: Through mist swirling like cigarette smoke, I hear Rod Serling's voice: "You have walked down the Way of Faith, a trek through another dimension, a dimension of body and soul, a land of shadow and light, a place where substance and spirit cleave together and apart, where dimensions of time and space have no meaning. You have just walked into the Camino Zone."

The Aligot Theory: We like to think that a kilometer is a kilometer, but kilometer measurements changed between signs. *Aligot* explains why. We know a big bowl of *aligot* stretches a full kilometer, but if *balisages* measure kilometers with *aligot* made by different cooks with different recipes in different sized bowls, then elasticity and volume would change from one bowl to another and cause kilometer measurements to differ.

The Demonic Possession Theory: What if demons trafficking in anguish and despair possessed the *balisages*? Possession would explain the cruelty.

Malachi Martin began *Windswept House, a Vatican Novel* with a Black Mass, a satanic mockery of *Missa Sancta*. The Black Mass was celebrated by Catholic priests partly in the Vatican and partly in the Diocese of Charleston. A laywoman in the diocese wrote Malachi Martin and asked if he wrote about a fictional or historical event. He answered that a Black Mass was, in fact, celebrated in the Vatican with the parts of the Black Mass that could not be performed in the Vatican being performed simultaneously in the Diocese of Charleston. This is perhaps the most evil thing a priest can do, and a priest committed this heinous atrocity in my diocese. That would explain the culture of cruelty pervading the Diocese of Charleston.

Despite villainous signs, I walk into the village Gréalou. Wet cold penetrates my bones. I have not eaten since breakfast, six hours earlier. I need shelter. Tables covered by umbrellas offer too little protection, sheds sit too far back on private property, decrepit buildings with collapsed roofs look dangerous and porous. I turn a corner and find a small shed with benches along the walls and a table between them, all sized for kindergarteners. A man from a house across the narrow road asks if I want coffee. I have stumbled upon a *pausa café*. With Manon and Josée's talk of John Luc's fare replaying in my head, I get coffee and a pastry. The small cup of watery coffee tastes like it was brewed by melting half a coffee-colored crayon in the pot, but I wrap both hands around the cup to warm my hands. The pastries are stale, convenience store–style pastries. After half an hour, I force myself to walk. My muscles have cooled and tightened and need a half hour to limber and warm back up. Rain slackens to a drizzle, then stops.

In a forest, I pass a dolmen, a rock slab on two upright rocks. Dolmens date to the Neolithic age. Archeologists do not know who erected dolmens but speculate that they functioned as tombs or as altars of sacrifice.

I catch Retreating Cajarc at the top of a ridge where one last rocky descent separates me from rest. Halfway down, an underground stream surfaces in the back of a wide cave, forms a clear pool, then bounds into a cataract and plunges to the valley floor below. Mary appeared to Saint Bernadette in a grotto, and in folklore, fairies dwell in grottos. Neither Mary nor fairies appear to me.

I arrive at the *gîte municipal* first, then Brian, Mary Claire from California and Wilfred from Austria.

While Mary Claire and I sit at table talking, Wilfred walks back and forth to the shower wearing a T-shirt and tighty-whities. Mary Claire winces. Women suffer the same unwelcomed sights as men. I lean over to her and whisper, "Modesty is a lost virtue." She nods.

"Does the *gîte* provide a hair dryer?" Wilfred asks. The question announces "rookie" in flashing, red neon letters. The walk from Figeac to Cajarc is his first day.

I answer with a laugh and a "no."

Miza walks in last, walking twelve kilometers more than her twenty-kilometer average. She gets into bed and is so still I wonder if she is alive. I look in on her to make sure she is breathing.

Brian invites me to cook with him. I decline and feel uneasy about my answer. Worn out again, I want to be alone. Wearing sandals, I go out to a restaurant, feast on a substantial, thick, medium rare steak, and for dessert enjoy flan with a coconut crust.

The *gîte's* entrance is a small nook with stairs to the second-floor dormitory. We left our boots here, and for hours, five pairs of wet, sweaty boots have emitted vaporous odors that have pooled in the nook. The stench nauseates me.

Amid the stench that pooled all night long, I lace up wet boots with dread. Within the first kilometer, my boots soak my socks. It portends to be another long day.

As I walk through a forest on trails and roads, a Frenchman driving a vintage Renault van stops. He has a shotgun and two hunting dogs. I gesture as if shooting a rifle and ask, *"Chausseur?"* I learned the word from "no hunting" signs.

"Oui," he answers. He talks about hunting, but I cannot follow his French.

"Chien?" I ask. Again, I cannot follow his French, but he speaks proudly about his dogs, and they look happy.

He asks if I am *"un pélerin."*

"Oui, je marche á Santiago."

We part with *"au revoir."* A kind man, he is probably lonely and wanted to talk to someone. I understand. I feel lonely and enjoyed the company and the conversation despite its brevity and linguistic challenges.

I walk among woods and pastures with sheep munching on grass. In the quiet of the late morning forest, sheep chewing grass sounds comparatively loud. I imagine a shepherd lying in the bright sun and soft grass with the peaceful voices of nature lulling him into dreamy slumbers, which is what I want to do. Exhaustion clings to my soul, but I keep walking.

At an outdoor café in the village Limogne-en-Quercy, while eating lunch, Brian walks up the road. I wave him down, and he sits with me. Wanting to make up for declining his invitation to eat the night before, I offer to buy him something, a coffee or anything, but he declines. He bought food at a grocery and plans to picnic.

We leave town together and walk into a forest. A sign directs us to a dolmen half a kilometer off trail. I want to see it but cannot stomach an extra kilometer. I hate going off the Way. So does Brian. He stayed in a *gîte* advertised "as three hundred meters off the Way, but it was more like seven hundred." He looks at me with a wry smile. We both know the owners advertised a shorter distance to lure pilgrim money to their *gîte*.

Pilgrims develop a feel for distance and measure tenths of kilometers with their feet. Unnecessary distance adds up; a couple hundred meters here, a couple hundred there adds up to a kilometer; an extra kilometer every day for twenty days adds up to an extra day's walk.

Brian stops for lunch and sits on a stone wall. I offer to sit with him, but he shoos me down the Way.

"Good man. You go. I'll be along."

As I walk away, I think about the appellation "Good Man." I am not sure if I was a good man. I feel like I failed as a pilgrim when I declined his invitation to eat together.

After walking through fields and forests, the last march of the day passes from the small village Varaire to the smaller village Bach. Guidebooks disagree on the distance by an exasperating 700 meters. Worn out and with feet raw and beaten, I walk into the courtyard at the *gîte La Grange Saint Jacques* and speak French to a man who steps out of the house.

"You can speak English to me."

Mike is English. Michelle, his wife, is French. He offers me a drink, but I explain that I need to settle in and rest. When I take off my boots, I have a new blister and coin the trademark phrase "New Day, New Blister."

Christian from France who lives in the French alps shares the *gîte* with me. He speaks as much English as I speak French, but we communicate. He has an infection in several toes, takes penicillin and walks with pain. He asks if I want to visit the local church. With the admonition not to walk extra meters echoing in my head and despite misgivings about my physical condition, the need to pray supersedes other concerns.

With walls of rough-cut grey stone, a stone floor, interlocking Gothic arches supporting the roof and clean lines, this unpretentious yet beautiful church has the first statue of the patroness of France that I have seen: Sainte Jeanne d'Arc, adorned in breastplate and a blue cloak with a sword in her right hand and a French flag in her left. The beautiful Joan is one of my favorite saints. I ask for her prayers.

Back at the *gîte*, I talk with Michelle in the kitchen mostly in English but a little in French. Then I sit outside at the dinner table. Mike sits down, then Christian.

Mike walked the Way and wrecked his feet crossing the Pyrenees. Initially happy that he found an excuse to quit and go home, he sobered up and kept walking.

"All pilgrims go through that experience," he says

"Not me. I had a physically identical but emotionally opposite experience. I felt distraught when I thought I had to abandon because of my physical condition," I say.

He says Spaniards distinguish between *peregrinos* and *tourigrinos*. *Tourigrinos* carry a day bag and have their luggage transferred by car. *Peregrinos*, like me and Christian, drag themselves into *gîtes*.

Mike, Christian and I switch between French and English, with Mike sometimes translating. When dinner comes and Michelle sits down, I wonder how we will bridge the linguistic gap. Michelle orders, *"Ne parler que français."*

After struggling with French and working hard to communicate with people from many countries with words from any language scattered in my head, and with those same people making the same efforts, Michelle's order to only speak French is more rude and more contrary to the Way than anything I have encountered. Her order infuriates me.

As it happens, Michelle launches into a diatribe, during which Christian repeats *"Oui"* and her husband eats in silence.

When Michelle goes back to the kitchen, I ask what she talked about. Mike answers, "Politics." For all I know, she denounced Americans who don't speak French.

I see my parents in Mike and Michelle. My mom dominated my father to the point where his mind was hers and he did not have independent thoughts except in his work. She even micromanaged my dad's relationship with me. When I first saw the *Oresteia*, which begins with Clytemnestra murdering Agamemnon, her husband, and eating his brain, I watched with stunned horror the mythic representation of my homelife.

Not surprising, considering my parental model, I am in an imbalanced, unequal relationship with Anna, although I argue with her and even left her at times. I do not know if Anna and I can reorder our relationship. What I do know is that our relationship will not be lived in disorder and that I will not be passive, compliant or submissive. But more than that, I do not want a relationship in which I have to fight for balance.

Kicking the Goad

DAYS 15 - 17

In early morning haze, Christian leads us through town and down a highway with no space for pedestrians. Turbulent air from passing trucks and cars buffet us.

"We've walked off the Way," I say.

"No, we have not," insists Christian.

I lead us down a dirt road between green pastures, where we find a faded *balise* on a fence post.

"See, I did not lead us wrong," Christian says.

"The *balise* is faded. We are on an old path, and the road was dangerous," I point out.

We soon find brightly painted *balises* on a side path that intersects the road we walk on.

"See, I led the right way," insists Christian.

"The new *balises* are coming a different direction, a different path," I explain, thinking the conclusion obvious.

"I led us the right way," Christian says again.

I glance at him askance. I have never felt comfortable with people who cannot admit to obvious mistakes.

In woods, an older black and white female dog with long hair and a white Labrador puppy, whose ribs show, look at us with hope. My heart goes out to them. I speak to the older one. She lies down and rolls on her back, and I rub her belly.

The only food I have is two squares of chocolate, which is bad for dogs and which I keep for myself. Thoughts of walking to Santiago with these dogs swirl around my head, but I am struggling to take care of myself.

I walk up to the trailer, and Anna is sitting on the porch with a jet-black Staffordshire bull terrier named Onyx. Anna dog-sat for him before.

"I'm going to adopt him," Anna says.

"How are you going to take care of him? You need to get off heroin and get a job."

"Don't be mad. They were abusing him. I had to get him out of that house. They kept him in a cage all day. They kicked the cage. They yelled at him."

"I'm sympathetic. All my animals are rescues. But you can't afford to have a dog."

"He won't cost much to feed. It is just one little thing."

"No, it is not one little thing. I pay for your rent, your food. I pay for everything. You need to stop doing heroin and get a job. This dog will be another excuse why you can't get your life together. He will cost a lot."

Weeks later, Anna admits she cannot keep Onyx. She cries when she says goodbye. I take him to a shelter and pay the fee to ensure his adoption.

With a heavy heart, I walk away from the two dogs, who follow with hopeful expressions until we cross a road, where the older female leads the younger one toward a village.

As we walk through lightly wooded green hills, Christian asks, *"Catholique?"*

I smile and answer, "Yes."

My answer does not satisfy him. Later, he asks again, *"Catholique?"* "Yes."

Still not convinced, he asks, "Godfather François?"

"Oui, el Papa," a mix of French and Spanish.

"I am very Catholic," he says.

I have known lots of very Catholic Catholics (and very Protestant Protestants) obstinate in error, arrogant in obstinacy, who make the Christian Faith a scourge to beat people. "Very Catholic" does not impress me. Saints say the first step on the journey to God is humility.

I hope to lunch in the village La Pech, but La Pech sits one kilometer off the Way. I am not going to add two kilometers to my walk, and the guidebook indicates that the trail passes through the edge of Flaujac-Poujois three kilometers ahead. Christian hugs me good-bye as if it is a grand parting, but uncomfortable in his presence, I am happy to separate from him. Christian limps toward La Pech. I walk with painful steps up into light brown, rocky hills, covered with dry grass, scraggly brush and stunted pine trees.

I do not find Flaujac-Poujois, and I eat one square of chocolate. An hour later, I still have found nothing, and I eat my second and last square of chocolate.

The sun comes out in force and cooks me and the plateau. I run out of water and empathize with the trees. Famished, exhausted, walking on empty physical reserves and pained feet, those two dogs are not the only hungry pups lost in the wilderness.

Driving near St. George, South Carolina years ago, I saw a dead dog on the road, a flock of vultures around that dog, and another dog asleep by the road. With pork I grilled the day before, it was easy to coax the exhausted Walker hound into my car. I named him George. Thinking about that day, I cry as I walk.

The descent to the outskirts of Cahors follows a small, narrow asphalt road through neighborhoods and straight down the steep, convex face of a hill. I descend with pained feet and two thoughts: I need to take a rest day, and I want a beer.

I planned to take a day off every Sunday but altered my schedule in Conques to be with friends. Now I am altering my schedule because my body is worn to nothing and worry that more, inevitable physical trauma will force me to abandon. The decision to stop for a day disheartens me.

Foremost in my mind is beer. After a hike, nothing satisfies like a beer. Beer quenches thirst, feeds the body and calms the mind without inebriety. An after-hike beer is a blessing. I plan to enjoy two beers, a double blessing, at the first bar I find.

I pass residences, apartments, businesses and intersections but find neither cafés nor bars as I drag myself through the beerless desert of Cahors. I cross the river Lot on a four-lane bridge and step into the medieval city limits. *I am close to beer.*

Someone yells from across the road. I ignore it. The yelling persists.

"Monsieur, êtes-vous un pèlerin?" An older woman waves at me.

My head drops. *I'm never going to get a beer.* I cross the road and step into a small pilgrim office staffed by two older women. They give me lemonade.

God, I know you have a sense of humor, but I am tired of being the butt of your jokes.

After the lemonade, I say, *"Merci beaucoup"* and start to leave to find beer. They stop me. *"D'où êtes-vous? Où allez-vous? Comment vous appelez-vous? Arrêtez-vous á Cahors? Voulez-vous un hôtel?*

Pouvons-nous réserver une chambre pour vous? Où? Pour combien de jours?" French exacerbates my frustration, and I simmer as I resign myself to no-beer martyrdom and a second cup of lemonade.

"Je voudrais une chambre pour deux nuits."

They give me a city map, locate a hotel near the cathedral and make reservations. As I leave, they look disappointed. I think they want me to make a donation. With emotions pricked by exhaustion, I harbor a no-beer resentment.

Because of the lemonade, I forgo beer until I find my hotel, *Le Coin des Halles*, where, at table, under the shade of an umbrella, with an e-cigarette in hand and a glass of wine in front of her, looking off into the distance as she ponders something, sits Suzy. We said goodbye in Conques, expecting never to see each other again.

"I don't believe it," I say.

Had that lady not waved me down, had I not stopped, had those ladies not given me lemonade, had they not made me reservations, and so on, I never would have found Suzy in Cahors. God's providence was at work, and I did not see it. In the Ancient Near East, ploughmen used goads—long, pointed sticks—to prod oxen. In the Bible, the goad represents God's labors to prod his people to walk his Way, with resistance imaged as oxen kicking the goad. I laugh at myself because I was a beast, a goad-kicker. I also feel like a cad because I was not more gracious to those sweet, helpful ladies.

I join Suzy and down a beer and another beer.

I comment that my feet throb, even as we sit. She says that the rocks pounded her feet too. I also confide that my boots stink so badly that they "offend all of France and half of Spain." She laughs. At 4 p.m., when her *gîte* opens, she leaves. Too exhausted to stand for goodbyes, I remain seated when she kisses my cheek.

"We'll probably see each other again, so this is not really goodbye," she says.

"I'm sure we will see each other again."

Everything in my room—walls, ceiling, Art Deco furniture, fixtures—is white. I love the room. Even better, when I shower, I recognize the faucet system. When I take off my boots, I have four new blisters, and my feet still throb.

Mass is celebrated in the cathedral's former sacristy. The cabinetry for vestments and vessels is still in place. The priest says the first Eucharistic prayer, the longest option, and we stand throughout Mass. My legs shake as I stand.

That evening, I sit on a bench in the half-lit square. On the cathedral's façade are thirty-three shallow arched vaults designed for statues, each one empty. I stare at the silent, dark, closed cathedral and wonder about the providence of God, which confuses me as much as surprises me, which I sometimes recognize but oftentimes miss.

What is providential about God's call to the priesthood and the subsequent abuse I received in the Catholic Church? What is providential about my relationship with Anna? What good will God bring out of these nightmares?

With a day off, I tour Cahors.

A section of Cahors' medieval city gates with ramparts and parapets remains. The stone walls rise high, the towers much higher.

The Arc de Diane, a Roman bath, has interlocking pools with mosaic tiles below a massive stone arch, which suggest a building of great prominence once stood here.

Cahors' First World War monument memorializes soldiers of the war, but not Marshall Pétain, regarded as a hero who saved

France in the First World War and a traitor who capitulated to the Germans in the Second World War. Called out of retirement as French armies reeled under the German onslaught, France asked too much of him, and unable to conjure a miracle, the French blamed him for not salvaging what others lost. After the war, the French made him a figurehead of blame and never forgave him.

I know about the titanic struggle to forgive.

In one of many homilies on confession and forgiveness, I asked the people, "Of the three forms of forgiveness: forgiveness by God, forgiveness by others and forgiveness by self—which is the easiest and which is the hardest?" Everyone knew the answer: forgiveness by God is easiest, forgiveness of self the hardest. I then asked, "Why are we not as merciful to ourselves as God is to us?" I know the theological solution: the grace we receive in confession, when God forgives us, includes the grace to forgive others and self. I do not know how to let that grace operate in my life. Neither did I ever imagine as a young priest that God could hurt someone as badly as he hurt me. Never did I imagine I would have to forgive God. How do I forgive myself for saying yes to God's call for me to be a priest? How do I forgive God for calling me to be a priest in an abusive Church?

I have no answers.

The façade of Cathédrale Saint-Étienne de Cahors evokes the character of a medieval castle. Three massive domes, the largest in France, form the roof of the rectangular church. Inside the church, I stare up at a dome and catch myself from falling over. An organist practices, and I enjoy a serendipitous recital of grand, classical, religious music.

In the cathedral's cloisters, I rest on a bench and enjoy peace and quiet. In a hall beside the cloisters, Xie Lei, a Chinese artist, exhibits his oil paintings. A painting entitled *Leading* enraptures me. Against a forest of slender trees and pinkish spring foliage, people walk single file down a trail. They wear black, except for one dressed in white, who turns off the path to follow his own way. I have followed my own way in my life but with half steps.

Being more tourist than pilgrim feels odd, like a shoe that does not fit. Even with broken feet and wasted muscles, I look forward to a return to the pilgrim life. Walking constitutes incontrovertible and measurable physical progress and gives me a modicum of reason to hope for spiritual progress.

I also hope my body will heal while I sleep.

Loud, obnoxious drunks hang about the square until early morning. Garbage trucks arrive to empty metal dumpsters, and metal clangs against metal. Talkative vendors arrive to set up booths for the Cahors market. I crawl out of bed exhausted.

I leave Cahors via Pont Valentré. Built in the fourteenth century, with six Gothic arches over the walkway, diamond piers, three square towers, wide enough for a horse-drawn carriage, all stone, the bridge is an architectural masterpiece.

I cross the pedestrian-only bridge, then climb stairs carved roughly in rock, then up natural rock. The climb tops out high above Cahors in a forest of stunted trees. In hot but not miserable weather, I stroll on tree-covered trails, trails lined with stone walls, and narrow footpaths through rolling terrain with thick brush, open fields and forests with trees grown to full height.

In the village Lascabanes, by the door of a house, stands an ingenious statue of Saint James. A weathered, aged, twisted remnant of a tree stump forms his torso and arms, broken scrap his legs and feet, a black oval disk his face. For eyes, he has light colored disks, one larger than the other, and a light-colored rectangle for a nose. Two roots, fat on one side, drawn to a point on the other, form lips. He wears a straw hat. In his right hand and for a staff, he holds a cut sapling upside down. With his head cocked to one side and propped in a corner to maintain a precarious balance, he stands awkwardly. The statue gives the impression of a pilgrim dumbfounded and in need of help, distorted in body and soul, but with open arms welcoming whatever and whomever comes. His left arm points to a destination, a goal, the journey down the Way. We look at each other as if in mirrors.

To be kinder to myself and merciful to my feet, I am determined to stop in Lascabanes, after walking twenty-two kilometers. The *gîte municipal* is locked. As I sit on a wall under a shady oak tree musing on this twist, Maddie and Trisha from California walk up. They have arrived in Lascabanes with the same intention as me and for the same reason—to stop after walking too far too many days. They call the telephone number of the *gîte* and get no answer. We debate a backtrack to a private *gîte* but walk to a fancy hotel on a nearby hill.

"We can sleep out. I have the gear," I joke.

"We don't have the stuff for that," Maddie answers.

I bust out laughing.

"That's not funny, Jeffrey."

"Everything is funny out here. The Way is the Way of laughter."

The paradisical hotel has a pond, manicured grounds and verandas. When we ask for a room, with hands folded in prayer, I add, *"Nous sommes fatigués,"* hoping the owner might take mercy on us. She offers us a two-bedroom apartment for €290 for a single night. I look at Maddie, say "no" and walk out. Maddie said the woman called me rude.

"What does etiquette prescribe when someone says 'no' to highway robbery?"

Maddie admonishes me. "You and all your *fatigues.*"

We laugh, then start a humorless ten-kilometer march to the small town Montcuq.

Halfway up a rocky, wooded hill, I run out of water. At the top, trees and shade disappear, and for nine and a half kilometers, we walk on a black asphalt road under the afternoon sun and roast.

They pepper me with questions. "Where do you live? What do you do? Are you married? Do you have any children? Have you ever been married?" I feel like they are interviewing me for a position—like husband.

I ask if they noticed the phenomenon of the treacherous time/distance signs. They coined their own phrase to describe it: "French Kilometers."

Two kilometers from Montcuq, they run out of water.

We take rooms at *Hôtel la Barguelonne,* run by a wonderful, sweet, friendly lady, who, after we handwash our clothes, lets us use her dryer. We throw clothes in the dryer and, after several cycles, pull out partially dry clothes.

Johanna and Meththild, two female German pilgrims in their forties, join us for dinner.

Meththild walked the Camino twenty years earlier when the Camino was little more than a dirt path and often not even that. Johanna hitchhiked the last six kilometers of today's section to Montcuq with a man whose brother runs the *gîte municipal* in Lascabanes. His brother took a day off to pick grapes in the family vineyard, and the mystery of the closed *gîte* and why Maddie, Trisha and I made a ten-kilometer forced march is revealed to ironic laughter and groans.

We also learn that the hotel is open this night because the German women had reservations. The next day, the hotel closes for the season.

Once when Maddie and Trisha wanted to finish the day's walk with a taxi, Maddie made a driving motion with her hands, as if steering a wheel, to communicate with a villager. The man led them to a stable with horses. Laughter and more laughter.

Trisha regularly hikes in California and expected the Camino to be a walk. "After two days, I decided that this was no walk. This is a hike." We all concur.

When we talk about the next day, the German ladies say that they must consult their "itinerary."

"Itinerary? You have an itinerary?" My face scrunches with incredulity.

"What do you expect?" Johanna says. "We are German." More laughter.

When Johanna says she is a doctor, I joke, "Doc, I need you to look at my feet."

"I'm not that kind of doctor." After several minutes struggling with accents and with the help of a smart phone slowed by reception problems, we translate *"psychotherapeut"* into "psychotherapist." When we clear that up, Johanna remarks, "Your feet are a long way from your head."

"Well, doc, I think my head needs to be examined," I say. Everyone laughs and says the same thing.

I want to laugh myself to sleep, but the mysterious tragicomedy of God's providence—a *gîte* closed for one day, a punishing forced march, a hotel open for one last day, how we learned the second half of the closed *gîte* story—mingles with the laughter at dinner and too much wine and the aches and pains of a bruised body and a lost soul.

The Stone Scream

DAYS 18 - 21

To make sure I get to Sunday Mass, I linger in Montcuq for the 11 a.m. Mass. To pass the time, at the town market, I kiosk-shop at booths with fish, bread, cheese, wine, meat, vegetables, honey, clothes, women's bags and belts, and crafts of many different sorts. The streets crawl with people.

The church sits on a high point, so to go to Mass, I climb a knoll. Mass feels awkward. Lay women sing the penitential rite, which is permitted, but they look uncomfortable, which makes me uncomfortable. Liturgical discomfort accompanies me throughout Mass.

Afterwards, I wait for the priest. I forgot to get a stamp at the hotel. As we walk over to the parish house, he tells me that he comes from Romania and has been assigned to this parish for a month. To my surprise, he confides that he has to make changes but follows his own counsel: "Look first, then change." A new priest/new parish relationship might explain awkwardness at Mass. He stamps my *créanciale* and gives me a miniature of Andrei Rublev's icon *The Trinity*, which depicts the three "men" who visited Abraham, except these "men" were the "LORD," God himself in human form. In Old Testament theophanies, God also appeared in storms and as fire; he spoke in silence and with both human words and thunder. I wonder how God will appear to me as I make my Way.

As I leave Montcuq, Jean-Marie from France is photographing the town's name, because *"mon cu"* means "my ass," and he wants to send it to his friends. I ask him about Condom, a town ahead. "Do the French know what that means in English?"

"They know," he assures me.

I hoped morning rest and a late start might help my body, but out of rhythm, I feel even more tired. Severe elevation changes damn this short fourteen-kilometer walk as much as gorgeous scenery blesses it. The most gorgeous scenery and the most severe climb come at the end.

Lauzerte, the veritable town on a hill, sits atop a steep, high hill, a pilgrim's cross. As I approach the base of the hill from the flat farmland surrounding it, the beautiful cross of Lauzerte grows bigger and bigger. I huff and puff uphill, step by interminable step, several times stopping to breathe.

I injured myself playing golf when I was young. I dug an iron too deeply in the grass and pulled a muscle under my left scapula. I told my mom that I needed to go to the doctor. She was chatting at table with her sister. "I don't believe you injured yourself," she said, then went back to her conversation. I never got medical attention and have lived with pain in that muscle my whole life, a daily reminder of my mother's neglect, a cross I have carried since I was a child. That spot has pained me off and on as I walk, but as I climb this hill, the pain worsens.

At the peak of the almost flat, rounded hilltop lays a large square, made of cut stone and surrounded by stores, cafés and the three-hundred-year-old Église Saint-Barthélemy, where a flyer advertises a chamber music concert that night. I find Maddie and

Trisha in a bar, where we register for the *gîte municipal.* They have also seen the concert flyer and want to attend.

We meet at the cathedral a few minutes before 6 p.m., and no one is here. Without exhausted eyes, we read the flyer more closely. The concert is at Église des Carmes, on the edge of town, at a lower elevation. We debate about going. Nobody wants to walk down and back up another hill. I observe that the serendipitous discovery of things like concerts are part of the journey, and we go.

As we descend, I confide to Maddie, as if it were a great secret, "I'm starting to hate downhill."

She looks at me, with wide eyes and her head drawn back. "You're only now starting to hate downhills?"

In the small, dark, Baroque church, we listen to an organ, piano, choir, violin and cello concert, a paragon of chamber music that transcends the travails of *Le Chemin* however briefly.

As the only man at the *gîte*, I get my own room and look forward to a good night's sleep. A cat caterwauls all night long.

Skipping breakfast, I walk out of Lauzerte in darkness, and among large, modern buildings, *balises* disappear. I make an intuitive turn on a narrow footpath behind a house and, at the bottom of the hill, find a *balise.*

The sunrise brightens the cloudy sky, and from flat farmland, a hill rises before me. *Le Chemin* bends left across it, and I look left to assess the climb. Sharp, intense pain flashes like lightning across the middle of my back. I drop my backpack. I walk around bent sideways. I try to straighten but stop moving, hands on knees, my head hung between my shoulders. I breathe laboriously. I straighten slowly, awkwardly and walk it out. A car comes, and I drag my backpack out of the road. That small action requires tremendous effort. Tears wet my eyes. After ten minutes, the agony spends itself, and I recover enough to hoist my backpack and walk.

I look straight ahead, wary of causing pain to erupt again. To look sideways, I glance with my eyes or rotate on my feet. I do not feel normal for an hour, but fear of that pain stays with me.

I traipse through gently rolling hills in a leafy forest pierced by sunlight. After one and a half hours, I arrive at Saint-Sernin-du-Bosc, a Romanesque church almost swallowed by the forest. My guidebook says the distance from Lauzerte to Saint-Sernin is four kilometers. Even with a ten-minute injury time out, I cannot figure out how it took an hour and a half to walk four kilometers. I maintained a decent pace after the spasm. A "trust myself versus trust the guidebook" debate surfaces.

Two hours later, I arrive in the small town Dufort-Lacapelette, which, according to Michelin, is seven and a half kilometers from Saint-Sernin, a pace just under my four-kilometer-per-hour average. The walk, over low rolling hills and through shallow valleys under a cloudy sky, was easy. I am sure I ought to have reached Dufort-Lacapelette sooner. The "trust myself versus trust the guidebook" debate resurfaces.

When I was about six years old, my parents took me and my sister to a drive-in movie. I wanted to wear clothes so I could play with the other kids. My mother made me wear pajamas, because she said no kids would be playing and she wanted to put me and Sara to bed as soon as we got back from the movie. At the theater, kids were playing in a playground. I was upset that I could not play since the other kids would make fun of me for wearing pajamas. My mom made me go and play, when I did not want to, and all the kids made fun of me. I walked back to the car dejected. My intuition worked perfectly. My mother forced me to act contrary to my intuition. As I grew up, my mom's unrelenting, controlling beatdown of my intuition taught me not to trust myself.

So, the internal "trust myself or the guidebook" debate incites intense angst. With my feet as canon, I decide the guidebook is wrong, and I am right.

Beside *Ruisseau de Loujol*, a stream by a road lined with tall sycamores, a Bally shoe bag lays on the trail. Inside I find a map, stamps and a train and bus schedule. I hook it to my backpack thinking the chance of finding the owner slim, but also that it depends more on God than me. *All I have to do is pick it up and walk.*

Chapelle d'Espis presents an architectural conundrum. Part chapel, part house where a family lives, and with three roof lines, the building looks Trinitarian by accident. The architecture does not inspire a visit, but something inside says visit. On a low wall by the locked door sit two Frenchwomen. After greetings, I walk away, then remember the Bally bag. It belongs to one of the women. Neither one of us believes it. I beam, happy I followed my intuition and trusted God.

I timed my morning departure from Lauzerte for a 1 p.m. arrival in Moissac. Because restaurants in France open for lunch at noon and close at 2 p.m. and because I skimped on breakfast, the timing is especially important. Because of the injury time out, an extra kilometer before Saint-Sernin, and an extra half-kilometer before Dufort-Lacapelette, I run late. The distance between Chapelle d'Espis to Moissac is five kilometers, according to Michelin. It is 1 p.m. In a hustle, I can walk five kilometers in an hour. I have done it before on meager rations. I can do it again. So, I hustle, on asphalt. I reach the outskirts of Moissac, and the spandex in the outskirts stretches out for an extra kilometer. I reach center ten minutes after two.

In a town with dozens of restaurants, the only open restaurant is also the most expensive and offers a limited menu. I enjoy an excellent salad, and as compensation for extra kilometers, I eat dessert. On the Way, any excuse justifies dessert.

I find Ultreia, a *gîte* run by an Irish couple, and walk through the foyer and into a large grass courtyard with lawn chairs, laundry lines, a kid's bicycle laying in the grass, and a garden with tools leaning against the wall. A large, old house sits in the back.

"Bonjour, bonjour."

Aideen comes out from the house. Because I have not had a good night's sleep in days, I take a private room with a comfortable bed and a sitting area with upholstered chairs and a couch. I then take an afternoon coffee at the outdoor table where I ate lunch. The sun comes out, and I enjoy its light and its warmth.

The massive Romanesque Abbaye Saint-Pierre de Moissac sits across the square. Corbels[4] high above the entrance catch my eye. To view them, I use my camera's telephoto capability. My exhausted arms shake as I hold the camera. One corbel depicts a beast with horns. Several depict human faces contorted with perturbation and abject sorrow. The most remarkable corbel depicts a man with hands on either side of his face, a distended jaw jut to one side, and an open mouth loosing a scream from the pain that torments his barren soul: the medieval stonemason's version of Edvard Munch's *The Scream*. I understand the scream. The scream ever wells within me.

The earliest memory I have of my father is of him yelling at me. One of the earliest stories of my childhood that my mother tells is

---

4 A structural stone that juts out from a wall to support a roof.

of her yelling at me so viciously that I squatted in the corner to get away from her. When I was around six years old, my cousin Anne was playing and broke an upstairs glass door. She was around four. Parents, aunts, uncles and cousins screamed. I was downstairs, and when I heard the commotion, I froze in place. I was afraid that I might have done something wrong but concluded that I had done nothing wrong. However, I had become so sensitized to yelling and screaming, associating it with punishment, that I froze in place, thinking if I did not move, I would not get in trouble: no one would yell at me. My cousins told my mom that I was standing still downstairs. So, my mom came down and yelled at me for doing nothing, as if a six-year-old is supposed to do something about a four-year-old breaking a glass door.

No one notices the corbels.

As Rom, Aileen's husband, cooks dinner, I mention the discrepancy between the distance between Lauzerte and Moissac indicated by my guidebook, twenty-four kilometers, and what I think the real distance is according to my feet, twenty-six and a half kilometers. Rom says the distance is twenty-six kilometers. I am proud that I trusted myself and not the guidebook, although I wish I did so with less angst.

As I lay in my bed, I think about the lengthy debate I had with myself. I have to rediscover and recover my intuition, that internal gyroscope, given by God and polished by evolution to guide our way on earth and orient us to the truth about ourselves, the world and God. I wonder if that might subdue the scream.

Msgr. Charles Rowland charges into my office and yells at me. All base anger and without any faculty of reason, that which forms us in the image and likeness of God, nothing he says makes sense. His words have no connection to anything that I have said or done, and the sentences

*little connection to each other. I had been sitting quietly in my office
working on a homily and remain seated as he yells. Finally, he stops.*

*With a nonplussed tone, I say, "I have no idea what you are
talking about. Nothing you have said makes any sense. Why in God's
name are you yelling at me?"*

He yells another apoplectic something and stomps out.

*It is not the first or the last of many incidences, just one of many.
The instinctual movement in my soul is to drive down to the bishop's office and say, "Either you move that asshole Rowland to another
parish or me or I am leaving the diocese today." I was taught that
the bishop articulates the will of God for his priests, and in seminary,
"obedience" was drilled into us. So, I stay at Saint Joseph's where the
bishop assigned me to serve God.*

At breakfast, Rom stamps my passport, and when he sees the
stamp I got in Montcuq, he exclaims, "Where did you get that
stamp? I have seen thousands of stamps and have never seen that
one." He goes on and on about that stamp. Apparently, no one
gets stamps at the church. Because of my forgetfulness and because I went to Mass, I have a rare Camino stamp.

Under a crystal-clear blue sky and a glorious sun, I walk beside a long canal lined by poplar trees. Its placid water exudes
peace. It occurs to me that this is the first walk of my walk.
Everything else has been a hike.

I catch Reinev from Germany, who wears a dark green
Bavarian Tyrol hat with a feather, and Xiomara, his wife, from
Honduras. Reinev speaks German and English. Xiomara speaks
Spanish and German. And I speak English, a little Spanish and
less German. We have a funny, triangular conversation.

Hills to my right and north of the canal give way to flatland. The Way turns south, crosses the canal and adjacent river, and makes straight for Auvillar, another town on a hill. The ascent is not as steep as and without the endless feel of Lauzerte. Even with a late start and a twenty-kilometer stint, I arrive an hour before lunch.

In the old cobblestone square stands a grain market, a circular, open building, with a tile roof supported by circular stone columns on the outer edge and intricate wooden arches in the center. A cupula rises in the center of the roof. The day has turned hot, and I stretch out on a bench in the shade of the market.

I eat a leisurely lunch, but after too long a break on too hot a day, I feel sluggish when I restart. The short, nine-kilometer stroll through farmland to Saint-Antoine feels longer than it really is. I wear my boots loosely, and my toes jam against my boots on a rare descent. My right big toe starts to throb.

In the dark, musty Église de Saint-Antoine, a mural of Saint George, my sweet hound dog's name saint, adorns the wall. I ask the saint to look after George until we can be reunited.

I find a *gîte* at an old farm, west of the village. Several times along the Way, I have dropped equipment to reduce weight. Here, among a few other items, I leave the multitool with the corkscrew.

Wilfred arrives, then Jean Marie. Because the *gîte* does not offer dinner, our hospitaller makes reservations for us at the local restaurant. Wilfred and I drink an after-walk beer, then a before-dinner beer. Wilfred only drinks beer and complains that beer glasses in France are "too small." Jean Marie joins us, and when he learns that I come from Charleston, he becomes excited. He visited Charleston on business and took the Ghost Tour. For reasons having nothing to do with him, the thought that he might have obtained Anna's services haunts me.

"Come back any time." The store manager at a convenience store on Remount Road wears a nametag that says Jonathan. Anna smiles like a child trying to pretend something away.

In Charleston, we run into a man at Walmart. "This is Alan."

In Walterboro at Walmart, "This is Mike."

As we dine at a restaurant in Charleston, a man walks in and Anna lowers her head and pulls a hat over her eyes. He gets takeout, and when he leaves, she says, "I know him."

At the methadone clinic in Charleston, I park my truck by another truck. An old, scraggly man keeps trying to get Anna's attention, as if he knows her. "Let's leave," she says.

Everywhere we go, we meet her tricks.

The sun rises on the cloudless horizon and illuminates the underside of clouds above in shades of purple, blue, orange, yellow and red. The morning is cool, perfect for walking.

Michelin says I will find food in the village Castet-Arrouy. I find no café and have walked thirteen kilometers on bread and coffee. I now must walk another ten kilometers to the next town to find food.

From Bach to Cahors, I walked twenty-seven kilometers on bread, coffee and two squares of chocolate. Between Moissac and Auvillar, I walked twenty kilometers on bread and coffee. Now, to reach the town Lectoure, I will have to walk twenty-three kilometers on bread and coffee.

Jeffrey, this nonsense has to stop. If you can't trust guidebooks, you have to carry food that will last for days and that you will enjoy as you walk.

I have become accustomed to walking tired and hungry, but acute, intense pain erupts in my big toes, especially my right one.

Every step tortures me. The pain feels catastrophic. If not resolved, I cannot walk through it. That thought reverberates in my head and overlays the physical pain with a greater pain. I harden my face and keep going. Several hours later, I near Lectoure.

A woman lies in the grass. Her head rests on her backpack, and she faces the sun. I consider saying hello, but the moment looks too precious to disturb.

A young Frenchman sits on a stone wall. His boots lay on the ground, and he rubs his feet.

"*Bonjour. Ça va?*" I ask with an upbeat tone I do not feel.

"*Ça va,*" he answers half-heartedly. "*Et tu?*"

"*Ça va,*" I answer, with a flat tone.

The approach to Lectoure begins with an asphalt dive into a valley, then goes up a steeper climb. I limp down the descent. With every feeble half-step, I bang my *bâton* onto the road and lean on it. I hear the young Frenchman's footfalls behind me. Thinking anyone can pass me, I am surprised he does not catch up. I have that unshakable feeling that he watches me and think him a voyeur into my sufferings. Tempted to self-pity, I decide that regardless of what he does, I alone control my feelings. I hold my head high, feel better and limp to the bottom. I glance backward. He limps downhill with an expression of dismay that mirrors mine. He watches me—I felt his eyes—not as a spectacle of pity but as a fellow pilgrim suffering and enduring.

At the tourism office, I mask my pain and suppress my emotions with an excessively forced, deliberately quiet, matter-of-fact voice. I obtain a town map and directions to *gîtes* from two helpful, friendly ladies. I muster an exhausted *"merci beaucoup,"* then go to Cathédrale Saint-Gervais-et-Saint-Protais.

I set my backpack on a pew and circle the interior of the cathedral, limping slowly. Suppressing sobs, tears roll down my cheeks. Alone, self-pity floods my heart and mind. The physical pain is horrible. I need to stop for a day to give my feet a chance to heal, but I do not think one day will be enough or even one week.

My Camino has ended.

I circle the ambulatory again. I need to weep, want to weep but hold back my tears. Someone has entered the church, and I do not want him to see my tears or hear my sobs.

I have to sober up, I tell myself. *I have to think through the problem. I have to keep going. Focus on the immediate: eat, find a place to sleep. Food and sleep will help. Solve the practical problems step by step.*

I regain control of my emotions, hoist my backpack and limp out.

The woman in the grass passes me smiling. I talk to the young Frenchman, who speaks English. Rafael heads to *Gîte Halte Pélerin*. After lunch, I go there.

Veronica, once a pilgrim herself, runs the *gîte*, which is located on the first floor of her house. She lives on the second floor.

Rafael and I sit in lounge chairs in the backyard and enjoy the sun. He has torn his Achilles tendon and endures great pain. The daily distance he walks has dropped precipitously. He describes the experience as an opportunity for "humility." I tell him about my toes and that I might have to take a day off to save my Camino.

Rafael does not remember the name of the woman in the grass but says that she is out of money. The ladies at the tourism office sent her to a local convent, where the sisters will feed and house her. My intuition tells me that I will help her at some moment on her Way. When she hits a crisis and her Way is in danger of ending, I'll give her fifty euros to continue her Way.

Our conversation eases into silence, and we rest in the sun. Pablo de Camino and Pastry, Veronica's cats, also lounge in the sun: one on a chair, one on a stone wall. Unrivaled masters of the nap, the cats repose with aplomb. I feel too conflicted to rest.

Condom

DAYS 22 - 23

Torn between walking and resting, I feel like I have no alternative but to walk. I lace my boots tighter to protect my toes.

As I leave Lectoure, at the bottom of the hill, I come up behind Rafael, who limps. We cross a stream, turn into woods and say goodbye. He again mentions "humility" and wonders that I am able to walk so fast when the day before I thought I had to take a day off to recover.

"I think my body has adapted to punishment during the day and recovery at night." I do not say it, but I have also adapted to walking in pain.

I adapted to a lot of pain in my life, but the adaptation formed a deep malformation within my psyche. As a child who suffered verbal and emotional abuse, I thought punishment the normal life experience. I became accustom to a life of pain and did not know a life of happiness. I debate whether walking in pain constitutes maladaptation or perseverance. Perseverance through pain became habituated in my life. Deeply wounded, I wonder if I am wounded too deeply to recover. I wonder if I am inflicting similar, untreatable deep wounds to my body as I make my Way. Tears water my eyes as these thoughts course through my head.

The present day presents a more proximate problem. Condom looms ahead. To avoid Condom, I have to choose between too short a day or too long a day: stop at La Romieu or take a shortcut to Condom and walk to Larressingle, the first place with a *gîte* after Condom. I loathe the thought of sleeping in Condom. I have to avoid it.

"Do you have a condom?" asks a prostitute.

Some prostitutes insist on condoms. Some do not. Sometimes I insist on condoms. Sometimes I do not. Because this woman is new to streetwalking, I decide that she is worth the risk, and I can have my way.

I realize I am using her and treating her the way I treat myself. I think, 'What does it matter if I catch something and die?' Because the Church is one with Jesus, the God-Man, and by the power of the Holy Spirit, is both human and divine, I experienced abuse in the Church as if meted out by God. Ecclesial abuse constituted God's divine judgment on me and formed within me a divinely sourced self-hatred. God hates me. So, I hate myself and think, 'Why not commit suicide by sex and hide the fact that I have committed suicide?'

"No, we're really going to fuck. We're going to enjoy it," I say.

Occasional light showers and sprinkles fall from a dark, overcast sky as I pass through flat, pastoral countryside. Despite the easy walk, hotspots on my feet precurse new blisters.

I come to Chapelle d'Abrin, which sits a hundred meters off the road. Days before I accepted extra meters to pray in a church, but weariness in my flesh has eroded those intentions. Now, not wanting to add unnecessary steps to my walk, I do not visit the chapel.

Here the Way and the alternate split. *Le Chemin* turns down a dirt road toward La Remieu. The shorter alternate follows an asphalt road toward Condom and is the best option to avoid that town by walking past it to Larressingle.

A sign advertises the village La Romieu as *Cité de Chats*. When I left for the Camino, I left behind two cats. I feel like I abandoned them even though I ensured that they were cared for. I worry less about Little Bob, who interacted with people, and more about Miss AJ, who interacted only with me. I fear she might not survive the transition.

I walk toward Condom, stop, walk back to the La Remieu turn. I think about my feet, my legs, my cats, and the loathing I have for sleeping in Condom. I walk toward Condom, stop and ponder. I want God to know how much I love my cats, and I want him to look after them. I want them to have good lives. I think about Jesus' admonition that he desires mercy, not sacrifice.[5] Will prayer be enough? Was adoption of George, Little Bob and Miss AJ enough? Or must I walk to La Romieu? I have little experience of God's mercy but endless experiences of merciless sacrifice. If I am merciful to myself and take the shortcut, will God be merciful to my cats?

For fifteen minutes, I walk back and forth, debating about mercy and sacrifice, measuring exhaustion in my limbs, trying to discern if habituated pain governs my decision or something greater, like wisdom. I walk a kilometer in fifteen minutes, and these fifteen minutes feel like an eternity. I revert to my default setting, chose sacrifice over mercy and turn toward *Le Cité de Chats*.

Le menu complete in La Romieu incudes sweet white cheese in a champaign flute with prunes at the bottom and Armagnac liquor on top, a dessert that almost justifies extra kilometers.

---

5 See Matthew 9:13.

I depart La Romieu at 2 p.m. and am sixteen kilometers and four hours from Condom. Larressingle lays four kilometers and one hour beyond Condom. With a decent lunch and fast feet, I am determined to bypass Condom.

Clouds hide the sun, the day heats up, and the heat cooks me. Then, as I traipse up and down hills, the sun comes out and roasts me. On the last stretch, I walk fast on gentle terrain, but heat and pace push tiredness toward exhaustion more quickly than I expect. After walking thirty-five kilometers, the last sixteen in three and a half hours, my body is blown. Despite my desire not to stop in Condom, utter physical exhaustion overwhelms my emotional motivations. Stopping in Condom has become a matter of survival.

A two-story building covered with backpacks, *bâtons*, old boots, gloves, hats and so on advertises itself as a *gîte*. Inside, pilgrims have written poems, greetings, admonitions and quotes in eight languages on the white walls. There are also dozens of drawings. Laurant runs the *gîte*. I take a private room.

I limp to 6 p.m. Mass at the Cathédrale de Saint-Pierre. Throughout Mass, celebrated in a small chapel, the African priest keeps looking at me with a worried expression. He is right to worry. The walk exhausted me. Pain in my feet sucks out what little life remains in me. I feel and look horrible.

As I drink my revival beer at an outdoor café, Jean Marie walks up. He is finishing in Condom, and for me, Condom marks the completion of five hundred kilometers, one-third of my journey to Santiago. We toast our success with beer.

Two groups of female pilgrims, with native English accents, sit beside us. Jean Marie says goodbye, and I chat with the women: three Americans and four Australians. Beneath the sociable conversation, I sense undercurrents of tension between the Australian and American women and among the Australian women.

My feet are wrecked again. I tightened my boots to save my toes, and blisters erupted on my heels. I have callouses on blisters, blisters on callouses. Even with tightly laced boots, my toes hurt badly.

Lying in bed, I say to God, "Give me wisdom." I need to take better care of myself. I have to walk fewer kilometers. I have to figure out how to make my boots work. I have to be kinder, more merciful to myself.

Rain falls in a steady, moderate shower. I accept the rain as a blessing and rethink my schedule. There are two good places to stop: Montréal-du-Gers, seventeen kilometers distant and Éauze, thirty-three kilometers distant. Another long day is out of the question. I decide to rest, start late and walk to Montréal-du-Gers.

I give myself permission to rest. All a sudden, I feel exhaustion like I have never felt it before. Exhaustion penetrates marrow and wrings out my ragged soul.

I wash my clothes in a washing machine and toss them in the dryer. After one cycle, they are wet. After a second cycle, they are still wet. I wring them, then run them through a third cycle and a fourth cycle. After a fifth cycle, my clothes come out damp. This is the third time European dryers have failed to dry my clothes. I begin to suspect that they labor under a No-Heat Curse.

Laurant stamps my passport, which clearly identifies Condom, then takes a red felt pen and draws a heart around the stamp. Here I am, a Catholic priest traveling incognito, who did not want to sleep in Condom because it reminds me that I tried to commit suicide through sex because of divinely engendered self-hatred, who now has a red heart, symbolizing love, around Condom. My eyes pop. My mouth drops open.

Ideas flash through my head: rent a car, backtrack and redo my passport from the beginning, throw this one away and start over, erase, remove or hide the heart; maybe Laurant is homosexual.

I do not know about Laurant. I do know I cannot alter my passport without doing violence to it. I also know that I do not have time to backtrack and cannot get in a car without violating my code. Moreover, my code includes accepting what the Way gives me. The red heart around Condom is now and forever an indelible, embarrassing part of my Way.

On a wall, I write *"ne capistra bovis,"* my favorite Old Testament Law: "Do not muzzle the ox when it treads out grain."[6] The Diocese of Charleston suffocated me while I labored to serve God and his people. But I will not be muzzled.

In the main square stands a statue of the three musketeers and d'Artagnan. I have an idea for a photo but need someone to take it. As people walk by with city-busy paces, there stands Wilfred. The four musketeers stand with the points of their swords touching. I stand in the center and touch the end of my *bâton* to the point where their swords touch. Wilfred laughs and photographs the Five Musketeers.

With the memory of walking without food etched into the lining of my stomach like an indelible sacrament, I take a table at Restaurant au Théâtre and enjoy a fantastic *plat du jour:* mushrooms in a thick sauce, salmon on pasta, and a rich, dark (not cakey) chocolate cake with pear slices secreted inside. Another fantastic meal in France.

Passing through suburbs, I cross a street. A young man starts his motor scooter a hundred meters up the road, then guns his engine and steers straight for me. I cross the road and walk a dozen steps before he reaches me. He yells something. I raise my arms

---

6 Vulgate Deuteronomy 25:4, NAB, Deuteronomy 25:4

in a "what-the-fuck" kind of way and say the same. He slows and turns as if considering coming back, then changes his mind. I name him The Condom Jerk.

Happy to put Condom behind me, I walk onto dirt trails rain has transformed into streams of mud. The mud clings to my boots as has no other mud. I scrape my boots against rocks to remove the mud. Ten meters downtrail, thick mud again clings to my boots. I scrape off the mud with my *bâton*. Ten more meters downtrail, thick mud clings to my boots yet again. But the mud does not just cling to my boots. The mud clings to itself and extends from the edge of my boots and under my boots. I give up scraping off the mud and wear mud clogs. Back on asphalt, I walk on the mud that clings to the bottom of my boots. Asphalt does not remove the mud. So, I wash my boots in water. A kilometer later, I walk off asphalt into more mud.

Sharp, shooting pains pulse through my right big toe. Off and on, rain falls in light showers and sprinkles. The weather turns hot and humid. Sweat soaks my already rain-besodden clothes.

Thinking about how I washed my clothes repeatedly to keep them fresh, the thought, *I have not washed my hat*, pops into my head a mere moment before a stench descends from my hat with an olfactory face slap and hangs about my face like a veil. My hat does not just stink. Three weeks of sweat, rain and sunscreen have fermented into a putrid, revolting effluvium. A non-pilgrim would collapse facedown in the mud where his body and bones would petrify, to be dug up by anthropologists studying ancient man. I trudge on, escape the mud, walk the last hour in a steady shower and, as the rain stops, walk into the small town Motréal-du-Gers.

At the tourism office, I obtain a map of the town that identifies *gîtes* and a map to Serviac, Roman ruins outside town.

Too tired for French, I ask the woman who runs *Gîte Napoleon* if she speaks Spanish. Maria de Fatima grew up in Portugal on the Spanish border. I leave my boots at the front door to keep out mud, and Maria gives me Homer Simpson slippers to wear.

Before I fall asleep, I tell God, "I am tired of suffering." I forget to wash my hat.

Angelique

DAYS 24 - 27

Maria de Fatima and I breakfast on fresh bread, assorted jams and coffee. We hug goodbye, and she wishes me, *"Bon Camino, Menas Agua."* We laugh.

I find the Roman ruins Seviac at 9 a.m., but it does not open for another hour. On a wooden gate hangs a sign: *"Attention au Chien!"* I drop my backpack and climb the fence, carrying my *bâton*. There is no dog, just one affectionate calico cat. Ancient Romans associated cats with divinity and were the only animals permitted in temples. Of course, a cat, not a dog, guards Seviac.

A woman drives up, and I cross back over the fence. In English, she apologizes and tells me Seviac does not open until 10 a.m. In French, I explain I am a pilgrim headed to Santiago and cannot wait. After several minutes, during which she talks non-stop and without pauses—I can't figure out when or how she breathes—she gives me a guide and tells me I can visit Seviac without paying. I thank her and stroll across the grounds.

Seviac was the villa of a wealthy, upper-middle-class Roman couple. Stone outlines of rooms and an extensive Roman bath have been excavated. Mosaics, with geometric designs and images of grapes and radiant suns, cover the floors. Archeologists discovered two skeletons: the man and woman of Seviac.

In the end, Anna and I will be dead, and what will our lives mean? The theological answer—love leads to eternal life—I well know but is difficult to believe after the Church that preached "God is love" practiced hate.

I say goodbye to the cat, and the woman sends me down a nondemarcated shortcut. With compass in hand and after a couple kilometers, I return to the Way.

I pass the Australian women in vineyards. I then pass a house with an unrestrained dog, more scared than aggressive, who lunges and barks at me. I hold my *bâton* between him and me. I feel sorry for him with his unhealthy disposition. I walk into woods and pass hunters with happy, wire-haired hounds who bay at me. I come across another hunter with a wet, muddy, tail-wagging dog beside him and, in thick brush, another dog baying every minute or so.

When George and I first walked together, he glanced at me and growled when we did not follow the scents of animal trails. He was a true hunter. I weep quietly and softly, thinking about our walks.

I walk into the small town Éauze, and because the next day is a rest day, my spirit lightens. I join Rainev and Xiomara at table in the square, order a beer and relax.

I ask Rainev about his opinion of beer mugs in France.

"Too small," he answers. I chuckle to myself.

I refer to the Way as "the Way of Mud." Rainev describes sections as "mud lakes."

Xiomara asks if I am married. When I tell her no, she says, *"Yo rezaré que encuentres una esposa en El Camino."*

Bemused, I answer with a straight face, "I am open to whatever God brings me as I make my Way" and wonder what she would think if she knew she prayed for a priest to marry.

The Woman With No Money walks by barefoot, shoes in hand, smiling and in happy spirits.

I get a room at Hotel Henry IV on the third floor, accessed by a spiral wood staircase. I climb with tired legs and feel like I am about to fall over when I reach the top. I lean against the railing and look down. The white, top newel plunges straight down. The natural stained banister, with white balusters, forms an inner spiral and curves down. The newel and balusters frame a lit table lamp, which looks like a suspended globe. The stairs darken as they descend, and the dark spiral frames the globe of light, where the last steps disappear in shadow.

Back in the square, I meet the American and Australian women. We push tables together, and the seating falls out with the Australians at one end and the Americans at the other.

I mention that I jumped the fence to visit Seviac. The Australian women laugh. Karen, one of the American women, rears back, looks down her nose and, in a judgmental tone, says, "We know. We know. She told us." I feel put out.

When the Australian women talk about how much they enjoy wine, Karen rears back, looks down at them and says, "We know. You have a reputation. You have a reputation." The Australian women look put out. Why I sensed tension between these two groups of women when we first met is obvious.

After more pained efforts to be polite by me and the Australians, Karen and her cohorts excuse themselves. The tension leaves us, and we order more wine and beer and laugh away the afternoon.

A man walks by with three German shepherds off leash. All three walk close to their master. Two older dogs focus on the direction their master heads, but the younger dog's eyes wander.

The Australian women have reservations at my hotel and ask, "Does the hotel have an elevator?"

"No, but there is a beautiful spiral staircase ..." Groans drown out my description of the stairs.

I enjoy the company of the German couple and the Australian women, but I still feel lonely. How different the Way would be if I enjoyed it with someone I love and who loves me.

I wash my hat first thing.

Sitting in the square, I watch people walk by and pigeons fly about the church. With strong lines, the tall, narrow church has potential, but the exterior is a mishmash of brick and stone of different sizes and colors, which gives the building a sickly appearance. I try to appreciate the appearance of the church through the lens of chaos theory that posits that a deeper order subsists beneath apparently disordered events, but the distorted appearance retains its distortion. Inside the church, I find the same erratic, disturbing patterns.

I retreat to my hotel and spiral up the staircase. My tired legs feel heavier with each step. In a room more ordered than the church, I take a morning nap.

I arrive at Mass just as the Woman With No Money walks up. I introduce myself as a fellow pilgrim, and we attend Mass together. Angelique from Belgium sings with energy and a sweet, ethereal voice. She kneels during the consecration and the prayer "Lord, I am not worthy," smiles throughout Mass and, even with little money, places a euro in the collection basket.

When Mass ends, I want to talk to her and give her money to continue her Way, but she talks to the man with the wonderful German shepherds—the dogs lay outside the church without leashes during the whole Mass—whom she must have met the day before. They leave together. I am glad she found someone to help her. Nevertheless, my intuition tells me that a crisis will come, and I will step in and help her along the Way.

After a delicious *plate du jour* at Loft Cafe, I again spiral up the staircase to my room. With rest and food, my tired legs feel even heavier than they had that morning. I take an afternoon nap.

I wander back down to the square, and the owner of Loft Cafe directs me to Musée Archéologique, which traces the ancient history of Éauze with a focus on Roman history. Le Trésor d'Éauze, dated to the third century AD and found outside Éauze, includes 28,000 Roman coins and fifty other precious objects, artwork, necklaces and earrings, all on display in a vault. Two attractive women in their thirties work here, a blonde and a dark-haired brunette. Both friendly, the dark-haired brunette acts especially friendly and invites me to stay after they close. When I leave without accepting her invitation, she pouts. She is beautiful, funny, playful, interested and interesting. The temptation to stay is great, the decision to walk out difficult.

"You have time to make love, or you don't have time?" Anna steps toward me. Her head moves from side to side as she frames my changes of mind. Long brown hair, brown eyes, pretty lips, and a quizzical, desirous expression, she knows how to make me want her.

She kicks off her heels, unbuttons her knee-length skirt and blouse and lies on the bed. I take off my clothes and lie on top of her. We interlace our fingers. She wraps her legs around me. We breathe each other's breath. Our lips caress.

I wake refreshed, and to keep that feeling alive, I tell myself, *you have to walk slower.*

The decision about where and how far to walk is daily occupation. Spacing between towns, elevation changes, attractions, the condition of feet and legs, where friends are headed and consideration of the walk a day in advance are factored into a mysterious algorithm. Today, the decision is again simple: long today, short tomorrow or short today, long tomorrow. I choose to get the hard part over with first and walk twenty-nine kilometers to the village Lanne-Soubiran.

I stroll among cornfields, vineyards and woods. In an open field, I stop and turn to my right. I do not hear or see anything but feel something. Two beagles walk out of a cornfield, and soon, a hunter with a shotgun. Thick chains around the dogs' necks weigh down their heads. Links hang between their legs and force them to take awkward steps. The dogs look thin. One dog shakes. Having never known a life without abuse, they appear happy.

Deep down though, animals know something is not right when they are mistreated. Looking at the hunter and thinking about my parents and prelates in the Catholic Church that I dealt with, I doubt that abusers possess any degree of self-awareness.

Chains hang around my neck and weigh me down. For my whole life, I accepted the chains as normal. Deep down however, I knew something was wrong, and as I walked through my life, my steps felt awkward. I have no idea how to throw off my chains.

I arrive in the village Manciet around 10:30 a.m., too late for breakfast, too early for lunch. With Nogaro eleven kilometers away and worried about missing lunch, I persuade a reluctant hostess at a café to persuade the cook to make an omelet. The cheese, potato and ham omelet, accompanied by a green salad, tastes great.

In the town Nogaro, I find the Australian women at a café. When I say I intend to walk another eight kilometers to

Lanne-Soubiran, they tell me excitedly their guidebook does not indicate a *gîte* in Lanne-Soubiran. They look worried. Michelin says there is a *gîte*.

I shrug. "I'll see what the Way gives me or does not give me."

As I walk, the omelet burns out of my body, I have no energy to fuel my steps and I rethink my decision to walk to Lanne-Soubiran. It does not help that Michelin betrayed me before, which makes the Australian women's adamancy about no *gîte* a worry that sucks psychic energy out of me.

In the village Arblade-le-Haut, where Michelin says I will find a *gîte*, I find a faded, weather-beaten sign for a *gîte* but no *gîte*. I consider retreating to Nogaro, but pride, shame, determination and the unappetizing thought of a five-kilometer backtrack drive me forward. However, worry about the nonexistent *gîte* in Lanne-Soubiran and second-guessing accompany each step and increases fatigue.

On a raised farm road, something rustles down in a cornfield. Startled *sanglier*, wild boar, disappear into woods.

I trudge down a shady path lined with trees and roofed by limbs, where a sign points to a *chambre d'hôtes* named Castagnére advertised as eight hundred meters off the Way.

A moment of decision has arrived. Trust Michelin, trust God, discern and follow my intuition, trust the sign, walk off the Way in violation of my code, stick to my code and possibly sleep in the woods without food: I make an agonized turn toward Castagnére. After a kilometer, a second sign directs me onto a rough tractor path through a cornfield. After another kilometer, I step out of the cornfield and onto a road across from the *chambre d'hôtes*. With tables in the dining room set with a five-piece silver service and three glasses, the place looks nice, too nice for a pilgrim. I sit on semi-circular stairs to rest. A man appears, takes one look at the pathetic wight on his steps, and says in French he does not have a room. Since he is treating me like a vagrant, I decide to be one. I sip water and remain seated. He repeats his statement several times.

"No chambre, no lit," I say. I accept the situation, the extra distance I have walked, the extra distance I still must walk, the rejection, the biblical connections. I stand and say, *"Je voudrais un gîte."* He says something about *"presbytére"* and gives me baffling directions in French. Frustrated with my French and my presence, he walks me to another cornfield, points down a farm road and repeats *"Gîte du Presbytére."* I thank him without enthusiasm and continue my ill-chosen, several-kilometer sidetrack through more cornfields.

I find a church and by the church a large house, and I wonder, reason, realize that the *gîte* might be the former rectory. I knock. No one answers. I walk into a house with black posts and beams, white plaster walls and hardwood floors. Several people cackle and clank pots and pans in a kitchen. Again, I call out, unable to penetrate the din. I walk to the kitchen where three people prepare supper. Indeed, I have found a *gîte* near Lanne-Soubiran, not the one Michelin named, and *Gîte du Presbytére* sits by the Way. Had I kept to the Way, I would have found it with ease and saved myself a lot of effort. That I ended up at a former house for priests after a sidetrack and being told there was "no room at the inn" is so in-my-face obvious that it is impossible not to wonder about its prophetic import.

Marinette, who owns and runs the *gîte*, gives me a bed in a room with four beds. Maria, a dark-haired woman from Switzerland, has one bed. I then sit at an outdoor table in the sun and enjoy an after-walk beer.

Jean and Ann from France arrive and join me. Jean worked for Michelin and visited plants in South Carolina. They have a daughter who is a nun, and a home by *Le Chemin* in Argagnòn, three days ahead. They are walking home.

A faint pig farm smell wafts around us. Jean detests it, but I accept it as part of the Way.

When I tell them about the *sanglier*, Jean says they are dangerous and that I was lucky. I explain that the pigs were no threat, were more afraid of me than me of them and only wanted to escape. Nothing I say dissuades him from his obstinacy. He has not spent much time in woods.

Ann's rosary, which hung from her backpack, fell off. Also tied to my backpack, my rosary has not fallen off, but the links have slipped, and it looks tattered. I have not prayed the rosary once. Praying the rosary exhausts me. I fetch my disjointed rosary, lay it on the table and count beads. Every bead is still there. I reconnect the links as Jean and Ann watch with silent curiosity and give Ann the rosary, which she accepts with profound gratitude.

They ask what I think of France. "I love France. The food is great, the people friendly, the countryside beautiful."

Echoing other Frenchmen, Jean criticizes the French. "The French always see the negative," which explains the comments of the Precious Frenchman and Jean's own misappreciation of my encounter with boar. He repeats a common French joke: "The only problem with France is that French people live here."

We come inside for dinner, and the pig smell remains outside. When we finish soup and bread, I think we have finished the first course, but realization that soup constitutes the main course sends shock waves through me as depleted cells in my body scream for more.

Twice, to kill a mosquito, Jean slams his hand down onto the table so hard that the table and everything on it and everyone around it jumps. In a heated exchange, his wife corrects him, but he defends his slaps with characteristic obstinacy.

Maria does not join us and is abed when we retired. We have a brief, whispered discussion about snoring. We swear we do not snore, and no one snores. I sleep well.

I stroll through a small forest and listen to birds. I do not remember hearing birds chatter as I walked, which surprises me. I love woods and the sounds of woods. I wonder if I have been so self-absorbed with internal conflicts that I have missed their wondrous songs. I walk slowly and enjoy their music.

After the woods, the Way follows roads that take me to Lelin-Lapújolle, a village not named in the profile in my Michelin guide. The trail superimposed on the map follows a road half a kilometer west. I have gotten sidetracked by old *balises* that have not been removed and walk the old Way.

Balises disappear altogether, and I reach a highway that leads to the town Aire-sur-l'Adour, but the highway looks dangerous, so I cross it, go south and end up in the hamlet Gee-Rivière. I turn west and follow an asphalt road that turns into a gravel road, a dirt road, a grass path, a leaf-covered farm road that winds through the woods by the river and ends.

A heron glides upriver ten feet above the water. I say to the heron, "God gave you wings, but he gave me a brain."

I walk into a maze of streams, pools, mud, thick brush and clusters of both dead and living trees. A deer looks at me and bounds away. I follow the deer through more mud and weave through trees, cross a water-filled ditch and climb a steep bank to the edge of a field, then walk through thick grass and come to a shallow creek. I throw my backpack across, lay a dead tree across the creek and cross, balancing on the tree while untangling myself from briars. I throw my backpack through trees interwoven with briars and into a field, then crawl through the entanglement. I walk along the edge of a field with tall corn and through thick grass to a stream with steep banks and deep water. I backtrack around cornfields and through grasses sometimes as tall as me and too thick to walk through. I walk down cornrows and find a dirt road that leads to the asphalt road I was on before.

Yep, God gave me a brain, which would be quite useful if I made use of my brain as well as the heron made use of his wings. The heron went where he wanted. My brain got me lost. I do ask myself, however, if getting lost on the Old Way constitutes a prophetic face-slap.

I return to the highway that has no place for pedestrians. When vehicles pass, I step off the road and stop. It takes me forty minutes to walk 1.5 kilometers and return to the Way.

It is 1 p.m. I am five kilometers from Aire-sur-l'Adour. Since restaurants close at 2 p.m., I teeter on the cusp of another day without lunch. The clock ticks, my exhausted body starves, I hustle on spent legs.

I walk into center five minutes after two, ask for lunch at different restaurants and am told no. Desperate, I go to the tourist office and explain my plight.

"I need lunch."

"It's after two," the woman answers.

"I don't care what time it is. I haven't eaten since breakfast. I have to eat lunch." I am emphatic.

"In France, it is not possible." She answers with a flourish.

I drink a beer at a café and, with less emotion and more sobriety, return to the tourism office to ask about accommodations.

"Most *gîtes* do not open until four," she explains.

"I don't care what time they open. Where are they and do you have a map?" I speak with a flourish. She gives me a map and notes locations of hotels and *gîtes*.

I have turned an easy twenty-kilometer day into a hard twenty-five-kilometer day. I am tired, sore and hungry yet again. I begin to feel sorry for myself and want to be alone. I consider getting a hotel room to comfort myself and give myself a better chance for undisturbed sleep. The argument favoring a *gîte* is that fellow pilgrims are part of my pilgrimage. I decide to stay at a *gîte* because *God has something for me there.* I get a bed at a *gîte* at 3 p.m.

I eat lunch—*deux pains aux chocolat et deux cafés*—then realize I left my camera at the *gîte*. I have often forgotten my camera when switching from hiker to tourist and kick myself because I have added a hundred meters to a painful day I intended to be a relaxed stroll.

When I walk into the *gîte*, someone sobs. To the left in a narrow kitchen sits Angelique. Her sobs border on hysteria. Tears roll down her cheeks.

"Angelique, what's wrong?"

With swollen, red eyes and a breaking voice, she says, "My father is dead."

I put my arms around her and say, "Angelique, I am so sorry."

With plane reservations the next morning, her Camino is ending.

I go to the river, sit on a bench and watch water flow and ducks swim. I go to Mass celebrated by an African priest with ritual scars on his cheeks. I eat something, somewhere but do not think about food. All my thoughts revolve around the astonishing fulfillment of the story of me and Angelique.

So many things went wrong: I got lost, didn't eat lunch, starved, walked into exhaustion, ran late, forgot my camera again. In my debate about where to stay, my intuition said *gîte* because God had something for me there. Both despite of and because of my stupidity, and because of my intuition, I ended up in the right place at the right time.

Days before, my intuition told me I would help Angelique at a moment of crisis, with money when her Way might end. My intuition was correct; my rational appreciation was wrong. I saw perfectly yet was blind. I did not help her when her Way was in danger of ending, but when it ended in a life-changing event, the death of her father, a crisis I never imagined. The help I gave her was not money but something of inestimable value: a friendly, familiar face and a hug, a simple act of kindness, love and compassion. My intuition was fulfilled beyond expectations and far better. The fulfillment of my intuition—tragic yet beautiful—can only be the work of God. The divine is at work in my humanity. Stunned, I want my whole life to be like that.

Martin's Wisdom

DAYS 28 - 29

The Way presents another "too short–too long" conundrum: either sixteen kilometers to Miramont-Sensacq or thirty-four to Arzacq-Arraziguet. Because the Way is mostly flat, I leave before sunrise to make the long walk to Arzacq-Arraziguet.

As the sun brightens the day, I walk around Lac du Broussau on a ridge ten meters above the lake. Through leafy trees and between dark green hills, on the distant horizon, I see a peaked, bluish grey wall: the Pyrenees. My heart lifts. I take a photograph, and to remind me to be mindful of the present day's walk, the camera focuses on tree limbs in front of me and blurs the distant mountains. The trail weaves through hills that take this edifying sight from my eyes. Nevertheless, I smile as I walk. The Pyrenees lay within my grasp, a mere 125 kilometers away.

Once out of the hills, the Way rolls through forests with tall trees, then turns south, and I walk among thousands of acres of harvested cornfields. Here I have a long, wide look at the Pyrenees. I whoop. I holler. I congratulate myself. I raise my arms in victory. I skip, but my feet object. I also thank God. But I celebrate alone.

The Way turns uphill to an unnamed hamlet where God placed a cat to humble me. On a roof, facing up the pitch with a cedar tree to his back, a black cat rests with his legs under him. The cat slowly turns his head and opens his eyes wide enough to see me through a slit, then just as slowly turns his head back and closes his eyes. I am beneath the cat spatially and in the hierarchy of being.

Several kilometers later, at a farm, I see calves raised for veal. They stand in small pens with a doghouse to sleep in and enough space to turn around. I worked hard to give my dog, cats and chickens as close to a natural life as possible. As a child, seeing animals in cages saddened me because they did not have the freedom to live their lives. I empathized with them because I had not had freedom. I am searching for freedom.

As I traipse through woods, I ponder on the question of the Tool of the Trip. Before I started, I imagined bestowing this honor on my boots but now damn the boots as the Worst Tool of the Trip. My *bâton* served its purpose well, keeping me balanced as I crossed creeks and negotiated steep descents and protecting me from barking dogs and the Condom Jerk. Also in its favor, my *bâton*, purchased in Le Puy, has a carved image of a chamois, a European mountain goat. I have always identified more with goats than sheep. My bandanas have served humble, ignoble functions: blowing my nose and wiping sweat off my face. As a record of my journey, my camera has no equal. In a flash, a photograph captures part of the story. And a few photographs are good. I entertain as viable candidates: socks, journal, compass, multitool and so on. I wonder if my hat ought to be honored, and at that moment, an acorn falls from a tree, hits my head and bounces off. *Well, duh.* The hat wins Tool of the Trip.

Without complaint or objection, my hat has protected me from sun, rain and acorns. My hat is light, wears well and looks good. Moreover, my hat suffered neglect and, with a rank stench, descended into hell—an intimation remains—and even that signifies the Way, a journey as coarse as often as beautiful.

Walking on meager rations, I wear down. Kilometers drag. Time drags. I drag myself to the small town Arzacq-Arraziguet. The last ten kilometers, which should have taken two and a half hours in rough terrain, took three hours in easy terrain.

I wander around worn out and lost. It does not help that the tourism office is closed from 2 p.m. until 4 p.m., and I arrived at 3 p.m. I find the Australian women at their hotel, and they give me directions to the *gîte municipal*.

The lovely female hospitaller, patient with my French, which suffers more than normal in my exhaustion, gives me a bed in a room with four beds. As I settle in, I chat with Martin from Germany, a thin man with grey hair and who stands a little shorter than me.

I then search for an after-walk beer and find one of the Australian women at an outdoor table. I sit down, and the other three arrive. They finish one bottle of wine, a second and start on a third. They encourage me to stay and keep drinking, but having drunk too much with them before, I excuse myself because of "exhaustion."

With two beers on an empty stomach and too tired to think about doing anything, I doze in bed. Jean and Ann arrive and take the empty beds.

I wake tired and cranky and feel disoriented. I walk through town, look at restaurants and chat with the Australian women. I want to photograph the church and again forgot my camera. So, I return to the *gîte*.

I say hello to Martin, and he offers to cook his leftovers for me. I accept his kind offer. He sautés leftover pasta and fries three eggs in a skillet.

I ask him if he thinks beer glasses in France are too small like every other German. He says beer glasses in France are smaller than ones in Germany, then adds that he does not drink. A member of Alcoholics Anonymous, he has been sober twenty-six years.

I tell him that I have a friend who is an addict, that I attended Al-Anon and AA meetings in the last year, which were good experiences. I fetch my hat and tell him that my friends from AA gave me the hat for my trip and that I remember them when I wear it.

I show him Anna's photograph and describe the addiction, the fights, the manipulations, the enabling, the attempts at sobriety. I omit telling him that she is a prostitute and I am a priest.

"Is she your girlfriend?" he asks.

"I am not sure how to answer that question."

Martin straightened out his life, has a good job, sings in a choir and has a girlfriend. I ask him how he did it. He wrecked his life, lost jobs, tried to commit suicide, had physical problems. His thinking was all screwed up. Martin took years to admit that he was an alcoholic, then years to turn his life around. At some point, he decided, "I want to live. I want to be happy."

"We can only be sober today," he continues. "We can't be sober for tomorrow. We can only be happy today. We cannot be happy for tomorrow. These simple thoughts are too simple for addicts. Addicts think complicated."

My cellphone rings.

"Hey babe," Anna says. "I need $200 for heroin."

"No, you went to methadone clinic this morning."

"I didn't make it."

"What do you mean you didn't make it?"

"I overslept. We stayed up too late talking."

"I told you this would happen. I said, if you go to the beach with your girlfriends, you will not get to clinic, and you'll call me up and ask me for money."

"I know baby, but I overslept, and we were having a good time, and I'd have to wake everyone up early to get back."

"You knew that before you went. I pointed that out, and I told you this was a bad idea, but you promised you would go to the clinic."

"I know. I'm sorry."

"Sorry? I've taken you to the clinic for weeks, and if you skip a day, the whole process starts over. You know that. My God, I can't afford this bullshit."

"Well, what do you expect me to do now? Do you want me to go trick? Cause that's exactly what I'm going to have to do."

"I am not giving you money for heroin."

"Fine, then I'm going to trick. I'm going to dress up in something that shows off my legs and let the first guy who pulls over do whatever he wants between them. Is that what you want?"

"No, what I want you to do is get your life together so that we can have a life together."

"I am getting my life together. This is just a little, one-time slip."

"No, this happens all the time. You fuck up, then you call me for money for heroin."

"Don't you love me? Do want me to trick?"

The argument goes on and on. I become exasperated and send her money.

"I have gone crazy," I tell Martin, "and my life has become complicated, which is as much my fault as hers and, in some ways, more my fault. I struggle with the habit of living in the moment as much as any addict."

"The best you can do is look for yourself. You need to seek mental sobriety. You cannot help her. One crazy cannot help another crazy. Not me or you or anybody can help her decide to be sober."

He asks about my "higher power." In the second step of AA's Twelve Steps, the addict accepts that only a higher power can restore sanity.

"God and I have a difficult relationship."

The room is quiet, but my mattress has a divot that swallows half my body when I stretch out and two-thirds when I pull my legs closer. The sleeping position pains my back, hips and knees. Yet again, I wake tired, sore and hungry.

Often the first person out, I gather myself slowly and leave last. A kilometer out of town, I find Martin enjoying the tranquility of a lake. We walk together and, in the small town Louvigny, catch Jean and Ann by a church.

"I am very happy," Ann says. "I got everything I wanted in life."

Stunned, I mumble something about being happy for her.

In my life, I have gotten nothing of what I wanted. When I graduated high school, I wanted to join the army because the army said, "You Can," the opposite of my father's "you can't" and "Be All You Can Be," the opposite of my mother's "you are not." I knew I needed to remake myself, and I loved history, especially military history. Seventeen years old, I had to have my parents' permission to sign up. My dad taught me that the military reshapes young men. He also taught me about investments. I discussed these things with my father: let the military shape me for a career, first as an enlisted man, then as an officer. I could invest my salary, the army would pay for college, and my dad could invest the money he would have spent on my college in a small endowment for me. Nothing I said mattered. Nothing he taught me mattered. Nothing I believed mattered. His only thoughts were my mother's thoughts. "Your mother wants you to go to college," he said. So, "Honor thy father and mother" and not having a choice, I went to college, and my life fell apart: dysfunctional relationships, physical problems, failing grades, undiagnosed depression, acceptance of verbal and emotional abuse from so-called friends, drug and alcohol abuse, marriage, divorce.

When God called me to be a priest, I thought God had taken my ugly life and made something beautiful. I believed God could write straight with crooked lines, that my suffering had meaning, that God could bring good out of evil not as a theological principle but in the deep reality of my life. None of this happened. I gave up everything I wanted to become a priest and serve God and his people, and my life became worse.

I struggle to live in the moment as I walk with Martin. Sorrow overwhelms my heart and floods my mind.

We walk among rugged undulations and scattered houses. At one house, in the corner of the fence, lies a dog. He has worn a deep path in the grass by the fence but lies with a look of dejection. The dog does not even look at people walking by his yard. He glances at me with furtive eyes. Not able to exercise his gifts, intelligence and instincts, beaten down and trapped by a fence, he has collapsed on himself.

After years fighting against abuses of power in the Diocese of Charleston, I gave up. I stopped attending events. I did not talk with priests or diocesan officials unless forced to by circumstances. Abuse defined my identity, and ashamed of myself, I hid from everyone.

Martin and I discuss the dearth of picnic tables on *Le Chemin*, and half a kilometer later, as if God answers a prayer with a mockery of abundance, we pass dozens of picnic tables. He stops for lunch. We say goodbye and promise to pray for each other.

Martin's pace is kinder than mine. He walks twenty kilometers to Pomps, while I walk twenty-nine to Arthez-de-Béarn.

The morning has been humid and overcast with occasional sprinkles. In the afternoon, the sun comes out, and the day turns hot. I run out of water, and my mouth becomes dry and pasty. The last climb ascends a steep pitch to a ridge and Chapelle de Caubin. Churches often have water faucets for pilgrims. Desperate for water, I find no faucet at the church.

In the cool, quiet, dark church, thirsty, tired and hungry, I feel lost and confused. I need an answer from God. I have attached myself to Anna. Yet God called me to be a priest, and after the abuse I endured, I have no idea why. I hate the priesthood, and I do not want to be a priest anymore. The dilemma torments me. The answer I need can only come from God. I have more than eight hundred kilometers to walk to find that answer. The proximate walk to the small town Arthez-de-Béarn is two kilometers.

Arthez-de-Béarn sits astride a ridge and has a triangular-shaped square. Here, I drink a revival beer. Tired but not wiped out, I have accustomed myself to walk without lunch.

I register at *La Maison des Pèlerins* and meet a Swiss group, André and Stephanie, a married couple who chaperon three youth walking in preparation for receiving the Sacrament of Confirmation. We get takeout pizza and eat together. The youth speak decent, unpracticed English. When André speaks English, he rolls his eyes back in his head which scatters to recesses inaccessible all the French and German in my head.

With a room to myself, I anticipate a good night's sleep, but restless, I toss and turn as blustery gusts and rain beat on the windows.

The Lone Pilgrim

DAYS 30 - 31

Unable to sleep, I rise hours before sunrise. The storm has spent itself.

I walk out of town, onto a dirt and gravel road and into countryside. Every so often, I turn on my headlamp and check my map against my compass and the bends of the road. *Le Chemin* turns south, and I descend into flatter farmlands with tall, standing corn.

Through corn tassels, on the edge of the horizon, the light of the sun glows in shades of gold, brightly polished and brilliant, dull and subdued. Above me, the light paints dark clouds in reds and purples. The sunrise is brief as if God thinks its beauty too great for man to behold for more than a moment. The sun rises higher, and glory dissipates into the flat light of day.

As I leave the bucolic farmland, I hear factories toil with an unceasing mechanical drone, as if a great beast rumbles and, with a giant metallic hammer, beats a slow rhythm.

I walk into the town Maslacq between France's customary mealtimes: too late for breakfast, too early for lunch. When I step into Hôtel Maugouber, my intuition says, "Speak Spanish," but in broken French accentuated with facial expressions and hands folded in prayer, I beg, cajole and sweet-talk an older woman into persuading the chef to make me breakfast. I have a light, fluffy ham and cheese omelet with fresh French bread and crude oil coffee. To drink it, I add milk repeatedly. I love the coffee.

When I pay, the woman counts in Spanish. My head pops back. *"Usted habla español?"* She is from Spain, and we converse in Spanish. The coffee is Brazilian.

As I leave, I admonish myself: *Jeffrey, your intuition worked but you didn't listen. You idiot. You have to listen to it.*

The day is hot, hot, hot, especially for mid-October. Drenched in sweat, my clothes cling to my skin and hang off my body. Plasticized water from my CamelBak does not sate my thirst.

I walk into the village Sauveleade parched and step into a bar permeated with a tomblike quiet that suggests nothing has happened here since the days of the Pharaohs. A surprised woman turns on music.

"L'eau, s'il vous plaît." I drain a glass of water, a second glass of water and drink a beer slowly. Leonard Cohen's "Hallelujah" plays. A song about being overthrown by beauty, the pain of love, the darkness of faith: had I not sweated so much water out of my body, I would weep. Even so, tears flow in my soul.

I walk out emotionally distraught and beer-sluggish. I want to lie down in the grass by the road and sleep and forget. Navarrenx is twelve kilometers ahead.

The Way follows asphalt roads and foot trails that pass through open country and patches of woods. In the cool forest, an undulating descent on asphalt with steep sections pains my feet. I walk the last couple kilometers under the sweltering sun. After soaking up sweat for weeks, the straps of my backpack emit a stench. The stench also re-emanates from my hat.

In Navarrenx, a small town, I almost step into a bar for a revival beer but bypass it to search out a *gîte*. After a convoluted search, I find the *gîte municipal* hidden on the second floor of a building complex. To register, a sign on the door directs me to a bar: the bar I bypassed. In front of the bar stands the sign for the *gîte d'étape communaux*. Searching for signs and learning to attend to instinct, I walked right past the sign for which I searched and ignored my instinct to walk into that bar.

Jeffrey, you're an idiot.

The narrow *gîte* stretches down one long hallway, with bedrooms and showers off the hall and a kitchen at one end. No other pilgrim is here.

At Mass at Église Saint-Germain-d'Auxerre, a young man in his twenties assists. I talked to him outside before Mass. He is a seminarian. I pray for him: *Lord, please give him a happy priesthood.*

Another seminarian and I are eating lunch with Father Henry Barron, the vocation director for the Diocese of Charleston. My fellow seminarian says, "Seminarians are not treated well."

"It will end when you are ordained," Father Barron assures us.

I am skeptical but take his word for it, thinking that it is part of trusting God.

I depart at dawn, and after the sun lightens the day, I cross into a dense forest that holds the cool of night in the shadows of dusk. Here men hunt mushrooms. I enjoy the cool, quiet walk but enter open country, where the sun burns fiercely, and the day boils. The sun and heat weary me.

At crossroads, a food distributor has a resting spot for pilgrims: tables with generous awnings, a detailed menu at a bar, but there are no people, no food, no water, no coffee, no nothing, except tables and awnings, the bar and the menu. I rest in the shade and drink water, thinking that being hungry and tired is the *norm de rigueur* of the Way.

Back out under the sun, I traipse through rolling hills with long valleys and vistas. A heron glides down a gently sloped valley, and I understand man's yearning to fly and why the flight of birds enraptures his imagination. The heron and its flight are beautiful. With black toenails and reddened blisters, my feet are ugly.

One kilometer from Aroue-Ithorots-Olhaïby, a *balise* indicates a left turn before the village, but the village holds the promise of lunch, if I climb a hill. Walking without lunch has been a hardship. So, I head uphill.

I find a pizza joint closed permanently and the locked *gîte communal*. I sit in the shade, drink water and ponder my doom. I am condemned, damned to walk another day in heat without food.

I check the Mass schedule at the local church. No Sunday Mass is scheduled.

The *balise* on the road indicated a turn before Aroue-Ithorots-Olhaïby, but the superimposed blue trail on the Michelin map indicates a turn after the village. What to believe? I dread walking back downhill, which will reinforce the uselessness of my ascent, but that is what I do. At the intersection, I recheck the *balise* and turn south.

The road does not feel right. *Balises* disappear. People driving past look at me as if I am out of place. I check my direction with my compass and my map's topography. Either I walked off the Way or onto the old Way or onto the bicycle Way. Either way, I have to decide: go back, keep straight or cross country. To go back admits stupidity. To keep straight will take me from an elevation of 110 meters to 347 meters. To go cross country means navigating farm roads not on my map.

I head cross country. I climb steeply, the road flattens, then I climb steeply again, and so on. I pass pastures with no animals and no shade, except for a rare tree. As I climb under the sun, my head hangs down, and I stare at dirt and gravel.

At the high point, a draft horse stands alone in a pasture without shade. The sun bakes us. He walks over to the fence. I extend my hand to him, and he touches my hand with his nose. I rub his forehead and neck and talk to him. After a couple minutes, I walk down the road. He follows along the fence. At the end of his pasture, I pet and talk with him again. He is lonely. I understand him.

With no *balises*, I make reasoned, gut-prodded decisions about turns. I take a rock-strewn path that descends dead west and end up on an asphalt road by several houses. I follow the road to an intersection, where a *balise* sends me back the direction I just came.

No, no, no.

I pull out my compass, check my map and keep a westerly bearing. I come to the hamlet Olhaïby and, with great relief, return to the Way.

Another day without lunch and with unnecessary climbs in blistering heat, I am baked, fried, sautéed, grilled. I am not done. I am well done, overdone, a charred piece of desiccated flesh.

I am also six kilometers from the village Larribar-Sorapuru, which according to Michelin, has a *gîte* at a farm. Under the merciless sun, I hustle, wanting to get this walk over with. I find no *gîte* in Larribar-Sorapuru and continue at a slow pace to conserve what little energy remains in my body.

I reach a two-lane highway leading to Uhart-Mixe, where Michelin says a *gîte* is located. I have seen signs to *Albergue*[7] *Duhalde Ostatua* in Uhart-Mixe, signs that promised shortcuts I was too wary to take. Now I make my own short cut. The Way leads into hills. I walk down the highway.

The highway comes to a river with a bridge about one hundred meters long, with enough space for two cars but no space for pedestrians. The highway curves downhill on both sides, which means cars will come upon me quickly. Cars from different directions will converge. I wait until the road is silent and jog. Three-quarters across, a car rounds the turn in front of me. I sprint and get off the road before the car reaches me. After several minutes, my nerves settle. I hope the worst is behind me.

The road winds through woods, then wraps around a steep hill above a river with no space for pedestrians. Against the hill rises solid rock; on the river side of the road stands a waist-high stone wall. I walk against traffic. When no vehicles approach, I walk on the road. When cars and trucks approach, I walk on top of the stone wall with the vehicle-filled road to my right and a twenty-meter drop into the stone-filled river to my left. I talk myself across this nervy transit. "Jeffrey, don't think about the river, don't think about the cars. Don't think." Although, I do think if I lose my balance and start to fall, choose the river, not the road. Once across, the sense of relief competes with nerves that do not want to settle.

In the hamlet Uhart-Mixe, I talk with two women who clean the church. No Sunday Mass is scheduled, and they do not know Mass times in churches down the Way.

Gîte de l'Escargot sits across the street. Duhalde Arño, the proprietor, pours me a glass of lemonade with the patient discipline

---

7 *Albergue*: the Spanish equivalent of *gîte*.

of hospitality, but hungry and exhausted after almost forty kilometers, I am desperate to know if he has a bed and food. He has both. I relax and enjoy two glasses of lemonade, without objection.

He puts me in a two-room suite: one a bedroom, the other a shower/bath. To move from room to room, I walk outside. With half doors and low ceilings, the rooms were once donkey stalls.

How befitting! As I lug my rucksack, I feel like a beast of burden, and when I make stupid mistakes, I feel like a jackass.

Aunélie cooks dinner, while I sit in the dining room at a long wooden table. A hutch holds dishes, and on top sits bowls and an espresso machine. Above a fireplace is a mantel with family photographs. Portraits hang on the walls. Two young girls sit at the end of the table and practice reading in Basque, which is darling entertainment.

I ask Aunélie if one of the girls is her daughter. She looks after them for a friend, then puts her hand on her belly. She is pregnant for the first time.

"I need $500 for an abortion," Anna says.

"What?"

"I'm pregnant and need $500 for an abortion."

"It's not my child. We've always used a condom."

"I know. I wish we never used a condom."

"You always use condoms with your tricks."

"Accidents happen, and it has happened to me."

"I am not going to give you money for an abortion."

She blows up. "I am not going to bring a baby into this fucked up world."

"Well, I am not going to pay to kill a baby."

"I have to have money today. I have an abortion scheduled tomorrow."

The next day is Tuesday and the abortion clinic in town performs abortions on Saturdays. It is just another lie to get money for heroin.

Aunélie and I talk in French, Spanish and English. A couple times when we have trouble communicating, she resorts to "show and tell." I have no idea what an *"œuf"* is. She goes into the kitchen and comes back with an egg. After the three-language comedy and culinary "show and tell," Aunélie writes down the menu: *soupe de légumes, pipenade-jambon saucisse, fromage brebis confiture, gâteau Basque* and *Patxaran*, an after-dinner *digestif.* Her traditional Basque cooking tastes wonderful.

For a second day, I meet no pilgrim. I have often felt alone. Now, I really am alone. I sit in the dark by the church, then sleep in my stall. In another Anna nightmare, she tricks.

Saint-Jean-Pied-de-Port

DAYS 32 -33

For breakfast, I enjoy toasted bread lathered with local honey, fresh squeezed orange juice and great coffee. Toasted bread and fresh squeezed orange juice are gastronomical signs that I am close to Spain. Duhalde stamps my passport with an image of a snail with two eyes, then draws a smile under the eyes.

Today, I have one overwhelming priority and one great goal. The priority is Sunday Mass. Because Jesus rose on Sunday, attending Sunday Mass is mandatory, and since becoming Catholic twenty-five years earlier, I have only missed one Sunday Mass. The goal is Saint-Jean-Pied-de-Port, the start of Camino Francés, the midpoint of my Way, and the completion of 750 kilometers. I am eager to walk.

I start up a small road that goes into the hills. The steep climb burns breakfast out of my body and energy out of my muscles. The sun rises, the day wakes up, the trail descends, and I enjoy a cool morning walk among pastures and wooded hills.

At 10:30 a.m., I arrive in the village Ostabat-Asme and find yet another church with neither Sunday Mass nor a posted schedule. Because 11 a.m. Mass is common, my next best chance is in Larceveau-Arros-Cibits, a village three kilometers away. If I hustle, I can make it. I hustle. In the heat and under the sun, sweat drenches my clothes.

The Way comes down out of the hills and parallels a two-lane highway. I see a steeple in southeastern Larceveau-Arroz-Cibits and make for the steeple. I hope to arrive at 11 a.m., then as if I drag and time hustles, a couple minutes after eleven, then five after eleven, then seven minutes. I walk into Mass fifteen minutes late. From Aroue-Ithorots-Olhaïby to Larceveau-Arros-Cibits, I have walked twenty-four kilometers and checked four churches to find Sunday Mass.

Outside the church, people mill about the square for a fiesta. There is music, chalk drawings and food booths. I would love to enjoy the fiesta, but no food is yet served, and I am driven. After more than seven hundred kilometers, Saint-Jean-Pied-de-Port sits less than twenty kilometers away. I follow *Le Chemin* back into the countryside and, even without food, walk with great energy.

Half a kilometer before the hamlet Gamarthe, two German men study their guidebook as they rest in the shade. They are the first pilgrims I have seen since I dined with the Swiss group in Arthez-de-Béarn, seventy-three kilometers and seventy hours earlier.

I wind down an asphalt road with spotty shade, then walk onto a long stretch of asphalt unshaded and baked by the fiery sun. My feet burn in my boots.

I imagine my arrival in Saint-Jean-Pied-de-Port. I will loose a primal scream of victory and dance in the main square. I will walk into the church and fall on my knees in thanksgiving. I will walk into town silently, touch the statue in the square and collapse from exhaustion. Many times on the Way I have imagined what was to come, and my imaginings were wrong. I wonder what manner of entry I will make into Saint-Jean-Pied-de-Port.

Walking on emotion and adrenaline, I eagerly cover the last several kilometers of turns, dips and climbs in sunlight and the shadows of trees and buildings. A couple hundred meters from the church and with Porte Saint-Jacques, the town gate through which pilgrims have entered Saint-Jean-Pied-de-Port for eight hundred years, in sight, someone calls, "Jeffrey, Jeffrey." I look uphill, and under a shade tree sit Rainev and Xiomara.

I bow my head and walk uphill. I want to keep going but sit down and wait while Rainev rolls and smokes a cigarette. Mere meters from completing a great goal, so tantalizingly close, I feel antsy, and the longer we sit, the more antsy I become. After twenty uncomfortable minutes, we hoist rucksacks and walk through Porte Saint-Jacques and down to the Église de la Notre-Dame. There is no square to scream or dance in, no statue to touch, and the church is closed in preparation for a concert. Tourists fill the streets.

We toast our accomplishment with beer in German-sized mugs, and a strange silence descends. I am not sure why: maybe we have too many emotions, maybe I am too tired or too antsy. The silence feels painful.

After beer, Rainev and Xiomara leave for Huntto, a hamlet a few kilometers up the mountain Collado Lepoeder, and I search for a hotel.

Someone calls, "Jeffrey, Jeffrey." I turn, and there stands the Indomitable Miza with her big smile. I throw open my arms and yell out "Miza" so loudly that tourists turn their heads with expressions of surprise. The life of a pilgrim differs from that of a tourist. Pilgrims make friends, encounter each other in different places, share a common life. Tourists walk past each other as if they drive to work in automobiles. Miza and I hug and talk excitedly. She intends to cross the Pyrenees tomorrow, finish two days later in Pamplona, then complete her Way the following year. We hug goodbye and wish each other *"Bon Chemin"* and *"Buen Camino."*

I find a hotel, get a room, shower and collapse on the bed.

I wake in time for the choral concert. Three choirs sing in several languages. For the encore, a choir sings a song in French, and the audience sings along. A woman tells me the song is about two separated lovers who long to return to each other. I wonder if Anna and I are those lovers or if we live an ill-fated lie.

Anna and I grocery shop, then go back to the trailer I rented for her so that she does not have to live on the street or trick to put a roof over her head.

"I am feeling so much better," she says. After starting back at the methadone clinic for the third time, the dosage had been raised to the maintenance level, and she has not used heroin for a week.

"That is a great feeling, I bet."

"Oh, it is. But I am not finished though. I have to stay on the maintenance level for several months, then withdraw from methadone."

"You can do it. I know you can."

Anna prepares supper: grilled chicken and a salad of green lettuce, walnuts, cherry tomatoes and scallions. I sit at the kitchen table. Everything seems normal. I think, This relationship might work out.

I breakfast in the hotel's dining room with pilgrims set to cross. All of them send their bags and carry day bags. One group walked up to Huntto the day before, took a taxi back down to Saint-Jean-Pied-de-Port, then scheduled a taxi ride that morning back up to

Huntto. Two women vacillate between walking and taking a taxi. Everyone else plans to take a taxi, either because of the steepness or the asphalt.

"If y'all start the Way taking a taxi to avoid climbs and asphalt, don't walk. Climbs and asphalt are part of the Way," I say.

A Swiss man, who boasts about hating the French and walking the Way "a dozen times," brags about using motor transportation. I think him more interested in justifying his own laziness than in giving sound advice. The two women take a taxi. Everybody collectively psyches themselves out and starts their pilgrimages with motor transportation. *I am in the wrong place with the wrong people.* My code forbids transportation by any means other than foot, and even with all the challenges that accompany my code, I love my code. I want to be with people who share my principles.

I happily return to my room to wash clothes. I also wash my backpack, which has putrefied. To dry it, I hang it out my window.

I buy sandwiches for the crossing since there is no place on the mountain to get food. To avoid the agony of walking without food when guidebooks beguiled me in France, I also buy dark chocolate, almonds and dried figs.

At lunch, I sit beside Abby from England and Maria Sophia from Greece, who walk together. I introduce myself, but glancing sideways when they speak to me, they make it clear they are not interested in a conversation.

I return to my hotel for a nap. The bells of one church ring, then the bells of another church, then the bells of the first church answer, the bells of the second church rejoin and so on. As I lie in bed not napping, entertained by the church bell version of "Dueling Banjos," I rename the Way of Saint James, the Way of No Sleep.

At an outdoor café, I eat an average supper except for dessert: goat cheese with black cherry jam. A little dog walks with nervous energy on short legs across a bridge and up the road. Lost and anxious, he circles a small block of buildings and disappears. I hope he finds his home. I hope, as I make my Camino, I find my home.

I like the friendly locals in Saint-Jean-Pied-de-Port, but there are too many tourists. Most of the new pilgrims I have met are tourists. Something about the town does not feel right, or maybe I do not feel right because of something going on with Anna back in the States. Either way, I am ready to leave. I want to be alone or with pilgrims.

I feel sad to spend my last night in France. With few exceptions, I met lovely people and fellow pilgrims who enriched my pilgrimage with humor, generosity, friendship and wisdom. I suffered and despaired yet persevered. I experienced an adventure in which, sometimes, I followed my intuition and instinct to great benefit and saw the Providence of God.

I wonder what Spain will be like.

Crossing the Pyrenees

DAYS 34 - 36

Cruel is the fate of pilgrims who walk Camino Francés and, on their first day, suffer the most difficult, grueling and arduous section of the Way. I experienced that fate when I walked through the Gorges de Allier in ignorance. I was never ignorant about Collado Lepoeder: an essentially pure climb of 1,230 meters over 18.5 kilometers, then a descent of 480 meters over four kilometers. The whole distance from Saint-Jean-Pied-de-Port to Roncevalles is twenty-six kilometers with an elevation change of 1,710 meters, not counting undulations.

I know this climb hurts pilgrims. Pilgrims have died on the mountain and not just in movies. The majesty of mountains mirrors their peril, and this mountain rises in majesty, at least in my mind. I cannot see the mountain I have to climb. Even so, there is reason for a man to psyche himself out, as I witnessed the day before. Temptations of doubt flit at the periphery of my thoughts.

Part of the preparation is practical: equipment, food, water. Part is physical: muscles worn into shape and abused feet will carry me up and over. The biggest part dwells in the realm of the spirit: will power and prayer. Starting off in the early morning darkness, I resolve, "I am walking up this mountain" and pray, "Alright God, let's walk up this mountain."

The first turn offers a choice between the high mountain pass to the left and the low valley pass to the right. A fear-inspired temptation whispers, "Turn right." I turn left.

A pilgrim walks ahead of me. I slow my pace but catch Wolfgang from Germany, a doctor on the city council, who walks to escape texts and phone calls. I breathe harder on the steeper sections. Nevertheless, he falls behind, and I creep ahead. Several times, I stop to rest, and he catches up. The sun rises, and in the sun's diffused light, outlines of ridges and trees become visible.

At a section where trees have been logged, the trail splits, and no markers identify the Way. Hank from Holland, in his sixties, with a Santa Claus beard and a big rucksack, has stopped, undecided about which direction to go. Intuition and subtle signs of a more worn trail suggests a right turn. I turn right, follow a contour, then climb straight up. A couple hundred meters up the mountain, I find a marker. I also see that the left trail leads to the same place. I stand atop a precipice, yell down and wave my *bâton*. Walking back and forth, Hank and Wolfgang do not notice me. I become cold, and knowing whatever decision they make will be okay, I start climbing. Wearing thin clothes and no jacket, I need to walk to maintain body temperature.

The morning sun climbs the sky and warms me, but the road passes into shade on the windward side of a ridge. I drop my backpack. The wind billows my sweat-soaked shirt off my clammy back, and the cold shocks my system. I put my jacket on, and my jacket presses my sweaty shirt against my back, causing another deep chill. After several minutes, exertion warms me just enough to ward off the cold.

I climb above the forest to a treeless ridge line at Vierge de Biakorri, where giant black boulders dot the grassy heights. Expecting to be alone, I come around a wide turn and see a mass of people with daypacks and cars parked around a tall, white cross. I want to visit the cross, but the cars and the tourists cheapen the place and the moment. Here the Way climbs upwards, but not steeply, which explains why the *tourigrinos* started where they did.

Pottocks, semi-domesticated ponies, live here. They have the mass and look of draft horses compressed into pony size: stout legs, barrel chests, huge bellies. They wear thick coats in bay, sorrel and palomino and have long manes. Herds of sheep with white wool on their bodies, black wool on their heads and curled horns live on the grassy heights without shepherd or guard dog. I stare at them, jealous of their wool.

I trudge through the milling tourist and come upon a young, Korean couple. The man holds the camera at the end of a selfie stick as they playfully rub against each other.

I walk up through a narrow, rocky col guarded by a flock of sheep. I pause to rest, eat and enjoy the view. The tourists arrive and mill about. I resent chatty tourists invading my peace and cross into Spain, the border delineated by a scraggly, two-strand barbed wire fence.

I pass under the shade of trees but walk mostly in the warm sun, which shines overhead. I reach the high point on Collado Lepoeder and wait for the Korean couple. They speak little English. With hand gestures conveying requests, we photograph each other.

I descend into a forest where dead leaves form a thick, spongy carpet. I expect walking on leaves to comfort my feet and knees. I step into camouflaged holes and kick hidden rocks. I happily step back on hard ground. I then descend through open valleys.

The map from the pilgrim office indicates an ornithology center by the Camino, and from atop the high mountain walls, I look down on a large building located about where the ornithology center is indicated. In the distance, several kilometers away, I see a village: Roncevalles! The end of the toughest day of the Camino is in sight. I feel ecstatic.

I descend through meadows, where pottoks, the last symbols of the high crossing, take more interest in grass than me. Once in the valley, El Camino winds over rounded shoulders of small ridges and down into scooped draws as it crisscrosses a stream. A thin layer of leaves covers the wide path. Old trees stand like cathedral columns. Sunlight dapples the forest floor.

After walking on a long straight grass road in the sun with tall bushes on either side, I reach the ornithology center. Out of water, I think I might get water here and continue to Roncevalles. I drop my bag and go in. I expect cold offices and metal cabinets indicative of an underfunded operation staffed by people who think more of birds than money. The floor is stone, the walls new and the entrance well lighted. Two sets of double glass doors stand to the left and right. I walk through the doors on the right and see hiking equipment in a glass cabinet. A woman sits at the end of a long desk where four people can fill out forms simultaneously.

"*Donde estoy?*"

"*Roncevalles,*" the woman answers.

"*Roncevalles? No es possible.*" I look at my watch, walk back outside and read the sign: "*Refugio de Peregrinos de Roncevalles.*"

I walk back in and say, "*Roncevalles? No es possible. Solo seis horas!?*" She gives me a thumbs up.

I am dumbfounded. I arrived in Roncevalles unaware that I completed the crossing of the Pyrenees, what I expected to be the hardest part of the journey. I wonder if I will finish my Way, not knowing I have reached the spiritual end.

I step outside and come face to face with a man I have not seen since Espeyrac in Église Saint-Pierre, twenty-five days and five hundred and seventy kilometers earlier. I recognize his face. I now learn his name: Pierre from France. When I photographed him in Saint-Pierre, he was praying to his name saint. I show Pierre the photo I took of him when he prayed, and he shows me a photo someone took of him that morning. He sat on a mountain spur, and before him lay great valleys, the far mountains and the glory of the sunrise breaking above the mountains.

I sit outside on a bench, considering my options: stop or walk. It is still early, and I am not exhausted. I rest, drink water, nibble on snacks and decide to stay. Crossing the Pyrenees is enough accomplishment for one day. My bunk mates are the Korean couple, Yu Hwa and Beong Mun, and a twenty-year-old woman from Canada, named "M," who uses the word "awesome" again and again and again.

Wandering around town, I find a statue that looks like a piece of paper torn from a sheet, rolled up tightly, then released to form a spiral, except this paper is made of copper-colored metal several inches thick and lays on the flat side of the loose end so that observers stare into the spiral. I wonder if the art means that pilgrims spiral into the depths of their true selves the further we pilgrimage or that we unravel as we walk and discover who we are. Or both.

I sit outside the *Refugio* on a bench as clouds, shaded from dark blue to white, sail in a rush, driven by wind blowing unhindered above the high peaks. The clouds hide and reveal sunshine, and I alternate between feeling cold and warm. Nara from Brazil sits beside me. On a ukulele, she plays Bob Marley songs. I enjoy her company and the private concert.

Many pilgrims have come down but not Wolfgang. I last saw him eight hours earlier. He walks in with four other pilgrims at 6 p.m. I am happy to see him, and he accepts my invitation to dine together.

The starter is a decent soup, the main course pitiful stuffed peppers and a small fish, dessert small and forgettable. As hungry after dinner as before, I certainly feel less satisfied.

Wolfgang, a Catholic, and I attend Mass together. Stone walls, floors and columns, a high arched ceiling, stained-glass windows, a bronze baldacchino and a wood statue of Mary covered with silver and decorated in gold: La Real Colegiata de Santa María looks stunning. Behind me, I notice a woman with dark hair and an intelligent face. Something about her attracts me.

After Mass, I introduce myself to her—Janey from London—then return to the dormitory and crawl into bed. As I lie here, a loud Irishmen uses the word "fuck" and "fucking" repeatedly.

I crossed the Pyrenees, I am in Spain in a dormitory with more than sixty people, I saw a man I thought I would never see again, I tried to make a friend, I introduced myself to an attractive woman, I am tired and hungry. My pilgrimage has begun anew.

Before sunrise, Gregorian chant starts softly, then becomes louder, and the dormitory lights brighten slowly, making the transition from sleep gentle and peaceful.

Awesome M and I sit at a bar. To order, she adds Spanish vowels to the ends of English words: "coffeeo, breado." The incomprehensible language confuses the man behind the bar. I translate, intermingling French and Spanish, but we communicate.

Awesome M worked at a farm in Ireland when she learned about the Camino. She made reservations the next day. As we talk, in the middle of one of my sentences, she looks away and sits with Irishmen at a table. My words trail off into a mumbling to myself.

Breakfast is as dissatisfying as the company: unsubstantial bread with a metallic taste left by a toaster, coffee in a demitasse, and orange juice in a child's glass.

It's time to walk.

As I leave, Janey and I almost walk into each other. Discomfited by bad food and bad company and feeling awkward because of my attraction to her, I blurt out, "Do you know where the Camino is?" As soon as the words leave my mouth, I kick myself for being such a dolt for blundering a conversation with someone I am interested in.

Flustered, she answers, "I don't know. I have not even had a cup of coffee."

"Neither have I," I answer in a vain attempt to restart the conversation.

I just need to walk. Walking solves lots of problems.

In the dark, with an educated guess, I find El Camino. Bini from Korea, a young, twenty-year-old woman, comes up, and we walk into a forest. To light the Way, I use my headlamp, and she uses her smartphone's flashlight app. After experimenting, we find that with one light pointed before our feet and the other pointed ahead, we walk safely, with shadowy outlines of pine trees and waist-high ferns to either side.

In conversation about why we walk, she asks, "How do we discern the will of God?"

"That is the question of the Way, isn't it?"

"I wish God's will for us was as obvious as the yellow arrows," Bini says.

Flechas amarillas mark the Way in Spain as red and white *balises* marked the Way in France. I did not see one yellow arrow crossing the Pyrenees, but Bini and I see them on signs, trees, fence posts, bridges, houses and the roadway itself.

"How did you come to believe?" she asks.

"I grew up with belief but have had experiences of God." I do not elaborate.

Bini and I walk through the town Auritz/Burguete on streets illuminated by streetlamps. The sun rises, and we walk faster, with more confidence. We talk about the Russian language and culture which she studied at university, and traditional Korean thanksgiving, which includes ancestor worship. She says that she struggles with the tension between respecting and obeying parents who come from a different generation and living her own life. She feels controlled and trapped by the older generation.

Back in the countryside, we come to an ingenious foot bridge—eight squarish concrete pillars, short enough for us to step across and separated by gaps to allow the water of a stream to flow between. We photograph each other on the bridge. Bini balances on one leg and raises her arms in the air.

She shows me the photograph of Pierre sitting on the belvedere and facing the rising sun. She was the person who captured that sacred, contemplative moment. Just before the village Aurizberri/Espinal, Pierre catches us.

The trail descends except for two climbs. At the top of Alto de Mezkiritz, pilgrims have woven hundreds of crosses made from sticks into a chain linked fence. The Way passes through villages, then climbs steeply up to Earrovide. Bini breathes hard and tells us to go on. She assures us that she is okay. Pierre and I assure her that she is doing well for her second day and keep climbing.

Pierre stops to snack, and I meet Giuseppe from Spain. With little money and little time, he camps out every night and plans to walk forty kilometers a day. He walks with a hectic pace, as if he hurries through a train station. He dresses to race: running shoes, blue support socks up to his knees, basketball shorts and an athletic shirt. He is impossibly thin and of small stature. As he disappears down the Way, he knifes through the air.

At a roadside café which consist of a van with tables set up, I take coffee. A man pushes a baby carriage, packed with his gear, down the road. I head downtrail.

Half an hour later, Pierre catches me. He is separated from his wife, and his son has just started university. The most important relationships in his life are changing. We talk about going home slowly. He can fly back home in half a day but intends to take the train home over two days. When I arrive home, all I want to do is sit at my farm and think. Halfway through our walk, we already know we have a lot to process.

In the village Zubiri, we stop in a small square with a water fountain along with Giuseppe, the Man with the Baby Carriage, and a pilgrim I have never met.

It is noon, and we have walked twenty-two kilometers. Larrasoaña, the next village, lays six kilometers ahead, and sixteen kilometers beyond lays Pamplona. I stand an hour and a half from Larrasoaña, where I plan to stop, but within striking distance of Pamplona. I feel good and have food left over from the crossing. Except for a few small hills, the Way to Pamplona descends gently. I say goodbye and walk. I do not know where I will stop, but my attention has been drawn toward Pamplona.

The trail crosses onto a long, straight, asphalt road, and the pilgrim I do not know walks half a kilometer behind. The road follows the contours of a ridge then descends. My left ankle and foot begin to hurt, a dull discomfort I do not want to worsen. Neither do I want to stop. The day is sunny without being hot, breezy without being cold: perfect weather to walk in the beauty of the foothills. It is hard to stop walking.

The land's character has changed. In France, the land was green and lush. In Spain, it is arid and brown.

The trail crosses a highway, ascends steeply, then parallels Río Arga. Down below, the river flows with its mysterious movement in which it ever changes and ever looks the same. Sunlight gilds leaves on trees that grow tall by the river. A gentle breeze flutters the leaves, which look like ten thousand golden hands waving at me.

I reach Pamplona's suburbs around 5 p.m. The pilgrim I do not know walks a couple hundred meters behind me. Waysigns change from *flechas amarillas* to brass *conchas* embedded in the sidewalk. *Conchas* appear to end when the Way turns, which makes missteps easy.

As I talk to a woman to confirm directions, the pilgrim behind me passes us. He now walks ahead of me and a truck that dusts leaf-filled gutters. I speed up to get ahead of the truck, the truck speeds up to pass parked cars. I slow down to let the truck get ahead, the truck slows down to work curbs. For a kilometer, I walk in leaf-dust fallout.

I cross the Puente de la Magdalena, a fourteenth century stone bridge, and come under high, medieval walls, cross a draw bridge, and walk through a gate into old Pamplona feeling a mix of accomplishment and relief.

The pilgrim I do not know sits on a bench. I walk up and give him my hand, and he takes it.

"Man, that was heroic," I say.

"When I was in Zubiri, I said to myself: just go for it," Chris from Brazil says.

"Which *albergue* are you planning to stay in?" he asks.

"I have walked eight hundred kilometers, and tomorrow is a day off, and on days off, I stay in hotels," I explain.

"I'm sure we will see each other again," he says.

"I'm sure we will."

I pass up a hotel that looks too expensive, then wander through the old city on narrow streets lined with buildings that rise like canyon walls. After walking through hamlets, villages and the countryside for a month, I become disoriented. I do, however, find the cathedral and, nearby, a pilgrim store.

After a two-kilometer circumambulation through Pamplona's historic district, I walk into Pamplona Cathedral Hotel, the hotel I rejected. At this point, exhaustion justifies the expense of four-star accommodations.

The hotel restaurant does not open until 8 p.m. I walked forty-five kilometers on minimal food and must wait two hours to eat. Spain's late mealtimes are another cultural adaptation I have to make.

The hotel was once a convent, and its dining room a chapel. A natural stained oak floor, white plaster walls, Roman arches supporting a white ceiling, backlit stained-glass windows, recessed lights illuminating columns, candelabras with small lights that look like stars: the dining room retains the character of a chapel.

The food tastes good. The Navarre wine tastes delicious, but a whole bottle is too much. I stagger to the elevator and to my room.

Lying in bed, I struggle with a dilemma. I often felt like I walked away from pilgrims to separate from them. Sometimes, I told myself that I walked to something ahead. I vacillate, unable to discern my motives or search my intuition with clarity. A second notion permeates my thoughts. Someone needs to tell me to walk slower.

In the *chapella*, I eat The Breakfast of Pilgrims: scrambled eggs, bacon, four kinds of fruit, four cheeses, smoked salmon and two croissants with blackberry jam, water, orange juice and coffee. That is a breakfast a pilgrim can walk on.

With a free day, I tour Pamplona.

At the gate to the Cathedral's courtyard sits a female beggar, who says, *"Ayuda me, por favor,"* with the most practiced, pitiful voice I have ever heard. Beneath the surface of her apparent pity, I sense intense anger.

La Catedral de la Santa María la Real is a monument to God. Its façade is neoclassical: massive, cylindrical columns, two tall towers with square lines and three doors at least five meters tall. Inside, the nave, three times taller than its width, creates an overwhelming emphasis on vertical space. The simplicity of massive interior columns reinforces the weighty impact of their size and the drama of the high space. A wrought iron gate separates the nave from choir stalls, an altar and the statue of Mary. A twelfth century wood carving with a silver-plated body, a porcelain face and adorned with a crown, Mary looks like a queen. The Spanish know how to build churches.

About twenty people, but no other pilgrim, attend Mass in a side chapel. After Mass, the sacristan stamps *mi passporto pelegrino* with a *sello* less dramatic and interesting than stamps at locations of lesser stature.

On Avenida Roncevalles, I find the life-size statue Monumento al Encierro, which memorializes the running of the bulls. Seven men run ahead of six bulls. Two bulls have lowered their heads to gore fallen men. The statue freezes a moment of tension and fear. It also captures the stupidity of man and the wisdom of the bulls who follow their instincts while the men ignore theirs.

I lunch at Café Iruña, Ernest Hemingway's favorite café, and like the thought of dining in the favored café of one of America's great writers.

I happen upon a statue of Saint Francis and the wolf of Gubbio. Francis's right hand opens to the wolf, who stands by his leg. As the story goes, a wolf terrorized Gubbio, an Italian village, killing livestock and people. Francis tamed the beast with a holy word and made peace between the wolf and the village, who adopted and fed the wolf. The story is hagiographic hyperbole. A realistic scenario is that the wolf preyed on livestock because he was old and that Saint Francis, with a gift of understanding the other creature, man or beast, domesticated the wolf, who was smart enough to figure out that he could survive more easily in communion with man than in opposition, which was how canines were first domesticated. This hypothesis looks beneath the overly pious story and says more about the man than hagiographic accretions say about the saint. Underneath the saint is the man, the clay of which the saint is made.

I tour the cathedral, and among its attractions, the brochure advertises that a tower, with a view of Pamplona, is open to visitors. As daunting as is the prospect of a climb, I want to see the city from the height. Halfway up, a locked door stops me. I laugh when I realize that my exhausting labors come to nothing. *A sign of life in the Catholic Church? Verily. A sign of how my Way will end? I hope not.* I return to my hotel for a siesta.

When I wake, the sun has set. I stroll down to the expansive Plaza del Castillo, pass up one restaurant after another, then hear "Jeffrey, Jeffrey." The Australian ladies sit at table with several empty bottles of wine. They finished in Saint-Jean-Pied-de-Port, then came to Pamplona to shop.

In the French Basque Country, they stayed at a *gîte* where the proprietor sang Basque separatist songs. At l'Escargot, they met the kind Duhalde. When I mention that I walked forty-five kilometers into Pamplona, as if answering my prayer, they caution me not to walk too fast, because "you will walk away from your friends." Liz also advises me not to stay in hotels because "it all happens in the *albergues,*" a lesson I learned well when I last saw Angelique. Liz also advises me not to expect too much when I arrived in Santiago, because I will set myself up for disappointment.

I do not disagree, but fed up, I say, "Stop mothering me."

They laugh, saying "We are mothers," and stop.

In France, they asked why I walked, and I stuck to my answer. Their minds did not stop working on the question.

"Are you a priest?" Liz asks. I bust out laughing.

Terri asks, "Do you think you might have a vocation to the priesthood?" Again, I laugh. They accept my laughs as no's.

"I know there is something," Anna says. "We've been together for a month. I'm not stupid."

"Alight, I'll tell you. But it is not what you think it is. There's no other woman."

I take a deep breath and close my eyes. Jumbled emotions roil me. Fear of her reaction, fear of exposure.

I am sitting on the bed of hotel room, wearing trousers and a button-down shirt. Anna is dressed in a business skirt and blouse and looks beautiful.

"Hold me," I say. She crawls onto the bed, with knees under her, leans on me and puts her arms around me. Her head rests against mine.

I breathe deeply and hold my breath. I feel my heart beating. "I am a priest."

She pulls away and asks, "You are a priest?"

"Yes. A Catholic priest."

After a few minutes back and forth, Anna says, "I am going to have to think about this. If I had known you were a priest, I would not have done what we have been doing. I am glad that I am Catholic, and I respect the Catholic Faith."

"I know it is a shock. I understand. But if you knew the hell I have gone through in the Catholic Church, you would understand. Those bastards who run the Church have done everything in their power to make it clear they do not want me to be a priest."

We hug and kiss goodbye. She goes to the clinic. I go back to my parish.

The Australian ladies stop inquiring and become introspective.

Teary-eyed, Terri says, "I walked because I am a fat, old lady. I only walked half the trail, but I walked it."

Liz says she wanted to have "the I-can-do-it feeling."

Helen and Liz walked Camino Francés three years earlier. During that pilgrimage, Helen's husband died, and she returned home. "I walked to complete what I did not finish before."

Jane does not reveal why she walked and leaves early. The other ladies relax and sigh. Jane is not a longtime friend, and early in their walk, she contracted pneumonia and was bedridden for a week. Liz, Terri and Helen rallied around Jane, and Jane did not say thank you once. The reason I felt tension among them the day we met is revealed.

Helen asks if I have someone waiting on me at home. I do not know the answer myself. She kisses my hand, my cheek. She pulls me to her, saying I am "wonderful." I look at Liz and Terri pleading for help. They howl in laughter.

"The Camino's the biggest hook-up walk on earth," Helen says.

I excuse myself with a comment about "an early start."

In another nightmare about Anna, she leaves me, and I am unable to get in touch with her.

Analisa of the First People

DAYS 37 - 38

As I rearrange my kit, my head lamp crashes onto the hardwood floor of my hotel room. Feelings of sickness and stupidity compete for primacy. I turn it on. Nothing happens. I take it apart and reassemble it. Nothing.

I go to the pilgrim store near the cathedral, but it is closed. I have not planned to attend Mass, but now near the cathedral, I go. Mass is celebrated at the main altar. About the same number of people attend as the day before, along with two other pilgrims. A woman with dark hair and a dark complexion sits on the other side of the nave. I cannot place her nationality. Another woman, a couple rows behind me, with fair skin and light brown hair, looks French. At the exchange of peace, I walk to her, shake her hand and say, *"La Paz."* Her accent confirms her French nationality. She has a beautiful, intriguing smile I do not know how to interpret. I return to my seat, and to my surprise, the mysterious woman has walked across the church to exchange peace with me. She speaks English with an American accent.

After Mass, I want to introduce myself to her because we both speak English, but she disappears. I also want to talk to the French woman, who is closer to my age. I am attracted but also restrained by my relationship with Anna, my priesthood, the

149

language barrier and fear of the attraction, which has gotten me into trouble before.

As I wait for the pilgrim store to open, the French woman walks by. We say hello, and I watch her walk away. I imagine chasing her down, walking with her and flirting. Instead, I wait for the store to open, then give up waiting.

A second pilgrim store does not have headlamps. A sports store has expensive ones, but when the salesman takes apart my headlamp and reassembles it, it works. He laughs because he lost a sale. I laugh at the irony.

I then walk into Parque de la Taconera, spacious with lots of grass and lined with trees and bushes. I photograph the park, and my camera battery dies. I kick myself because I could have charged it during the night. I cross the park and realize I have walked off the Way.

Everything is going wrong.

At a café, I drink coffee, sample truffles, plug in my camera, and wait. And wait. And wait, until my impatient self can wait no longer.

I search out where I stepped off the Way and realize I walked past a turn when I entered the park. I stand beside the brass *concha* embedded in the sidewalk, and within the space of a breath, as I stare at the *concha*, someone's feet step on it. I look up and into the mysterious, dark woman's smiling face.

Half-Mexican, half-Navajo, Analisa identifies with the Navajo People. She resents the labels "Native American" and "Indian." She describes me as a Native American since I was born in the United States. She defines her nationality as "First People."

"What does Navajo mean?"

"Knife carrier."

"Let's see your knife."

"I don't have one. Knives can't be carried onto planes." So, the multitool I dropped off had a purpose in God's plan. I could have given it to Analisa.

"How do you say 'white man' in Navajo?"

"Biligana."

She started at Lourdes, where she prayed that she might be a mother like Mary, then walked to Saint-Jean-Pied-de-Port where she learned that she was pregnant. She and the father, friends for years, got drunk and had sex once. Because of questions about her and the baby's health and their relationship, she does not want to tell him. Doctors told her that she cannot become pregnant, and if she becomes pregnant, she cannot carry a baby to term.

"Don't worry about the health of the baby," I say.

At St. Joseph's Church, in my first year as a priest, after the 6 p.m. Sunday Mass, a young couple asks to talk to me.

"We're have troubling conceiving a child and have scheduled in vitro fertilization this week. We want your blessing."

"I've got bad news for you. In vitro fertilization is not considered ethical or moral by the Church." They look surprised but not upset.

"We didn't know that, and we so much want to have a child. Why does the Church teach that?"

"In our mind, medicine enhances the natural processes of the human body but does not frustrate it or replace it. The simple example is that when we are sick, medicine restores us to health, the normal state of being. It's kind of strange, but when it comes to the conception of children, we're kinda old-fashioned. We think the only moral and ethical means is for couples to make love."

"But we want a child, and we want to do what the Church wants us to do."

"I know you do, and God wants you to have a child. Let's do this. Cancel the appointment, let me give you a blessing and give God a chance. What's the harm in waiting one month? Has any priest blessed you and prayed that you conceive a child?"

"No."

"Let's give God a chance."

I bless them, they cancel the appointment, and that month, they conceive a child. That same year, I bless another infertile couple, and within a month, they conceive. The babies are born healthy.

I pray silently: *Lord, when you made us in your image, you said "Be fertile and multiply." I ask that Analisa's baby be born healthy.* I also think, if the baby is born, it will be a sign from God for me to stay a priest. Of course, I may never see Analisa again after today, and the baby would be born after we return home. Nevertheless, I cling to this thought.

When Analisa crossed the Pyrenees, she walked in with Wolfgang and remembered that I waited for him.

"We have to look out for each other," I say.

"We are a tribe," she says, with a brightening face.

"Yes, we are a tribe."

Pilgrimaging with little money, she has slept in a tent and bathed in rivers. The night before, she slept in a homeless shelter. They washed her clothes, gave her a nice bed and, when she left, gave her two euros.

She considered abandoning her Way because she had not met any Christians but changed her mind when she saw me at Mass. Baptized Catholic, she had not attended Mass in decades, until that morning. She cried when she received Communion.

Walking with an unmarried pregnant woman, I feel like Joseph walking with Mary to Bethlehem and imagine walking to Santiago with Analisa but dismiss that thought as fanciful.

In the village Cizur Menor, we buy fruit and bread at a *mercado*, then walk out of the suburbs and into semi-arid countryside with little shade. We picnic under a rare tree, then resume the climb and summit Alto del Perdón. Black steel silhouettes of pilgrims walking with a dog, riding a horse and leading a donkey line the top of the crossing. We photograph each other among the silhouettes. As we descend, dust blooms around our feet, and rocks, disturbed by our feet, roll downhill billowing dust.

In the village Obanos, we photograph each other walking through metal artwork with a cut out in human form. At a farm, Analisa pets dogs, while I visit horses who nuzzle me and nibble my shirt.

We stop at Hotel Jakue in the small town Puente la Reina. Analisa does not want to stay here. Money is the problem, but I insist on paying. In my mind, paying for a pregnant woman to sleep in a bed instead of on the ground is a prolife act.

In the *albergue*, on the bottom floor, we share a room with Joseph, a Basque from Spain, Marcel and Leonard from Germany, and a Frenchman who keeps to himself.

Joseph is older, thin, half bald with close cut gray hair and a narrow, gray beard. Marcel has dirty blond dreadlocks, tattoos and a nose ring. Leonard has short black hair, no jewelry and no tattoos. Opposite in appearance, both are easygoing.

Analisa and I persuade Joseph to join us for supper. I buy food for a salad and spaghetti, and Analisa cooks. Beong Mun and Yu Hwa, whom I met the day I crossed the Pyrenees, cook an Asian dish. All five of us eat together, share our food, laugh and talk.

As I lay in bed, my restless mind wanders back down the Way and replays each event with hindsight that makes sense of the senselessness. Everything went wrong, and because of that cascade of blunders, I met Analisa and enjoyed a delightful afternoon. Analisa, about to abandon and return home, decided to persevere when she met me. This serendipitous confluence of events can only have been wrought by God.

Analisa taught yoga in the States, and I feel inspired to stretch. She gives me a few pointers, but my poses do not look like hers. Her poses look like human art.

Breakfast in the hotel bar constitutes a devolution of the French breakfast: a pitiful piece of insubstantial bread, a miniature glass of orange juice and a small cup of coffee, the second such gastronomically uninspiring breakfast in Spain in two days on El Camino—the Breakfast of Pilgrims on days off does not count. After adjusting to the paltry French breakfast, I cannot believe I must adjust to a breakfast equally meager but less satisfying.

We sit with Hank and Nicole from Holland, who met on the Way, and like me and Analisa, formed a Camino friendship.

"How are you doing?" Nicole asks.

"You know, I am pregnant and so happy to be a mother," Analisa says.

Nicole looks at me and says, "Congratulations."

"We only met yesterday," I explain. I put my arm around Analisa and say, "We're very happy." The table erupts with laughter.

As Analisa and I leave town, we pause at an *albergue*, where pilgrims have gathered in the entrance hall to listen to a pilgrim play his didgeridoo. I introduce myself to Lucas from Czechoslovakia.

He hopes to pay for his walk by working as a street performer in the cities.

Then Analisa and I head downtrail. The sun rises, and as the trail climbs, the sun comes out in full force. Atop the climb, I slather myself with sunscreen and show Analisa my whitened arms.

"Now, I really am *biligana.*"

In the village Cirauqui, I meet Santiago from Spain, a thin, older man with black hair and a short, black beard, streaked with lines of gray. He and Analisa shared a cubicle in Roncevalles.

"This is your trail," I say.

"Ahh, yes, this is my trail." He speaks in accented but intelligible English.

"Thank you for letting me walk your trail."

"Ahh, you are welcome."

Analisa buys bread in a *panaderia.* She and I then climb a hill, walk on a Roman road and cross a Roman bridge. An hour later, we cross a medieval bridge, where we chat with the Korean couple. Their playful, blossoming love is adorable. They met in Huntto. Yu Hwa describes them as "partners of the Camino."

Analisa and I picnic in the small town Lorca, then stop at the church, which is locked. In a shady spot by the church sits the French woman from Mass in Pamplona with her smile I do not know how to interpret. I go over to her. Caught between friendship with Analisa and attraction to this woman, I have no idea what to say or do. All I say is *"Bon Chemin."* She smiles her beautiful smile and says, *"Bon Chemin."* As Analisa and I leave, I hope to see her again, despite the conflicting thoughts.

We walk among huge fields and past hundreds of straw bales stacked together. The sun hangs high. The day burns hot.

We come upon Marcel and Leonard. Analisa trades sage, which she brought from home, for marijuana. Sage is used for ritual purification in her culture, and she brought it to trade and help pay for her Camino.

As we walk, Analisa tells me that her father died when she was young and her mother, an addict, beat her. She is angry with her father for his early death and his abandonment of her to abuse. She lights candles in churches to pray for him, for reconciliation with him and for forgiveness in her heart. Now pregnant, she knows a mother's love for a child not yet born, and the abuse with which her mother afflicted her makes even less sense.

Analisa dedicates each day's walk to a different person: a day for her father, a day for her mother, a day for her unborn child and so on. I stop, touch her arm and look at her.

"That's a beautiful way to pray the Camino."

We hike up to Ermita de San Miguel Arcángel, a small, high-roofed, stone chapel set atop a knoll and surrounded by olive trees. When we walk into the chapel, a couple is lying on a blanket on the floor. With an embarrassed look, the man jumps up and takes cigarettes off the altar.

In the town Lizarra/Estella, Neil from Ireland stands by the trail. Analisa knows him and his favorite word. "How are you doing fucking Neil? How the fuck are you?" She speaks without malice, but her effrontery stuns Neil.

Analisa and I find an *albergue* in a recreational center in the small town Ayegui. We know a little Spanish but have trouble understanding the man at the desk, which upsets him. When I ask for a receipt to track expenses, he answers, "No."

The *albergue* is a room in the basement with about sixty beds. While an indoor football game in the gym above us makes an annoying racket, we cook pasta for supper in a closet kitchen on a countertop stove with a single burner.

The hospitaller told us Mass at the local church was at 8 p.m. Something inside said Mass was at 7 p.m., but at 7:45 p.m., we head to church. We meet locals who tell us that Mass started at 7 p.m. Back at the *albergue*, we inform the hospitaller about the time for Mass. The inhospitable hospitaller shrugs.

Analisa sums up our experience. "We went from one of the best *albergues* to one of the worst."

In the basement, we meet Yuichi from Japan. At the beginning of every English sentence, which he speaks well, he draws out "Ahhh soo" in a deep voice. Two Chinese parishioners gave me a Japanese good luck sign to carry. The sign is a kanji, the Japanese writing system using Chinese characters. I show it to Yuichi, who translates the sign as "happiness."

I want to be happy, but the path to happiness has always been hidden.

Migration Rituals

DAYS 39 - 40

I dream about Anna. I do not recall details but wake unsettled. Analisa wakes with a cold. She coughs. She sounds stuffed up. Her voice is not clear.

"Our primary goal today is Mass," I say, but I worry about Analisa.

We start slowly and find a pace she is comfortable with. Because she normally walks fast, the slower pace is still good. We come to El Fuente de Vino, a fountain from which pilgrims can get free wine, and we drink breakfast wine.

After passing through a shady oak forest, where trees do not grow above ten meters, we cross into open countryside, then climb up to the village Ázqueta. The church is locked, and Mass times are not posted. I begin to worry that I might miss Sunday Mass.

We come upon El Fuente de Los Moros, a thirteenth century well in a shed-like building with stone walls, a gabled roof and a Mozarabic double arch entrance. Steps go down to a clear pool. The sun casts our shadows down onto the wall above the water-line. I take our self-portrait, and the photo is one of those rare great ones that just happens.

In Villamayor de Monjardin, a village on the arm of a hill, the unlocked church does not post Mass times. It is 9 a.m., and we are 12.5 kilometers from Los Arcos, a small town and the next best possibility for Mass. If Mass times in Spain match those in France, Mass in Los Arcos is at 11 a.m. We are running late.

The trail descends through farmland, vineyards and olive orchards. At crosses, pilgrims have left worn-out shoes, rosaries, holy cards, prayers and so forth. Analisa puts her whole foot, shoe and all, inside of one giant shoe.

We hear the rhythmic rev of engines. I check the Michelin guide. We are ten kilometers from a raceway. Against the songs of birds, boots crunching on the trail and human conversation, the mechanical noise sounds alien.

We top a mountain, then descend through a forest and into a wide, long valley, with mountains to the right and hills to the left. The Way parallels a stream that passes through the hills. Several kilometers from Los Arcos and close to 11 a.m., we rev our motors and all but run. I worry about Analisa, but she is a triathlete and tough.

After walking twenty kilometers in four hours with 480 meters of elevation change, the last 12.5 kilometers in two hours and fifteen minutes, we walk into a church empty of people but filled with architectural and artistic drama.

High up in the choir loft towers an organ. A three-story, Gothic, golden altar piece rises in the sanctuary. Statues form choirs around the tabernacle on the first tier and the statue of Mary on the second tier. On the third tier, angels surround Mary's statue. High above the altar piece rises a dome. The whole church reflects the altar piece, an attempt at glorious artistry that comes across as a busy, gaudy, overwhelming spectacle.

The other drama plays out prosaically. A woman walks in and tells us Mass is *"a la una."*

We rest at a table in the plaza and take off our boots. Victoria from England joins us. She was in an *albergue* the night before with Allan from Ireland who got drunk and used the word "pussy." When an Asian man asked him to be quiet so that pilgrims could sleep, he insulted the man with racial slurs. Analisa and I want to avoid Allan. Victoria says he heads to Torres del Río.

Analisa and I eat lunch, Victoria takes coffee, and I pay for everyone. When I buy Victoria's coffee, she pulls out a bag filled with oregano, rosemary, thyme and sage, and sprinkles the mixture into our boots. My boots smell wonderful, a treat I know will not last long.

Grand organ music complements the church, but in the overdressed church, the dressed-down celebrant wears an alb and stole but no chasuble, a minimal required vestment for Mass. After Mass, the three of us look at the artwork. I never become comfortable with the church.

Not feeling well, Analisa is done. She and Victoria stop in an *albergue* in Los Arcos. Analisa gives me a sprig of sage as a thank you. I give her twenty euros. We hug goodbye. I worry as I walk away, but her Way is hers to make as my Way is mine to make.

The effects of the morning's foot race manifest as afternoon shin splints and foot pain. The sun reaches its full might, and the barren land offers no shade. I swelter and run out of water. I slather myself in sunscreen which mingles with sweat to form an oily concoction not unlike hippo sweat, an oily secretion that protects hippos from sunburn. The seven-kilometer stroll to the village Sansol feels like a march twice as long.

Something says go to the village Torres del Río, half a kilometer beyond Sansol, but I want to avoid Allan. I register at *Deshojando del Camino*, a paradise in miniature: a walled courtyard, a cool, outdoor pool, a grassy yard with lawn chairs and tables under a canopy. In the downstairs bar, I drink a glass of water, a second and a third, then go upstairs to the dormitory and introduce myself to a pilgrim.

"Hi, I'm Jeffrey."

"I'm Allan."

I almost leave but stick it out. The saint in me wants to see what God has wrought in his providence. The impertinent sinner with a skewed perspective of God wants to discern God's joke.

I sup with Allan and Slavo from Slovakia, who walks with Allan. Conversation with Allan reveals more complexity than the story of his drunken behavior, which is entirely believable, even without his admission about being drunk and his complaint about a day-long headache. He walked for a year in places as far away as the Himalayas and Turkey. He started the Camino in Italy. After crossing into France, his mother became ill. He returned to Ireland to care for her, which says more about Allan than one night of obnoxious drunkenness.

He makes juvenile jokes, saying "fork" as if it were "fuck." Cynical and contrary, his jokes negate or twist everything I say. I think him deeply wounded and difficult company. Kind and respectful, Slavo drinks one beer a day. I wonder how they became friends and why they walk together.

"I always use condoms with my clients. You don't have to worry. I don't use a condom when I give blow jobs though. I hate the taste of plastic. Imagine what it tastes like putting your mouth on plastic."

I hate Anna's venal conversations but hope she will grow out of it, if she escapes heroin. Intelligent, with a college degree from a Catholic all-girls school, she is capable of conversing on many subjects but talks about what occupies her mind.

That night, I dream about Analisa. "Your child is intelligent," I say. She says, "I love you." I wake confident that her child will be born and be healthy.

At the bar, I order *"café au lait."* Allan, standing beside me, says, *"Olé, olé, olé,"* and it dawns on me that I have ordered in French. The previous day, when I spoke with the fun-spirited hostess, I laced Spanish with French. Now that same woman says, *"Su cuerpo está en España, pero su cabeça está en Francia."* I still have not made the linguistic transition to Spain. We all laugh.

Intelligent, capable of bright humor and always smiling, somewhere down deep in Allan dwells pain that surfaces in cynicism, a negative contrariness, which accompanies breakfast on the patio.

I reprovision at a grocery in Torres del Río and walk into the open countryside. The overcast sky gives relief from the blistering sun I have walked under since Pamplona. The Way turns uphill, and I surge ahead of dozens of pilgrims. Atop the climb, I walk into a cool, quiet pine forest and come upon a rock garden where pilgrims have built cairns and decorated them with relics and messages:

a brass AA badge from San Diego,

a photograph of a couple surrounded by a heart formed with rocks,

a cross made of sticks with a pinecone tied to the top,

"I would rather feel pain than nothing at all. Keep Walking. Alex" painted on a rock,

"God is with you" above a heart drawn on a rock,

a broken walking staff,

a holy card of Saint James,

"Love is Free, Forgive Her" painted on a rock, and many other articles and messages.

I contemplate the human offerings and feel the presence of the divine. Most pilgrims pass the shrine with a glance. Some linger for photographs and walk on. I half-hope Analisa will walk up the trail. I wait until I am again alone and reflect on "Love is Free, Forgive Her."

Anna undresses and lies naked on the bed, her left leg straight, her right leg rolled slightly to the side. I undress, crawl on top of her, and we make love, our legs and arms entwined, groaning and moaning.

"I want to spend the night with you," I say.

"You can't stay here."

We are lying on a bed in the back of a trailer where she is staying.

"Why not? You stay here."

"Look at this." She points to red splotches on her legs. "These are bed bug bites. I don't want to you to get bedbugs."

"I don't care. I want to be with you."

She insists I leave. I suspect she is getting rid of me so she can trick. I say goodbye on a wooden porch, and as I walk down the ramp, a man walks up. He is young and obese. Anna touches him and says, "Give me a minute."

"What are you doing?" I ask.

"Nothing, he's just a friend."

I drive away but turn around. I am sick of the lies. I knock on the door, and the old man who owns the trailer opens the door. He looks worried.

"I want to talk to Anna."

He disappears in the back, and Anna steps outside.

"I am sick and tired of your lies. I know what you are doing."

"You want to know what I am doing. Go and see."

I walk to the bedroom where Anna and I made love earlier. The man is pulling his pants up against rolls of fat. I walk back outside. Anna stares at me, her weight on one leg and arms crossed.

"So did you see what you wanted to see?" she asks.

"You think you get away with these stupid lies, but you don't."

"I have to support myself and my son."

"I give you money, so you don't have to trick to support yourself."

"It is not enough."

"Two hundred dollars a day is more than enough. The problem is you spend it on drugs, and you promised me you were going to clinic. You're not going to the clinic. That's another lie."

"You don't know how long it takes me to go to the clinic. I have to get on the bus, ride it for an hour, wait at the clinic, see someone for methadone, then wait for the bus, then ride it back. It takes all day to get methadone. Every day."

"Well, I guess tricking is easier."

I leave furious. The next day, I wake up and think, it's not her, it's the heroin.

I descend into a valley with shepherd huts made of stones and shaped like small domes, follow Rio Cornava, a deep, narrow stream, then climb uphill.

Someone calls behind me. Santiago, whom Analisa introduced me to, holds up a water bottle and asks if I forgot mine. I have not. He and I walk among valleys and hills with thick grasses and scrub brush in rocky, white soil and dark, arable farmland planted with grapes and hay.

"Spain is beautiful," I say.

Santiago says what many pilgrims say. "All countries are beautiful, just different kinds of beauty."

Santiago limps and supports the back of his right leg with his hand. He has strained his hamstring, which makes downhills especially hard. On a descent, he tells me to go on, and we say goodbye. I enjoy Santiago's company and do not like to leave him. I feel lonely and want a friend to walk with.

When I walk into the town Viana, I say, *"Bonjour, buenos días"* to a pilgrim I have never met.

Shorter than me, he puts his stern face in mine and says, "What did you say?"

"I said 'hello' in French and Spanish: *bonjour* and *buenos días.*"

Mikai from Romania backs off and explains, "I have trouble understanding short phrases."

Because of his aggressive demeanor, I feel uncomfortable in his presence.

In Viana, I chat with Joseph, whom I last saw at supper the day Analisa and I met. With an injured Achilles tendon, he intends to finish in Longroño. I then come upon Allan and Slavo, and they start walking with me, but I have no desire to endure an immature conversation with Allan for a stretch of kilometers. We come upon Neil, Abby, Maria Sophia, engaged in a self-absorbed discussion, and Janey, all sitting in a row of chairs in front of a café. Neither Neil, who is not using his favorite word, nor Abby or Maria Sophia, who treated me with minimal, polite tolerance in Saint-Jean-Pied-du-Port, acknowledge my presence when I say hello. I stand here weighing an irritating conversation with Allan, the disdain of this trio and the desire to talk with Janey, thinking *How and why do I get into these stupid situations?* I decide to tolerate disdain to escape adolescence. I get coffee and sit by Janey. We exchange pleasantries, but unable to conjure a conversation starter to overcome the last stupid thing I said to her and flustered by attraction and the uncomfortable feeling of being marginalized, I slug down my coffee and head down the Way.

As I leave Viana, Mikai scowls at me. He carries a big bag and walks fast. I slow my pace and let him put space between us.

In a wide field, thousands of black birds fly into the air, circle, then alight. The birds again rise, separate into groups, join back together. The flights and landings, separations and rejoinings happen simultaneously. Finally, a large flock turns south and disappears over the horizon. Then, a second large flock disappears over the horizon. Then, a third smaller flock does the same.

I cross a bridge and walk into the city Logroño with a bad feeling. I find the locked Cathedral de Santa María de la Redonda in the central square, and a little farther, the closed *oficina de tourismo*.

I sit down, depressed and lonely. My efforts to make a friend have failed, and something feels wrong. Again, I cannot discern whether my feeling is related to the Camino or something beyond the Way, like Anna.

Navarrete lays thirteen kilometers and three hours away. I think I should leave immediately, but the longer I think about it, the more unreasonable the decision to walk becomes. I do not want to walk in the dark.

I shuffle back to the main square, find a restaurant and order a hamburger, hoping a good burger might redeem the day. The burger comes without a bun, which is not a hamburger.

Portales Hosteleta looks good but feels wrong. Standing at the desk, I think I ought to leave. I passed up *albergues* when I entered Longroño because I wanted to sleep downtrail, thereby cutting the next day's walk by half a kilometer or more. Because backtracking feels defeatist, I ignore my intuition and stay. The three-story hostel caters to travelers but not pilgrims. I do not recognize a single person.

I head to a church for Mass and cross paths with Hank, whom Analisa and I breakfasted with days earlier, and Dae-Yung, a friendly Korean man. They invite me to eat with them.

I fall into a horrible dilemma. I failed to make a friend all day. Now, two men have invited me to join them as I head to Mass. To say yes to them, I have to say no to Mass. When he answers prayers, God's solutions to our problems are supposed to be more befitting than our own. My experience in the Church scourged that belief. Nevertheless, wanting to trust God and in a choice fraught with anguish, I choose God. Locals pack Iglesia María de Palacio, and the priest says a clean, simple, by-the-book Mass. I ask God to bring me a friend.

At a different restaurant, I order another hamburger, again hoping comfort food will revive my spirits. When I see the bun, I become excited. But it is untoasted.

Plato posited that all things have forms. For example, though tables have different shapes, colors and materials, we recognize tables as tables despite their variations, because we grasp the form of table. Saint Augustine christianized Plato's philosophy. Because all things have their origin and perfection in God, a perfect form of table exist in the mind of God. In Heaven, the perfect hamburger includes a grilled bun. In Spain, I would settle for a toasted bun. The untoasted bun and soggy fries make me feel worse.

Back in my hostel, the bad feeling remains. I preposition everything—rucksack, boots, *bâton*, clothes—for a middle-of-the-night departure. Something does not feel right.

The Providence of Snores

DAYS 41 - 43

Two men and one woman cut petrified wood with dull, rusty chain saws. When one stops, the other two start. When two stop, the third starts. I walk out at midnight.

Darkness lays upon the city like a thick quilt, but lights from streetlamps push up against its weight. I walk in shadows that vary from darker to lighter, but always the blanket collapses down on me.

In the Michelin guide: the Logroño city map shows the streets but not the Way; on the section map, the Way is imposed on streets that are tiny, unnamed lines. Under a streetlamp, I flip back and forth between the two maps, discern the route, turn down several streets, pick up the Way, and follow it to the edge of the city where a tunnel passes under a highway.

In the tunnel, a graffiti artist has drawn a Gothic arch that encompasses four smaller arches along the bottom and, above them, three circles arranged in a triangle. Each circle encloses an inner circle surrounded by six half circles. The art evokes a rood screen. In Eastern Christian architecture, rood screens separate the sanctuary of a church, where priests transubstantiate bread and wine into the Body, Blood, Soul and Divinity of Jesus Christ, from the nave, where the people dwell. Stars of white light, with blue and red auras, have been drawn on the arch, as if the light of Jesus pierces the screen. I wonder on which side of the screen I stand. I wonder which side is more illuminated.

The Way leads to a road in a park, with grass fields and pine trees. Here, I come upon a cabin with cut outs for a door and windows, a concrete floor and walls with two by fours covered with exterior wood siding. I roll out my sleeping pad, lay my backpack between me and the door, cover myself up with my woobie and sleep in my boots.

A jogger's footfalls wake me before sunrise, and in darkness, I walk out of the park. Haze hides the sunrise, and the day lightens gradually. I parallel the highway, then at the small town Navarrete, turn uphill into olive groves and vineyards. The day warms but becomes breezy and cooler the higher I climb. Intermittent shin splints pain me.

Around midmorning the combined effects of not eating breakfast and a bad night's sleep wear on me. The village Ventosa sits one kilometer off trail, and Nájera, the next town downtrail, is ten kilometers away. Torn between extra kilometers and food or fewer kilometers and hunger, I am drawn to Ventosa by images of eggs and potatoes.

After a couple hundred meters, I stop and reconsider my side-track, then look down. On the gravel road, at my feet, lay two five-euro-notes. *God just bought me breakfast.*

I keep on toward Ventosa, walk into a bar and see "the Reggie Girl." Nara has a big smile, and we talk with natural ease. She eats *tortilla espaῆa*, an egg and potato pie, the very food I imagined and food which redeems Spanish breakfasts. With an injured knee and short on time, Nara jumps part of each day's section by bus. I tell her about my one-star experience in Longroῆo, the snores and my midnight flight. She tells me about a four-star *albergue* in Azofra and an *albergue* that is part of a church in Grañon. I decide to head to those.

The sun comes out, and I welcome its warmth, but as I climb Alto de San Antón, the sun blazes with full force. I lather myself in sunscreen, then descend through farmlands.

Pondering on the previous twenty-four hours, I am tempted to despair, but I reason and pray. *God, you have surprised me before on the Camino. You can do it again. Jeffrey, you just have to keep walking.*

At a concrete plaza by a business park in the town Nájera, I meet Brandt from Tennessee. He interrupts every statement I make and brags about his forty-pound pack, a forty-eight kilometer start from Saint-Jean-Pied-de-Port—he just retired from the infantry—that he averages more than thirty kilometers a day.

I begin to tell the story of the night before. He cuts me off at "snoring."

"Snoring doesn't bother me."

I let my story go and say, "Snoring doesn't bother snorers either."

He laughs and tells me about a dream he had several nights before. A man snored, and between snores, he talked. In the dream, Brandt woke up, then woke the man. He never remembers dreams, but he remembered that one. For a moment, he looks introspective.

I walk back into vineyards and fallow farmlands and into the village Azofra, where I find the four-star *albergue*—high walls, a cold pool, a large kitchen attached to a dining room and rooms with two beds—and Nara sitting at table. We smile at each other.

I pay to have a room to myself. I need a good night's sleep.

Yuichi, Brandt, James and Christopher from England, and Nicole and Amanda from California arrive.

Nara and I make salad, spaghetti and bread. Nicole and Amanda also cook, and the four of us eat together. Everyone else goes out for supper. Afterwards, we all sit around and talk. Nara asks why we walk. James survived pancreatic cancer. Christopher, his adult son, walks with him. Nicole talks about love and forgiveness. Amanda wants to find a purpose to her life. Brandt, retired from the army, needs a new direction. Yuichi walks because he has time available. I say I walk because God and I have a lot to talk about. Nara likes my answer and makes it her own.

Brandt had a positive experience in Logroño at an *albergue* connected to the cathedral: after supper, the pilgrims went into the cathedral for a prayer service. I begin to think that my bad feeling is related to something beyond the Camino.

As I fall asleep, I think how my horrible experience in Logroño led to meeting Nara, which led to a great experience in Azofra. The awful snoring, the midnight flight, images of eggs and potatoes, the decision to step off the Way, euros on the road, meeting Nara. I cannot understand how God manages these things. The mystery of God's providence is beyond me. I lie in bed lost in wonder.

Brandt sits hunched over a table, with his hoodie pulled over his head. Yuichi and Brandt shared a room. For forty-five minutes, Yuichi slept quietly, then his snores "shook the walls." Then, he slept for forty-five minutes and snored violently again. Brandt got no sleep. I laugh—on the inside.

I limp because of a new blister but walk with greater weight on my heart. Something has changed. The Australian ladies said that the first third of the Camino is physical, the second third mental, the last third spiritual. I wonder if I have begun the last third.

Before I departed for Europe, I studied Saint Augustine's theology. He argued that friendship is the highest form of love, and on the Camino, friendship has become a paramount concern. I want a friend.

At the corner of Remount Road and Pilgrim Avenue stands a tall, long-legged woman, with long brown hair and small breasts. I pull into an empty parking space. She comes up to the passenger window.

"My name is Jeffrey."

"I'm Anna."

She needs money for her and her son to get a hotel room. She sounds desperate and honest. I give her twenty dollars and drive off.

I cannot stop thinking about her and the terrible last time with a prostitute and the desire to go out on a good note. A day later, I drive back to Remount Road. I resolve that I will be with her or no one, but I do not see her. The next day I again drive to Remount Road.

She crosses the street, wearing shorts, a top that shows her stomach and cowboy boots. She gets in my truck, and we buy half a dose of Suboxone from a drug dealer.

"It's a drug to help me get off drugs. It's easier to buy it on the street than to get it from a clinic." That's a good sign, I think.

We go to a run-down, unoccupied apartment building. One apartment has a door that does not lock.

The lights do not work, but dingy light comes through the windows. The living room has a television and a couch, both broken. In the bedroom is a bed with old sheets and enough light for us to see the outlines of each other's bodies.

We strip, and she lies on the bed. I kiss her feet, then move slowly up her legs. I kiss her stomach, her breasts, her neck, her lips, then I slip inside of her. We make love for a long time, and after holding my orgasm for as long as I can, I come, and she groans.

When I get off her, she holds her legs up in the air.

"I had an orgasm." Her smile radiates joy.

"You did?"

"Yes. Didn't you feel it? I am still having the orgasm." Enough light falls on her face, that I see the ecstasy.

I drop her off, and she walks up to a prostitute friend, who, worn and aged beyond years, looks like she has walked the streets for decades. Anna raises her arms as if signaling a touchdown: "I had an orgasm."

"Now, that was the way to go out," I say to myself. I swear it will be the last time.

Three days later, I track her down. "Let me take care of you."

I think about Anna, the twin nightmares of addiction and prostitution, manipulations, broken promises, exhaustive efforts to help her change her life, the many days addiction destroyed hope, infidelity, lies, financial ruin, the priesthood, the abuse I experienced repeatedly in my life, my desire not to be a priest, total loss about what to do with my life, the death of George, the abandonment of my cats, the loneliness in my life, the pain in my feet, the pain in my heart and soul, the loneliness. I cry as I walk.

I descend softly on rolling hills toward the town Santo Domingo de la Calzada. Brandt, James and Christopher catch me. We split into two pairs: Brandt and James, Christopher and me.

Christopher asks why I walk. To my stock reason, I add: "I have a difficult decision to make." Later, I talk about my farm, my dog, my cats, my chickens.

"Is getting rid of your chickens the big decision you have to make?" Christopher asks.

I bust out laughing. "No, and you will never figure it out."

"Do you want to go back?"

"That's a good question." I think a while and say, "I don't know."

Buildings in Santo Domingo are not more than three stories tall, except for the cathedral. From hills, we see the town; from valleys, we see the cathedral's spire.

I say goodbye to James, Christopher and Brandt at La Catedral de Santo Domingo de la Calzada.

In the fourteenth century, a young man pilgrimaged with his parents and stopped in Santo Domingo. A woman made advances toward him, which he rebuffed. Angry, the woman hid a cup in his pack and accused him of theft. The young man was hanged. His parents continued their journey to Santiago, and when they returned to Santo Domingo, their son, who still hanged, said, "Santo Domingo has saved me." The magistrate doubted the young man was alive and said, "He is as alive as the chickens prepared for my lunch." At that moment, the chickens came to life. So, a big, white rooster and hen live in a well-lighted second story loft in the cathedral.

I dismiss the story of the young man as hagiographic embellishment: maybe the hangman tied the rope improperly, the man's neck did not break, and in a clever, desperate attempt to save his life, the young man attributed his survival to Santo Domingo. I do, however, ask for Santo Domingo's intercession and wonder what that might look like in real life. I have no expectations. As my faith in God collapsed, so did my trust in his saints.

I visit his tomb, contemplate artwork, look at the chickens, take photographs, sit in the pews, watch tour groups and cry. To hide my tears, I hide my face in my hands. But more than the insanity of my life plagues me: something churns inside. Again, I cannot discern whether it is related to the Way or Anna.

Outside the cathedral, I sort gear on a bench.

"Jeffrey!"

I look up and see Analisa's happy smile and Mike from Belgium. Bulky muscles, no fat, a goatee, a nose ring, earrings and tattoos, Mike looks intimidating. He carries a big bag and a staff carved from a stick he found. Bent a little at the top, the staff looks like a pointed spear and has feathers tied below the point.

Mike has a protective soul—Analisa calls him "my Saint Michael."

"Will you be safe with him?" Mike asks, referring to me.

"Absolutely," Analisa answers.

"Are you sure you will be safe?" To me, Mike seems like he is overplaying a hand.

"Perfectly safe," she answers. Mike and I shake hands, then he continues down the Way.

Analisa met Nara at a bus stop and learned that I headed for the *albergue* at the church in Grañon and decided to make for Grañon herself. She and I follow a road that parallels the highway, then turn onto a small road that climbs to the village Grañon, where we find Nara in front of the church.

Pat and Christine, two married, Methodist, unpaid volunteers, run the *albergue*. Christine orients us. Pilgrims cook and eat together in the third-floor kitchen/dining room and sleep in the second-floor dormitory. The *albergue* is *donativo*: people who stayed the night before paid for our food; the money we donate will pay for pilgrims' food the next day.

Nara and I go in search of a beer, but no bar is open. As we discuss this predicament, Mike walks up, intent on walking through Grañon and camping out.

"Analisa would love to see you." I add, "Analisa told me you were a chef."

We go up to the kitchen, and Mike is appointed chef.

Nicole and Amanda arrive, then Rupert from Germany and Shanti from Spain, whose baptismal name is Santiago. He does not want to use the name of the Camino as he walks.

Christine buys food for salad, pasta and two soups—one vegetarian, one with meat—and apples for dessert. Analisa and I core the apples, and when finished, Christine leads us, carrying trays of cored apples, to a bakery owned and operated by the same family for three generations. Susanna runs the bakery which has a wood-fired stove. Analisa stays while the apples bake to learn how to make a Spanish pastry.

Back in the *albergue,* Mike works on pasta sauce, Nara plays her ukulele, Rupert sings a Bavarian yodeling song, and other pilgrims cut vegetables and set the table.

When time comes to fetch the apples, we line up in a semicircle outside the bakery. Susanna and Analisa step out. With Nara leading and Rupert as second vocals, we sing "Don't Worry, Be Happy," then a song for Susanna, who bakes apples as a *donativo.*

Three times we sing: "Oh Susanna, don't you cry for me. We're here for some apples from your bakery."

Then, Analisa picks me and Nara to carry the apples. Inside the bakery, Christine hands us wigs she covertly carried to the bakery. Nara wears long, wavy purple hair, Analisa a yellow and red Mohawk, me a big Afro. I feel stupid silly but go with it. We jump out the door and yell, "Dinner's ready!" Everyone laughs and cheers.

During dinner, we learn two critical pieces of information. To get a *compostela,* a certificate acknowledging that we walked the Way, in Santiago, we need two stamps on our passports for every day we walk from Sarria to Santiago. On one-hundred-year anniversaries of Saint Francis's pilgrimage, Franciscans issue a second *compostela* in honor of Saint Francis. Because we are walking eight hundred years after Saint Francis, we can obtain the rare Franciscan *compostela*.

After cleaning the kitchen and dining room, we file into the church and up squeaky, uneven stairs into the choir loft, where Pat leads a prayer service. He tells two stories.

"A week earlier, a young man from Germany passed through. He started at home, and when he left, his father advised him, 'Don't walk faster than your soul.'"

"When Saint Francis pilgrimaged to Santiago, he said, 'It is solved by walking.' He did not specify what 'It' was. 'It' differs from person to person."

Pat lights a candle. We take part reading a prayer service, which Pat ends, praying that we will have the best sleep of our Camino.

Rupert snores reverberate off the walls. The guttural sounds do not sound human. Neither do they sound animal. In my most feverish imagination, I cannot imagine a mountain gorilla could make these sounds if, on his deathbed, he struggles violently to breathe. Rupert's snores originate in the bowels of Hell and resonate with the Voice of the Beast.

I sit up and laugh. Nara wakes Rupert and tells him, "You have to stop snoring." He snortles and rolls on his side. His snores now sound like they are of earth.

Santi and I drag ourselves to the dining room with red, swollen eyes and droopy shoulders. Amanda and Nicole, who moved their mattresses upstairs to sleep, look half-alive, half-dead. Still sick with a cold, Analisa looks awful: dark, swollen eyes, a pale complexion. In the middle of the night, she came upstairs to sleep on the couch. Almost in tears, she says, "I didn't get any sleep. I have to sleep. I'm not going to get well unless I sleep."

Nara walks in, and I hail her. "You are my hero."

She puts her arm around my shoulder, and I put my arm around her waist. "Why?"

"Because you woke up Rupert and told him to stop snoring."

"Those were not snores. That was something else." She sits across from me.

Mike comes to the table. "If that snoring had not stopped in two minutes, I was walking out."

I motion toward Nara and say, "Thank her. She told Rupert to stop snoring. She's my hero."

"I had to," she explains, motioning toward me, "I didn't want this one to leave in the middle of the night again."

I recount my midnight flight from Logroño, then add, "When Saint Francis said, 'It is solved by walking,' 'it' was snoring." Laughter is uproarious.

Rupert walks into the dining room, and a pronounced, awkward, drawn-out silence befalls.

Nicole asks, "Rupert, how did you sleep?"

"Very well," he answers.

With tension a moment away from explosive, sarcastic laughter, I change the topic of conversation. "Where is everyone headed?"

Nara, Mike, Analisa and I intend to walk twenty-nine kilometers to Villafranca Montes de Oca. Amanda and Nicole take the most unpressured, low-stress approach to their days. They find a coffee shop and sit there for an hour or so, until they decide where they are headed. Sometimes they get there, sometimes not.

Analisa and I leave with Shanti. He started in Cap de Creus, the easternmost point of mainland Spain, where he swam in the Mediterranean and saw the sunrise. He plans to walk to Fisterra, the westernmost point of mainland Spain, swim in the Atlantic and watch the sunset.

Named *Finis Terrae*—the end of the earth—by the Romans, Fisterra is a popular finish for the Camino. Most pilgrims stop in Santiago, but many walk to Fisterra. I have mused on a Fisterra finish but plan to end in Santiago, the religious terminus, where I expect to get my answer from God. It also depends on how fast I walk. I have to catch a flight out of Paris.

Analisa and I walk through the countryside and several villages, and I feel comfortable enough with her to reveal more of my reasons for walking.

"God spoke to me once."

"When you read your Bible."

"No."

"When a friend spoke to you."

"No."

"In the silence?"

"No." I stop, look at her and touch her arm. She stops.

"I heard his voice." She looks uncomfortable. I have the impression that she thinks I am crazy, hearing voices and all that. So, I drop my story.

In a village, Analisa and I catch Nara, then in the next village, Mike catches us.

Hours on the trail under the hot sun in the shadeless countryside wears me down, but Nara's knee slows her. She limps and falls behind. We stop, but she tells us to go ahead. She plans to limp into Belorado, then take a bus to Villafranca de Montes de Oca.

On the outskirts of the town Belorado, Mike, Analisa and I find an *albergue* with a restaurant and a small pool. Mike drinks a beer, while Analisa swims. I keep walking, pass through Barrio el Corro, Belorado's old quarter with narrow streets lined with houses painted light blue, apple red, orange and turquoise, then walk back into the countryside.

Behind the village Tosantos, I climb a narrow, steep, grassy road to *Ermita de la Virgin de la Peña,* an ancient hermitage built into the side of a cliff north of town. The hermitage is locked, but two shallow caves are carved into the cliff. One shelters a bench. I take off my boots and socks and sit in the shade with my feet in the sun. Tosantos lays below, and beyond the hamlet, fields stretch across low rolling hills. I imagine living out my priesthood here, saying Mass and hearing the confessions of pilgrims. Too simplistic to be real, it is a false idyll. I descend back down to the plain and keep walking.

In the village Villafranca Montes de Oca, I check into *San Antón Abad,* a large stone building with a bar, restaurant, rooms and two dormitories: one with bunk beds and another with cubicles for a couple extra euros. Because I tread the Way of No Sleep, I pay for the chance that I might get some sleep.

Nara has already arrived, and we wile away the afternoon at an outdoor table. We check email, and I receive an email from Anna:

> "Darling, I am out of jail and am so happy. I can't wait for you to come back so we can start a new life. When are you coming back?"

The first time Anna was in jail, she wrote a letter in her drug therapy class entitled "Goodbye to My Addiction." I visited her often. We talked to each other through a video screen, and she swore she was done with heroin and prostitution. The day she was released she started reusing heroin and tricking. Later, she admitted, "Heroin was the only thing I thought about in jail."

She has been out of jail for a week. I know many things are going through her head, but I was always last. She used me more than loved me. When I read her email, I feel anger, suspicion and hurt more than happiness and joy.

I answer that I will return in a month. I suffered fifteen months of hell waiting for her to become sober. I wonder if she will wait one month.

Determine not to let problems with Anna cause me to fall into myself, I decide to accept what the Camino brings me.

Janey arrives, and the three of us go down to the bar where I meet Mike from the United States. A fallen-away Catholic who became Jewish, Mike insists that he does not walk for religious reasons but for "fun."

"I walk for religious and spiritual reasons and would never walk the Camino for fun," I say. "If I wanted to do something for fun, I'd sit on a beach."

"I'd sit on a beach and drink mojitos," Nara adds.

Mike and Janey know each other and have a testy relationship. Mike advises everyone to keep things dry in plastic bags. Janey condemns his suggestion because plastic rattles. Mike immediately switches from pontifical to supplicant, but that reverses itself just as quickly.

Mike insists men do not snore when they sleep on their side. Janey is adamant they do.

"Janey, you, you are always . . ." Mike points at her, then clinches his fist in a prudent, hold-the-tongue retreat. Janey has a sharp, quick mind and a sharper, quicker tongue. To defuse the tension, Nara and I talk about Rupert and that he snored when he lay on his side.

Alejandro from Spain joins us. He and his wife own an *albergue* in Sarria. His wife runs it. She thought Alejandro ought to make a pilgrimage because he never walked the Camino.

Mike and Analisa walk in. After the pool, they played on swings and took six hours to cover the distance I covered in three, which makes me suspicious.

At dinner, we drink more wine, tell more stories and suffer more conversational angst.

Janey tells us about her visit to Ermita de San Miguel. As she walked up, a young man ran out the open door embarrassed, and a young woman remained in the chapel. Both adjusted their clothes. According to Janey, she caught them *"in flagrante."* Mike from the United States defends the couple's behavior. Janey excoriates him.

Analisa and I bust out laughing because we have the first half of the story, which we tell. Janey has the second, climatic half.

Mike from the United States then reignites the debate about snoring. After more heated arguments, Janey ends the debate with the emphatic, "I've slept with a lot of men, and I know men snore when they sleep on their sides."

Silence cloaks the table as it does when someone wins an argument with an unassailable statement and indomitable spirit. And because of the implications of what she said. I do not think it came out the way she intended.

Conversational angst switches to me and Alejandro when we talk about the next day's walk. Mike from Belgium wants to be in Burgos for Halloween. Janey has to get to Burgos because it is her last day. I want to get to Burgos to attend the vigil Mass for

All Saints Day. Alejandro doubts that All Saints has a vigil or that there will even be Mass in Burgos on Friday night.

"All Saints Day is a holy day of obligation, with a vigil Mass like Sunday and Christmas. Even if it were not a holy day of obligation in Spain, All Saints is a solemnity and has a vigil Mass."

"Maybe in the United States, but not in Spain."

"No, this is true all across the world."

He asks the waitress if there is a vigil Mass for All Saints in Burgos. Unhappy to referee, she says she has no idea about Mass schedules in Burgos.

I think about revealing who I am but do not.

I suspect Alejandro is trying to find some issue on which to assert masculine authority. He invites us to stay at his *albergue*, but after his boneheaded intransigence, I have no desire to stay there.

The evening would be more enjoyable if Mike from the United States and Alejandro dined together and inflicted their personalities on each other. Even so, the rest of us get drunk and laugh the evening away, until the staff asks us to leave. We leave reluctantly.

I leave with great reluctance. I do not want to be alone with my thoughts, but exhausted and drunk, I fall asleep quickly and sleep hard.

Horror Vacui

DAYS 44 - 45

Nara, Analisa, Janey and I start out in the cold before sunrise. We climb steadily, sometimes steeply. The sun rises, and we become hot and shed jackets. Walking in rotating pairs, sometimes I walk with Analisa, sometimes with Nara, sometimes with Janey. Janey asks why I walk, and I give my stock answer: "God and I have a lot to talk about."

Monumento de los Caídos, an inverted, stone obelisk, memorializes three hundred Spaniards shot in this remote location by order of General Franco during the Spanish Civil War because of their belief in liberty. Pilgrims have left prayer cards, prayers, photographs and equipment. I lift the tip of a bandana tied to the chain that cordons off the monument.

"I lost a bandana yesterday. Maybe I ought to take one of these."

"You and God do have a lot to talk about," Janey remarks.

I smile at her and leave the bandana.

We descend into a valley. Janey bounces downhill. For me, downhills have become drudgery. As usual, I walk fast uphill. At Alto de Valbuena, we have our last pairing off. Janey and I walk down logging roads among pine tree farms ahead of Nara and Analisa.

Janey, an elementary school teacher, participates in an innovative program: philosophy for children. They ask fundamental questions: "Who are you?" and "What do you want?" The children begin with superficial answers, but more questions lead to deeper answers.

"The same process led Saint Augustine to God," I say. "He asked, 'What makes me happy?' Many transitory things made him happy but also left him sad because they went away. That answer led to a deeper question: 'What will make me happy and will always be there?' The answer is God."

The meaninglessness of the venality of my life opens a dark chasm inside of me. Depression clings to my soul and crushes me. I lie on the floor of my rectory, with two Bible verses to offer as prayer.

"Some deadly thing has fastened onto him, and he will not rise from the place where he lies,"[8] and "Cursed be the day of my birth."[9]

To get up off the floor, I put forth the energy a man needs to rise from the dead under his own power. Rising to a standing position drains me of everything in me, which is practically nothing. I get up to say Mass and, after Mass, go back to the rectory and lie on the floor for another day.

As depression crushes me, evil fills the nothingness within and twists the pain of the abuse I suffered in the Church. The depression, hatred focused inward, reorients itself. I begin to hate people.

This darkness I have never seen, experienced, understood or imagined could exist. Not the absence of good as theologians often define evil: a living, dynamic evil gnaws at the core of my soul, consumes it, and whispers in my pain that killing someone, anyone, will relieve the agony.

---

8 NAB, Psalm 41:8
9 NAB, Jeremiah 20:14

This active, violent evil shocks me, and as I watch it grow inside of me, I know I cannot give in to its call. Evil lies, and I know it. I hit bottom, the deep hole from which I begin to crawl out. After three days, I get up off the floor.

"What kind of work do you do?" Janey asks.

"I'm independently poor." She persists in her questioning.

"My work is to walk." She becomes more persistent.

"I've done lots of things," I say. "I had a farm with free range chickens. I worked as an engineer. I was an activist involved in stopping the placement of a coal ash landfill in the ACE Basin, a several hundred-thousand-acre environmental treasure. I wrote a book about that experience in which I argued that environmentalists and energy companies need to work together. I've done lots of things."

Janey asks me again why I walk. "All I can say is that God and I have a lot to talk about." I do, however, share stories. I started in Le Puy-en-Velay. I saw Pierre from France in Esperyac and did not see him again until Roncevalles, five hundred kilometers later. I walked two days without seeing another pilgrim. I wrecked my feet. Some days I starved.

"People at home don't understand what we are doing," I say. "Everyone said, 'Oh, you're going to have so much fun.' This is a pilgrimage, not a vacation."

Janey understands but adds, "I hope you are having fun."

"I'm having an adventure, and I'd rather have an adventure than a vacation. To me, adventures are fun."

Janey, an adventurer herself, biked across southern France and visited the Galapagos Islands. Not religious but spiritual, she likes things with a religious character such as the Camino. She is a kindred soul.

We come upon a waymaker. A pine log, painted red, blue, green and white, rests on an obelisk at an angle. On the obelisk, "2 km" written on a *flecha amarilla* indicates that we stand two kilometers from San Juan de Ortega, a remote hamlet that marks my completion of 1,002 kilometers.

"I just hit one thousand kilometers." I want to celebrate with a hug, but shy and afraid of a "no," I do not ask.

A sculpture welcomes us to San Juan de Ortega. I have no idea how to interpret metal, square-edged chain links, standing vertically with the top link cut in half. Janey has a great idea: "man reaching up to God while still linked to earth."

The four of us come back together at the village café, then Mike from Belgium arrives. We celebrate my one-thousand-kilometer achievement with pasties and coffee, except for Mike who drinks a beer.

We walk back into the countryside, and at a signpost, Janey wants to photograph Mike, Nara, Analisa and myself. "Now I want you to line up, side by side and in front of the sign."

I laugh and say, "Tell me you're not a teacher."

Obedient children, we line up as directed.

We then make a short, steep descent into Agés, a hamlet where we find a combination bar-café-grocery. We drink fresh orange juice and coffee, except for Mike who drinks a beer. Nara's knee pains her. She plans to take a bus to Burgos, then from Burgos to Sarria for the last leg of her pilgrimage. We hug goodbye, sad we will never see her again.

While relaxing at umbrella-covered tables, Janey gets a text message. "Dumped again!" she blurts out. She furiously punches out a return text with her thumbs. She boils but keeps the lid on. "Dumped by text! I don't believe it!"

Janey storms up the Way, while Mike, Analisa and I follow behind. We come back together before Atapuerca, but with Janey's
angst propelling us, we blast through the village and up a steep
hill, a cascade of rocks reminiscent of France.

Atop Matagrande lays a meditation circle with raised, grassy
furrows demarcating concentric circles. Mike wants me to photograph him in the center. Instead of a contemplative, introspective
journey, he cuts across every line and stands in the center with
head held high and a big smile.

We descend into low rolling hills. The Way bends around
them, but Mike runs uphill on a road, an amazing physical feat
with his massive pack.

"I have followed a lot of people off the Way without good
results," objects Janey.

"But you've never gotten lost with us, so this will be a new
adventure," I say, smiling at her.

The road disappears. We cut cross-country through thick grass
and scrub brush, then descend steeply to a gravel farm road.

In the village Orbaneja-Riopico, Mike wants to stop for a
beer, so we stop. Janey complains to me privately about his drinking. I share her concern.

Two pilgrim routes lead to Burgos. The pastoral route follows a river; the other goes through industrial and commercial
sections. We want to take the pastoral route but miss the turn.

In Villafria, a suburb of Burgos, we find a bar and all of us drink
beer and discuss taking a bus to the center or enduring ten kilometers of concrete sidewalks. No one wants to travel by bus. I am
especially opposed. So, for the next two hours, we pound concrete
sidewalks with our poor feet but laugh at ourselves and everything.

Mike puts on dark, wraparound sunglasses, ties a bandana
around his head and turbocharges down streets. With his nose

ring and earrings, a goatee, tattooed arms and a big bag, he looks scary and intimidating.

We come upon twenty teenage girls, dressed for Halloween and too busy talking to look where they are going. Mike yells "Boo!" The girls turn, look at Mike and part. We walk straight through them.

A father and son, five years old and dressed as Dracula, walk toward us. The boy looks at Mike with big eyes as if Mike is dressed for Halloween.

We pause for Analisa to go to the bathroom. A kilometer farther, she realizes that she left her water bottle on a bench. Because a friend gave it to her, she goes back for it, while Mike, Janey and I wait in a park. The sun begins to set, the temperature drops and we put on warmer clothes. As we talk about how unimportant a replaceable water bottle is, Mike describes Analisa as a "strange person."

Janey whispers, "Do you think he wants to reflect on that?" We both noticed boy-Dracula look at Mike with wide eyes.

Analisa returns, and we race on in the gloaming. The sun sets, and darkness falls. At the edge of the old quarter, down a long street and between rows of buildings rises the illuminated spire of the cathedral.

"The spire of the cathedral," I exclaim with a desperate sense of relief. We have walked forty kilometers.

"Oh my God," Janey says, "It's like seeing Jerusalem."

I laugh, impressed with her 2,500-year-old reference to Jewish pilgrimages.

We seem to walk forever through Burgos' elongated old section but reach the *Albergue de Peregrinos*, the *albergue municipal*. I intend to stay at a hotel because I plan a day off, but everyone else intends to stay here. When we step inside, I almost walk into

Pierre. We talk loudly and laugh. The woman at the desk yells at us. Immediately, Analisa decides not to stay here because the hospitaller exudes "bad energy." Janey asks me to stay at the *albergue* with her. I almost ask her to share a hotel room but hesitate because it might lead to sex. I do not want sex to derail my Camino.

I commute from Round O to Charleston to work at a parish, several campus ministries and a couple diocesan jobs, driving one hour each way for a sixty-to-seventy-hour work week. The Diocese of Charleston does not pay me or house me. Severely depressed, I feel like a failure. I pass women who hitchhike and start to pick them up. First, we talk, then we touch. One day, I pick up a leggy, light-skinned black woman and take her to her apartment.

"Can I come in?" I ask.

I step inside. We sit on the couch and talk. I lean over and kiss her.

"Our first time," she says, looking coy. "Let's go up to my bedroom."

We disrobe. I lie on the bed, and she straddles me. She lowers her hips, and about to touch, someone knocks on the door. I wonder if God stopped me from breaking my promises by this act of providence. We jump up, dress and rush downstairs.

She opens the door. A man walks in. He looks hurt, as if he wants a relationship with this woman.

"I am busy," she says. He shakes my hand and leaves.

We take off our clothes, and she lies on the couch. I get on top of her, but conflicted, I cannot have sex. She is understanding.

I go to Mepkin Abbey, a Trappist monastery in Moncks Corner, South Carolina, to make a confession. I sob as I start to speak. Between sobs, I say, "The diocese is not paying me. Bishop Baker and Msgr. Roth refuse to budget money to pay me. They made me homeless. I got in bed with a woman." I say more, a lot more between sobs but cannot stop crying.

"I know Bishop Baker," he says. "He cares about priests. He will be sympathetic."

I sober up. The priest has not listened to a word I have said. Baker is not the solution. He is the problem. The priest keeps talking, saying the same thing over and over. "Bishop Baker cares about priests."

"Just give me absolution so I can leave," I say.

I feel worse about myself and go back to the woman. I think, If I cannot be successful as a priest, at least I will be good at sex. Sex becomes easier, then easy. I have sex with many women and become good at it.

Moreover, saints tell us not just to avoid temptation but to avoid situations where temptations might arise. I decide to get a hotel room but agree to come back, get Janey and go to Mass at the Cathedral at 6:30 p.m., the time the woman at the *albergue* said Mass begins.

Mike, Analisa and I find a hotel. They take a room. I get a room with two twin beds pushed together. Mike stays in the room to clean up, while Analisa and I meet Janey.

We walk into Mass late. It started at 6 p.m. At the end of Mass, an old priest with a gentle soul, invites pilgrims forward for individual blessings. He asks us where we are from, blesses us and gives us a holy card with a pilgrim prayer.

As we stroll back to the hotel, I see Nara. Five feet tall, a small frame, not an ounce of fat, a limp, wearing a white knit hat with two wool strings dangling down either side of her face, she looks like a street urchin. "Nara!" I exclaim.

Nara visited the Cathedral, prayed in a chapel alone, burnt sage Analisa gave her and cried. Her bus to Sarria leaves at 4 a.m. She plans to walk the streets until then. "I was accepting," she says. I insist she throw her stuff in my room and take the second bed to get some sleep. Nara drops her bag in my room, and we get Mike.

We pass up several packed restaurants, find an empty restaurant and discover why: poor food, poor service, meager portions. With the pilgrim's menu, we get one bottle of wine per three people, a drought of wine. Nara fruitlessly argues with the waiter. I order more wine and pay for it. I want to get drunk.

Janey goes to the *albergue*, and the four of us go back to the hotel.

"Mike and I are going to take a walk and smoke a spliff." Nara's eyes are as red as a dragon's, and she speaks so languidly that I think she might fall over.

"I'll leave the door unlocked."

I shower, crawl in bed and fall right asleep. Later, the door rattles. I mumble "Nara," hear her voice and slip back into unconsciousness. She showers, changes and crawls into bed.

Nara and I wake as if from his wing, an angel let drop a feather that floated into our room to coax us out of slumber. The room feels bathed in peace. Sunlight shines through the window. I mumble something about dawn.

"It's early. We're on Camino time," Nara says.

"You did not catch your bus."

"No, the desk manager checked the bus schedule. I had the time wrong. My bus does not leave until noon."

We lie in bed and talk quietly for half an hour. Then I leave to get Janey. We planned to meet at the *albergue*, but she sits in the lobby. We go to my room, and few minutes later, Analisa knocks. After Nara explains why she is not on a bus the third time, I interject. "There never was a bus. Nara made up that story to get more goodbye hugs."

"There's nothing wrong with too many hugs," Janey says. We count the times we hugged people goodbye. Janey and Nara have hugged goodbye eight times. Pilgrims never know when goodbye is goodbye.

Mike gets up, and we take coffee at a café across from the cathedral. Mikai steps in. Analisa knows him and invites him to sit with us. He has lost his scowl. The day before, he walked fifty-two kilometers. Maybe exhaustion softened him. Maybe it is Analisa's infectious joy.

In London that night, Janey plans to go out dancing in "too short a black dress." We hug goodbye, but I want to kiss her.

Back at the hotel, I lie in bed while Nara packs and tells me why she walks. A woman she refers to as her wife is pregnant. They are not yet married but plan to wed. Nara is not sure if she is ready to be married or to be a parent. Tempted to reveal my priestly identity and pronounce the Church's teaching on homosexuality, I remind myself that I am not walking to preach to anyone. I just listen.

With a jump to Sarria and new friends, she says, "I'm starting a new Camino." We hug goodbye.

"Love," she says.

"Love always," I answer.

That's the best theology I ever articulated, the best preaching I ever did.

Mike and Analisa check out, and we eat second breakfast/first lunch in the same café. Mike and Analisa went out dancing the night before, and in a contest, Mike won a straw cowboy hat. He asks me to sign it. With a permanent marker, I write "J", then add two marks that turn the "l" part of "J" into a "K". Mike and

Analisa look perplexed. I explain my mark and draw it on the back page of my journal. "It's my initials."

I ask Mike why he walks. "I don't like my job. I'm young. Why not? I quit my job. I don't know what to do. There are lots of possibilities. I can only make one choice."

I hug them both goodbye.

"I love you," Analisa says.

"I love you too."

"I'll see you on the Way," Mike says.

"Yes, we will see each other on the Way."

Then I am alone.

The sprawling Santa Iglesia Basílica Catedral Metropolitana de Santa María de Burgos covers a city block, and its spires reach up to the heavens. A plethora of chapels, statues, artwork and so on fill the interior, but its immensity absorbs everything and preserves the cathedral from busyness.

The audio tour begins with a quote from Psalm 86: "In the midst of your temple, I will glorify you, because you do wondrous things."[10] God has done wondrous things for me on the Camino, but I have not experienced that in my life. In my life, I have suffered serial abuse, the worst in the Church. The discrepancy between this psalm and my life as a priest fractures me.

The sacristy architecture is *horror vacui*, fear of empty space. Something covers every part of the walls and ceiling. The poignant architectural term strikes me. My friends have scattered in different directions. Anna has likely hooked up with someone. *Horror vacui* envelopes me and opens deep within. I think about the absence of love in my life, from childhood to priesthood and think, *My whole life has been a horror vacui.*

---

10 Although many psalms express these ideas, I could not find this exact translation in any English version of the Bible.

At *La Favorita,* a packed *tapas* bar, I explain in bad Spanish, *"Yo nunca comer tapas"* and in good Spanish, *"Yo quiero comer seis tapas diferentes."* The *tapas* taste delicious. With background music and the chaotic din of conversations, the atmosphere exacerbates my experience of loneliness.

I return to my hotel for a siesta and doze with the window open. A gust of wind shakes my room and startles me awake.

With sunset, temptation toward depression grows more powerful. I pray in the cathedral chapel and attend Sunday's vigil Mass. Walking along dark streets, my stomach churns, as it has since Saint-Jean-Pied-de-Port. At another empty restaurant, I get greasy garlic soup, soggy French fries and lamb with fat and bone and little meat. I pick at a meal that sickens my already nauseous stomach.

I check email and have not heard from Anna. I email her and ask how she is doing.

My depression deepens. I walk around until exhausted enough to sleep. At my hotel, I ask about the weather. Cold temperatures and rain are forecast.

Today, All Saints Day, is the silver anniversary of my reception into the Catholic Church. Tomorrow, I will begin my Camino anew in spiritual emptiness and cold rain.

Kairos

DAYS 46 - 48

Moderate, steady rain slackens to a light shower, then turns into a heavy downpour. Thunder rumbles in the distance. The rain soaks my clothes and fills my boots with water. In a pedestrian tunnel, I say hello in passing to a tall, young man sorting rain gear. The rain slows, then stops as I depart Burgos and walk into the countryside on solid, well-compacted, dirt roads.

At an intersection, a *flecha amarilla* is angled forty-five degrees, half-way between "continue straight" and "turn left." I ponder this stupidity, turn left, and the absence of *flechas amarillas* tells me that I have walked off the Way. With compass and map, I decide I head the correct general direction and keep on under gray skies.

I cross a highway bridge, then step onto a dirt road on the edge of a huge construction site. I pull out my compass and examine the Michelin map which is not detailed enough for this kind of navigation. More by wit than orienteering skill, I dead-reckon across the site. Mud clings to my water-logged boots, and I walk with heavy feet.

I rejoin the Way, and in the village Tardajos enjoy a hot double-decker sandwich with ham, cheese, bacon and a fried egg. I have not drunk Coca-Cola in Europe, but Analisa said Coca-Cola tastes better in Europe because it is made with sugar instead of corn syrup. In memory of her, I drink a Coca-Cola, which does taste better.

In Rabé de las Calzadas, an ancient village, I find Santiago, Joseph and a pilgrim I do not know.

Smiling, I shake Santiago's hand. "Santiago! I don't believe it. Last time I saw you, you lay half-dead on the side of a hill."

"I'm better. I feel good." His leg mended as he walked.

I shake Joseph's hand. "Joseph! I thought you planned to finish in Logroño."

"I decided to keep walking."

A woman pulls up in a van and honks. Older women in nightgowns and house coats materialize, buy bread and vanish back into their houses.

Santiago and Joseph introduce me to Stefan from Germany.

"You were the pilgrim who passed me in the tunnel," he says. "When I saw you walk through the rain like you did, I thought, *That's fantastic*. You were the first pilgrim I ever met. I thought you were crazy."

"You're probably more correct than you know." Everyone laughs, but my self-deprecatory statement feeds the internal doubts I wrestle with and undercuts my confidence. So, I articulate the wisdom of the Way: "The only thing a pilgrim can do about the weather is walk through it."

Santiago and Joseph walk ahead of me and Stefan. For old men, they maintain a fast pace. We climb onto a *meseta* and enjoy expansive views of the grassy plateau.

Eighteen years old, intelligent, gifted, at a total loss about what to do with his life, Stefan says he wants to be a doctor, a lawyer, a priest or a theologian. He has no girlfriend.

"Good! Women create more confusion than clarity." That wisdom was forged in the furnace of experience.

He understands celibacy with more maturity than most people I have met. For him, it concerns family.

"The question is whether a man will have a traditional family or an ecclesial family. Both have challenges," I say.

The woman across from me in the confessional speaks about abuse in her marriage, the absence of love, the misery. She concludes with: "I put up with him for seven years, and something snapped."

She's describing me, I think. After seven years suffering egregious ecclesial abuses of power, something broke deep in my soul.

Another woman in the confessional says, "I put up with it for seven years, and I couldn't take it anymore." And another says, "I put up with him for seven years and then decided I had had enough." Each time they describe themselves, they describe me.

I think I should leave too, but God called me to be a priest, and so I stay. But the longer I stay, the worse I become. The break becomes a chasm, and because God called me to a life of abuse in the Church, my anger with God becomes volcanic.

We come down from the *meseta* and walk into Hornillos del Camino, a village with an *albergue* beside the church. We drop our packs on the church steps and rest in the sun. Shanti is here, along with a beautiful woman.

"I don't think we have met. My name is Jeffrey."

She smiles and says, "My name is Mar."

"What a beautiful name! *Mucho gusto.*"

"Igualmente," she says with a smile. Mar lives in Madrid.

The sun comes out, and we take off boots and socks and doctor feet in the sun's bright warmth. I switch to sandals.

We talk about whether to stay or walk ten kilometers to the village Hontanas. The moment feels surfeited with import.

Something powerful is happening. Ancient Greeks distinguished between two kinds of time: *chronos*, time measured with clocks, and *kairos*, with a secular definition: a befitting or opportune moment; and a religious definition: the in-breaking of eternity into *chronos*. *Kairos* is God's time made present in *chronos*, in our time. This moment is kairotic. I feel it in my soul. Confident of my intuition, I photograph everyone on the steps. The photo captures the physical scene, but only a creature made in the image and likeness of God can grasp the spiritual. Everyone decides to walk to Hontanas.

We climb back onto the *meseta*, and warmth cedes to cooler temperatures. A steady wind blows in our faces, and my face feels flush. The sun descends behind broken clouds. Backlit, the clouds appear dark, but through openings, sunlight shines like molten gold. In the dark clouds, thunder rumbles, lightning flashes.

Hontanas sits in a bowl on the edge of the *meseta*. When we arrive, the sun sets, and the temperature drops. Santi, Mar, Stefan and I go into one *albergue*. Santiago and Joseph go into an *albergue* attached to a restaurant. There we find Mike and Analisa.

They walked ten kilometers to Tardajos, with Mike saying he was tired and worried about me. Analisa says a hangover was the real reason he did not want to walk. They found an *albergue* that closed for the season one day earlier. The woman there gave them beds and bags of leftover food. Then they walked to Hontanas.

In the restaurant, Mike, Mar and I sup on beans with chunks of meat, a wonderful meal at the end of a long, wet, cold day. After supper, a bunch of us crowd into the small, pilgrim kitchen, drink beer and wine, and talk for hours.

One day after *horror vacui*, I become a member of a loose group of pilgrims.

Trees dot the long Arroyo de Garbanzuelo, and I walk on dry soil among tall grasses in cool temperatures with the wind in my face. I think about my sins and the decisions facing me, and cry.

The Way leads to *Convento de San Antón*, an ancient convent now in ruins. Two high arches connect two towers with a building overgrown with vines, shrubs and trees. Here I find Analisa and Laurence from France: beautiful, spiritual, happy, kind, friendly, a mother of six and in God's Providence, the perfect woman for Analisa to meet that morning.

"I lost my baby."

"What?" I say. "Are you sure?"

She chokes up, trying to hold back tears that cannot be held back. Tears flow as her heart breaks. I hug her.

"I did everything right." She stopped smoking and drinking. She prayed.

"It's not your fault." The miscarriage was a natural evil, the consequence of biology wounded by Original Sin, not moral evil, which requires a conscious choice.

"I don't understand," she says, "I loved the child I never met, and my alcoholic mother knew me and abused me. Why does God do these things to me?"

I know all the theological answers. Even the best answer, that God brings a greater good out of evil, sounds insufficient. I simply say, "I don't know."

Meeting Analisa seemed providential for both of us. Doctors told her that she could not conceive, then she prayed to be a mother at Lourdes, learned she was pregnant at Saint-Jean-Pied-de-Port. Doctors told her that she could not carry a child to term, and in Pamplona, she met me who had blessed infertile couples who had children. I hoped to see that miracle again. I even dreamed about her baby, and my dreams have often proved prophetic. I do not want to be a priest but thought that if Analisa's baby is born, that will be a sign from God for me to remain a priest. Everything fit, and everything fell apart. The tragedy confounds me.

Analisa tells no one else.

Santi and Mar arrive, and we cross a flat plain. In the western sky hang dark, tumultuous clouds.

In the village Castrojeriz, Analisa and I want and need to pray in a church, but all three churches are locked. We find a bar and in the bar Mike, Mar, Santi and Laurence. We take coffee and eat. When she leaves, Laurance puts her arm around Analisa and, with a compassionate, motherly smile, says, "You'll be okay."

"We will take good care of her," I say. "I promise you that."

Analisa wants to walk twenty-three kilometers to Frómista and a hospital. I offer to pay for a bus or a cab. Determined to walk there today, she refuses.

Mike, Analisa, Santi, Mar and I walk back onto the plain. With each step, an elongated hill rises before us. When we reach the top, we talk, laugh, rest, write messages on a board and take photographs. I topped climbs steeper and more challenging, but this is the first time I celebrate with friends. The experience feels strange.

We become cold and walk to warm up. We cross the ridge, then descend onto a broad plain. The wind kicks up and blows in our faces while rain sputters like an engine trying to start.

In the village Itero de la Vega, we find a brightly lit bar. Santiago and Joseph walk by. We wave them down. Stefan walks by. I wave him down. A couple, Patrick from Australia and Elisabetta from Italy, walk in. I persuade them to join us. We have a party.

It is not fun to leave the warm bar and step into the cold, but only six kilometers from Boadilla del Camino, we only have another hour and a half to walk in a light sprinkle falling out of the grey sky on a gentle breeze.

Once on the plain, the sky unleashes its fury. Torrents pelt us. The wind howls. Santi's poncho hangs below his knees. The wind wraps it around him. Mar's flimsy poncho blows up over her head. She holds it down with her hands. Mike, Analisa and I wear light rain jackets. Soon we are soaked, cold and miserable.

"Fuck!" yells Mar. "Fuck this!"

I look back at Santi and, over the wind and rain, yell, *"Buen Camino."*

"Buen Camino," he yells back.

"This is the real Camino."

"Amen, brother."

I worry about Analisa, but Mike is with her.

When we walk into the village Boadilla del Camino, the wind abates, but rain continues to fall as we search for an *albergue*. We check into *Albergue en el Camino*, with a grassy yard adorned with statues, rocks and other lawn decorations and surrounded by a high wall. Eduardo, the wonderful hospitaller, gives us rooms and tells us to get dry and warm. "We will take care of the money later." Mike, Analisa, Mar, Santi and I end up in a room together.

We lounge on beds and the floor. Mar wears a shirt and panties. Short brown hair, a pretty face and dreamy legs: when she walks in front of me, I tear my eyes away. She sits on the floor and invites me to sit beside her. She says she does not have a boyfriend. I try to keep cool, but all kinds of thoughts rampage through my head.

We talk about Fisterra. Santi and Mike plan to walk there. With only two weeks, Mar does not have time to walk to Santiago.

Analisa is on schedule to reach Santiago. For days, I have counted and recounted days, measured and remeasured distances, and each day it looks more and more like I have time to walk to the end of the earth.

Santi swam naked in the Mediterranean.

"Are you going to swim naked in the Atlantic?" I ask.

"Why not?" he answers.

"I'm only going to walk there once," I say. "If I make it to Fisterra, I'm jumping in the ocean naked."

I check email and have not heard from Anna. I email her again.

At dinner, we sit around one, big, long table along with two young Korean women, Jinyoung and Ara Cho. Eduardo's mother cooks lentil soup, hominy soup, beef stew with carrots and peas, and serves ice cream for dessert. We drink a lot of wine.

Our half-English, half-Spanish conversation whisks from language to weather to home to Spain to food to the Camino. Mike likes communal meals and says, "This is the right way to do the Camino."

"Let's get all the priests on the peninsula together for supper on Holy Thursday," I suggest to Msgr. Roth.

Jesus Christ instituted the priesthood on Holy Thursday, which is why the Chrism Mass is celebrated that day, but in the Diocese of Charleston, because priests are spread out across the whole state, that Mass is celebrated on Tuesday of Holy Week.

"We all will have just been together a few days before at the Chrism Mass," objects Msgr. Roth.

"Yeah, but Holy Thursday is the best day to celebrate the institution of the priesthood, and it is good for the priests on the peninsula to get together."

"We're too busy with the Holy Thursday Mass to have supper together."

"We can have an early supper."

No matter what I say, Roth rejects my idea.

A week after Holy Thursday, Father Basil Congro asks, "Why didn't you come to supper with the bishop on Holy Thursday?"

"What do you mean?"

"All the priests on the peninsula had supper with the bishop on Holy Thursday. It was Roth's idea, and he called everyone. It's the day the priesthood was instituted. You should have been there."

"He didn't call me."

When I wake, Analisa has packed. I chase her downstairs.

"You're not going to leave without breakfast," I say.

"I don't need breakfast."

"Yes, you do. You need to eat for your health. I'll pay for it."

Jinyoung and Ara Cho join us at breakfast. Jinyoung always wears a bright countenance, even early morning. I love her happy, smiling face. She has her Michelin guide in hand.

"I'm reworking my whole schedule to see if I can reach Fisterra, and it's all the fault of you and your friends."

I smile. "We recalculate our schedules day and night. It's a Camino addiction."

Analisa wolfs down the continental breakfast, hugs me and says, "This is not goodbye. I'll wait for you in Carrión."

As I sort my kit, Mar asks, "Where are we walking today Jeffrey?" Her invitation entices me. But the Anna-priesthood question haunts me like a dark shadow, and the loss of Analisa's baby occupies my thoughts and emotions. Moreover, I am trying to sort out my messy life and my broken relationship with God. I like Mar. I really like Mar. But I do not need more confusion. I have plenty confusion for myself and more than enough to share. I answer, "I plan to walk to Carrión," a factual but inadequate answer.

Downstairs as I lace up my boots, Jinyoung and Ara Cho leave. At the door, Jinyoung says, "I love you." Ara Cho, an introvert and a sweet, kind person with limited English skills, says, "Love."

Saturated from the day before, my boots soak my socks and feet, and temperatures have dropped. I start with cold, wet feet and dread.

A horse chained to a metal stake in a backyard charges me aggressively, but the chain restrains him. Chained my whole life, I became angry. I tell him how sorry I am for his abusive life and keep walking, knowing there is nothing I can do for him. Outside of town, two horses wander free in a pasture without a fence. I rub the neck and back of the friendly one while the skittish one stands apart.

After walking among pastures and fields, I walk into the village Frómista. A sign points to a medical center, and guessing Analisa went there, I feel relieved. Santi walks up. I ask where Mar is. He does not know. I regret not acting upon Mar's invitation, but it would not be fair to her. I have wrecked my life, and inner turmoil roils my emotions.

I walk past the café in the hamlet Revenga de Campos, but Mike steps out and flags me down. He has not seen anyone and waited in the bar for thirty minutes. I tell him that Analisa said she will wait in Carrión, and that I saw Santi in Frómista.

I eat breakfast, and Mike drinks a third beer. We soon go back into the cold. The wind blows steadily, and my ears hurt. I wrap a scarf around my head and tie it under my chin, as if it is a bonnet, then put my hat back on.

Outside the village Revenga de Campos, a kitten, grey with black stripes, walks out of a cemetery and cries. He rubs against Mike's leg, then mine. We look at each other. I hand my *bâton* to Mike, pick up the cat, put him inside my jacket and cradle him with my arm. He crawls around, settles down and cries for food.

"I know you are hungry. I know you need food. We're going to find you good food and a nice home." I have no idea what we are going to do.

Half a kilometer farther, a man sits beside the road by a nut orchard. He runs a roadside ministry.

"*Usted quiera un gato?*" I ask. He has a mouse problem and puts the kitten on the front seat of his van. The kitten stops crying and settles down.

"*Su nombre es Camino,*" I say. The man does not respond. Maybe he wants to name the cat.

"*El gato tiene hambre.*" He says he will feed him in an hour.

He gives us handfuls of nuts, stamps our passports, and writes "*Espere y ore*" on mine and "*Nunca haga a otro lo que no quitas parati*" on Mike's as Mike and I exchange questioning looks. At the van's window, we say goodbye to the kitten. Even with a few minutes of care, I feel an attachment to the kitten and a pain of loss when I leave.

Mike and I hustle across a flat plain, where nothing shields us from wind and cold. In the village Villalcázar de Sirga, we shelter from the elements in a café along with other pilgrims, several of whom mock the man who handed out nuts and wrote messages on our *passportos*. Nut job or not, he exercised a prophetic ministry. "Hope and pray" is prescient for me. I do not know the import of Mike's message: "Do not do to others what you do not want done to yourself." I wonder if the pilgrims' mockery eclipses the light of wisdom that might unveil God's messages to them. When God gives us a word, he gives us the grace to receive that word, but we can reject that grace. Israel rejected Ezekiel, who was insane, until his prophecy proved true.

Clouds blanket the sky, and rain showers course across the plain in the distance as we trudge all afternoon against a cold, steady wind.

Outside the town Carrión de Los Condes, we catch Santiago and Joseph. Santiago leads us to an *albergue* run by religious sisters. Santiago, Joseph and I register. Mike is unsure if he wants to stay or walk another sixteen kilometers. He cannot understand why Analisa ran off, and I cannot tell him.

"Let her go," I say. "She's crazy."

He leaves but comes back to celebrate Santiago's birthday.

The *albergue* is in a building in the back of the complex. Rooms are on the second floor up exterior black metal stairs and are named for continental sized areas. Santiago, Joseph and I are put in America. Mike goes to Africa as does Stefan, Mar and Santi when they arrive.

I meet Lucy from England, whose native English accent delights me. She is holed up here for the day with a wrapped ankle.

Mike, Santiago, Joseph and I find a bar filled with men, who drink, smoke and play cards and dominoes. Amid the din of conversations and clinking glasses, they slap cards and dominoes down on tables to cheers and groans.

We take a table, toast Santiago with drinks and sing Happy Birthday in English, German and two versions of Spanish. A local comes over and berates us. Santiago closes his eyes, shakes his head and with his hand, palm down, motions us to be quiet. The tirade ends, and the man walks away. A local catches my attention, taps his head with his finger, then waves dismissively. Mike and I ask what transpired. Santiago and Joseph tell us to forget about it.

"El señor no está contento porque cantamos muy mal," I say. We laugh—maybe our bad singing disgruntled the man—and order more drinks.

We speculate about Analisa. Did she get lost? Unlikely. Did she hitchhike or take a bus? Possibly. Did she go to a hospital because of the pregnancy? Hopefully. Did she walk farther down the Way? Likely. "Where's Analisa? Where's Analisa? Where's Analisa? Where's Analisa?" circles the table.

Then we talk about the Way.

Santiago says, "You have to keep an open mind to other people."

"And an open heart," I add and repeat what the Korean women said that morning. As I say "love," Jinyoung and Ara Cho walk in. We chat, but sideways glances at the male clientele prompt a retreat, as it had with several other groups of female pilgrims.

Santiago and Mike buy food for supper, while I go to Mass with Daniel from Germany and Pepa from Spain, whom I met in the *albergue*. The sun has set, and we walk through dark, cold streets to Iglesia de Santa María del Camino, a small church packed with locals. I sit apart from Daniel and Pepa, to hide my pain.

Overhead lights are so bright the light hurts my eyes. Two wood stoves, in the front and back, warm the church and overheat me. I disrobe: hat, scarf, jacket, fleece and shirt, until I wear silk under-layers, top and bottom, and pants.

Tired, hungry, teetering on drunkenness, my emotions spume to the surface in a frothy, roiling boil. Self-doubt plagues me. I wonder what my friends think about the fact that I go to Mass when they do not. Not hearing from Anna, I imagine her in bed with other men. Anna was always selfish, never faithful, never honest. I think about how much it hurts to love her and cry.

We return to the *albergue*, and when I walk into the kitchen, Mike is cooking pasta, so I check laundry. Before Mass, I washed my clothes and now put them in dryers. I run the dryer through two cycles and pull out wet clothes. The curse persists.

Around 11 p.m., a sister comes to the dining room and tells us that we have to go to bed. The Spanish speakers explain that we are late because we were the last to cook and it is Santiago's birthday. She accepts the explanation and leaves. We clean a little but talk and drink a lot.

At midnight, three sisters walk into the kitchen. Dressed in black skirts, white shirts and black sweaters, with short black hair and beach-ball bodies, they look like triplets. They advance in military formation: the superior in front, flanked by the other two, a step behind. The whole scene appears comical, but it is impossible to laugh. They lambast us. Under withering stares, we clean up beer and wine bottles, cake and cookies, and leave. We walk away like children who resent being scolded but also like inebriated adults who find the whole situation all too funny.

Tired, drunk and ready to sleep, I lie in bed thinking too much about too many things: I do not want to be a priest, why Anna has not responded to emails, the agony of self-doubt, emotional legacies of abuse, the rescue of the kitten, the horses that ran free, the abused horse chained to a stake, the new, strange experience of friendship, that I am drinking too much, the loss of Analisa's baby, Analisa herself, attraction to Mar, temptations, discernment, God's providence, *horror vacui*, my group, the crucible of love.

The Way is intense, concentrated, boiled down, a reduction to essentials. Superficialities that hide real issues with pretended illusion are stripped away. Only exhaustion brings me sleep and rest.

The Tribe

DAYS 49 – 51

On the edge of town, I catch Patrick and Elisabetta. In brisk weather, we walk past farms and fields. I enjoy their company, then surge ahead. I stop at a picnic table by a farm, and Mike catches me.

He and I cross onto Via Aquitania, a Roman road that tracks straight through a vast, empty plain. The wind picks up, making a cold day worse. The barrenness makes the walk a psychological challenge, exacerbated because the village Calzadilla de la Cueza is nowhere to be seen, after several hours of walking. Based on our pace, we know we ought to be close but see nothing. We check watches, compasses and maps and keep walking. Finally, a cross emerges above the plain. For another kilometer, we see only the cross, then we top a rise and hidden in a bowl of grass sits Cazadilla.

Directions to the only bar are painted on the road. Mike wonders if Analisa left a note and goes to the bar. I search for a *mercado* unsuccessfully, then go to the bar. Mike busts out its door. "A note from Analisa!"

"St. Michael: My name is Analisa, and I have
a problem. (She drew a winking smiley face.)

Missing you and headed toward Moratinos. I will be @ The Peaceable Kingdom." Under a heart, she signed, "Analisa."

Mike tells me that he once walked up beside Analisa and said, "Hi. My name is Mike, and I have a problem," and Analisa busted out laughing. I wonder if Mike knows that people in twelve-step programs introduce themselves the same way. Mike understands her note as an inside joke, but knowing Analisa lost the baby, I take the sentence in all seriousness.

A dozen pilgrims pile into the bar, including Santiago and Joseph. Although I cannot reveal details, I tell them that Analisa has a problem and where she is headed. For days, Joseph has walked with pain so bad that he has considered abandoning. Santiago's first instinct is to go, but concerned for Joseph, he wants to stay with him. Joseph resolves to walk to Moratinos.

I tell Mike that, if he sees Analisa, to call her "Big Medicine."

I depart first and alone. I need time to think. Analisa addressed the note to Mike and not to me, which bothers me. I have been instrumental in her pilgrimage. But she sees Mike as a lover and me as a father figure, and, of course, spousal relationships take precedence over parental relationships. In Burgos, when Analisa, Nara and Janey congregated in my room, on Facebook, Analisa wrote that I was full of love and wisdom and that I reminded her of Martin Sheen, a father figure, in the movie *The Way*. In my mind, the priest-father connection exacerbates my confusion.

The Way passes between low ridges and rock-strewn hills. On one section, pilgrims have arranged fist-sized stones on the trail to form names and messages. Amid the stones, I see my mark, my initials.

Outside the hamlet Ledigos, the Way splits. One path follows the road. One goes cross-country. I choose the scenic route.

I traipse through low hills and pastures with flocks of sheep and shepherds, until I reach Moratinos, a hamlet with four *albergues*. I stop at three before I find The Peaceable Kingdom. Rebecca, an American, opens the door.

"This might sound strange, but I am looking for Analisa."

"That does not sound strange at all. Let me take you to her."

In the kitchen sit Analisa and Mike. He took the quicker road route. Three ounces of marijuana lay on the kitchen table.

"I told you my friends would come for me."

From Boadilla, Analisa went to the hospital in Carrión. A sonogram revealed that she had the physically perfect miscarriage. Everything had been evacuated. From Carrión, she walked to Calzadilla, stayed in the *albergue municipal*, then walked to Moratinos and The Peaceable Kingdom. When Rebecca opened the door, Analisa burst into tears. In exchange for room and board, Rebecca put her to work trimming marijuana, a skill Analisa had mastered in the States.

When we are alone, she tells me that she told Mike she lost the baby, and Mike comforted her.

"I'm glad you told him. I kept your secret. I told no one. Even when everyone kept asking why you ran off, I kept your secret."

"I knew you would."

"I covered by telling everyone you were *loca*, a crazy woman." I tell her about Mike's reaction when he found the note. "He really likes you. But me? I was like, ah, it's only Ana-*loca*-lisa." I shrug.

She purses her lips into a wry smile, turns her head away, then turns back with the same smile. "You're just upset because I wrote the note to Mike and not to you. I wrote your initials on the road. Did you see them?"

"I saw my mark. I knew you wanted me to come."

"What did you mean by Big Medicine?"

"It's a First People phrase that means crazy."

"I've never heard of it." She looks borderline indignant.

"Maybe you should watch more Cowboy and Indian movies," I say smiling, then add, "Big Medicine means something more like 'powerful spirit' in several First People cultures, maybe not in yours. It is high praise. It is associated with crazy, since crazy and otherworldly powers are often synonymous."

She looks unconvinced.

Santiago and Joseph arrive, then Santi and Mar. Because of limited space, Santi and Mar register in another *albergue*.

One by one, Analisa tells everyone that she lost the baby, and everyone comforts her with hugs and expressions of love.

Patrick, Rebecca's husband, builds a fire, make drinks and plays jazz, light rock and classical music. Rebecca offers marijuana to everyone. Everyone partakes except me.

"I don't smoke," I say.

Analisa thinks our group needs a name. I suggest "The Tribe" because we came together because of her. Among different suggestions, we settle on The Tribe.

Half concocted with leftovers, Mike's ragu de boeuf tastes fantastic. What Mike conjures in kitchens borders on the magical.

At dinner, Rebecca tells us that many people journey from Sarria to Santiago by bus. The bus stops, they get stamps, get back on the bus and receive *compostelas*. Our eyes glass over as we replay the struggles of our walks. Our mouths open, but no words come out.

After dinner, we migrate over to Santi and Mar's *albergue* and talk a couple hours. Stefan arrived late. After not sleeping because of snoring in Africa, he napped in a field where sheep grazed. He fell asleep under the warm sun but woke in dark, freezing cold. When he reached the *albergue*, he was sick. Every so often, we hear him retch.

Mar tells us that as she smoked a cigarette that morning, one of the sisters berated her, saying "Is this the Way? Drinking and smoking all night? Smoking in the morning? Is this the Way?"

The sister has never walked the Way. The Way encompasses all life: the good, the bad, the tragic, the joyful. The same people who partied also walked twenty-nine kilometers because someone they loved needed them. Our loving response to the tragedy Analisa suffered transformed a loose group of pilgrims into a community. Jesus created the Church when blood and water flowed from his side when he hung on the Cross. In death, his love brought forth a community. Analisa and her baby are Christlike figures and Big Medicine.

I asked God for a friend, and he answered with a community. That the catalyst prompting the formation of The Tribe was the death of Analisa's child tempers my thanks. It is a sad truth of our fallen world that evil reigns before good triumphs. The price to be paid for good to triumph over the reign of evil in the Diocese of Charleston disheartens me. The triumph over moral evil sanctified by ecclesial self-righteousness demands a death, most likely mine.

We all depart, except Stefan, who takes a day off at The Peaceable Kingdom.

Conversations ebb and flow as if we are at a party, albeit a party strung out over a dozen kilometers.

Walking with Santiago, I admit, "You know, I've been out here a long time. This is day fifty. I've walked somewhere around

1,200 kilometers. The closer I get to Santiago, the more confused I'm becoming. I have more questions than answers."

I arrive at Ermita de la Virgen del Puente along with Claire from Canada. An arch marks the halfway point.

"Halfway between what and what?" I ask.

"Between Saint Jean and Santiago," Claire answers.

"We start in different places. My halfway point was Saint-Jean. Mike's halfway point was farther back. Stefan started in Burgos. Some people start at their front door." I'm on a roll. "Where's the spiritual halfway point? That's the important marker. I don't think I'm there yet. I don't think I'm close to that." *I am not even sure what that might look like*, I say to myself.

Claire's father-in-law has died. She is stopping in the town Sahagún, two kilometers ahead, to return home. The halfway arch marks the end of her pilgrimage.

"I hoped you have reached the spiritual end, whatever that is for you."

"There have been spiritual fruits," she answers and looks off into the distance.

In the corner of a bar in Sahagún lays a pilgrim's bag. I sit mine beside it, order breakfast and go down to the cellar to use the bathroom. A homeless man washes his clothes in the sink.

I wonder about the resolution and determination of the homeless man. What keeps a beaten down soul moving forward? Why does Anna persevere in her wretched life? Is it addiction or something deeper, a mysterious ember of hope buried under darkness ethereal yet heavier than lead? Why do I keep going? Why do I persevere in the priesthood despite suffering systemic abuses? Is it the human spirit or the spark of the divine?

I go back upstairs, and there sits Lucy.

"How's your foot?"

"I feel good, and my backpack feels light."

"Good, but if it makes you feel better, my feet are a wreck."

"It does," she answers with a laugh.

I laugh and say, "In my pilgrimage, everything has gone wrong, but I'm not stopping."

"I'm not going to let it get to me either."

I take a coffee and pastry with Lucy, then step outside, see The Tribe and join them at a second bar. Joseph and Santiago insist I try *"callos."*

"What is it?" I ask.

"Don't worry about it."

Santiago forks *callos* onto a piece of bread and puts a second piece on top to form a bite-sized sandwich. It tastes good. Joseph directs me to take a bite of *callos*, soak a piece of bread in the gravy and eat it along with the *callos*. It tastes great. I am eating cow intestines.

As we leave Sahagún, I fart involuntarily. It's the *callos*. Santi grabs his belly and cries out, "You got me." Normally, I would be embarrassed, especially with Mar here. But I have suffered enough angst on the Way, so I go with it.

"How do you say 'death by fart' in Spanish?" I ask.

"Muerte por pedo."

"Santi, they're going to put up a memorial to you. A cross with your photograph and under your photograph, your name, today's date and *muerte por pedo*. You'll be a Camino saint, and everyone will say, *'Pobre Santi, muerte por pedo.'* Pilgrims will leave rosaries, shoes and God knows what else to memorialize your martyrdom."

For the next few hours, we walk slowly, at times together, at times alone. To not think about anything serious, I write *poetica terribilis*.

I got ten more days to walk.
Time for me and God to talk.
I walk with *mis amigos*,
But we make our own *caminos*.

I got blisters on my feet.
The sun's aflame with ungodly heat.
I've had too much beer to drink.
I got too much time to think.

Snores sounded like a demon's howl.
Farts smelled like the devil's bowels.
But the stars above shone so bright,
I laughed myself to sleep last night.

The Devil's Bowel phrase bothers me. I have not been in a dormitory fouled by flatulence. Contrary to the common understanding of prophecy, prophets do not predict the future. Prophets unveil the present. God, who was, is and ever shall be and to whom all time is eternally present, speaks through the prophet to give the prophet's word meaning in the past, present and future. I worry that by uttering the Devil's Bowl phrase, slumbering evil stirs, and even now a Polluter of Dormitories stalks the Way, and we walk on converging paths. I fear bad poetry might be good prophecy.

We warm up at a bar in a village, then walk to another village, El Burgo Ranero, except Analisa who blitzes ahead of everyone. Mike and I find the *albergue municipal,* and speaking Spanish, I get The Tribe a room with seven beds.

As I sit on a chair and doctor blisters, Analisa pops in, sits up against the wall on the bottom bed of a bunk bed and announces, "I can't stay here."

She is emotional. I decide to be matter of fact.

"Why not?"

"Two men who have been prejudice toward me are here."

When Analisa told people she was Navajo, everyone thought she was "Indian." She informed them that "Indian" is prejudicial and that she is a member of the First People. Some people accepted the explanation, but others argued with Analisa about her own cultural identity. Two of those men stay in the *albergue*.

"You can't leave. It's too late. It's too cold. There's no other place to stay in this village, and the next village is too far away."

"I can't stay here."

"Well, you can't leave. It's too dangerous."

"You don't know what it is like to experience prejudice."

"That's not true," I counter. "I've experienced prejudice plenty of times. There's virulent anti-Catholicism in South Carolina. As a southerner, I have experienced pathological prejudice from northerners."

"Why is it always me?"

"It's not always you. We all experience prejudice. You're overreacting."

"I'm not overreacting."

"Yes, you are. You're emotional. You want to leave because of those two men. But look who you are with. Your Tribe. You are so upset about how those men treated you that you ignore the fact that you are with us. We're more important than they are, and we love you."

As we talk, I burn needles with matches, stick them into blisters, press out fluid, wipe blisters with antiseptic and apply Compeed. I have performed this task so many times that I do it by rote.

"One reason I came on the Camino was to learn not to fight so much," she says. Because of physical abuse she suffered as a child, I can see how her feisty nature developed an adversarial approach to problem-solving.

"That's good. How are you going to do it?"

"I'll kill them with kindness. Next time, we are at a table together, and they are there, I'll invite them to join us."

"Love will confuse them. Love certainly confuses me."

"I'll stay."

I walk through gently undulating countryside, broken up by arroyos, roads and a passenger train that parallels the Camino. I have not seen a train since Le Puy. With dark windows and intractable, the train looks anonymous, emotionless and moves with modern man's indifference to everyone else. The train looks like a modern Leviathan. Encased in metal and glass, people on the train travel in an environment immunized from the world. Pilgrims experience everything: the smell of manure, the beauty of flowers, the curiosity of a horse, the hardness of rock, the softness of a smile. A pilgrim lives in the world with all its pain and glory. A pilgrim's journey is human and divine.

Mike and Santiago catch me as I walk into the village Reliegos, and Santiago leads us to a bar he knows. The white exterior has writing all over it. The largest word is "Elvis." So, everyone calls the bar the Elvis Bar and the owner Elvis. Pilgrim messages also cover the white interior walls, along with pilgrim offerings hanging everywhere.

A second group arrives. They walk with Charlie the Dog, a half Doberman, half Rottweiler, who looks like a tall rottie with features softer than a dobbie. A man named Luca from Italy owns Charlie.

"Is Charlie walking all the way to Santiago?" I ask.

"All the way to Santiago," he answers.

"If he walks to Santiago, Charlie gets a *compostela.*"

"I will pay for him to get a *compostela,*" Luca says.

Charlie's group lays a T-shirt on the table and signs it. Mike, Santiago and I sign it as does Analisa who arrives. They hang the shirt on the wall. A signed leather pouch Santiago hung on the wall three years earlier is still here. In a blank book, I write *"Ne Capistra Bovis"* and make my mark.

The Tribe and Charlie's Group have a spontaneous party. We drink beer and wine. We eat cheese, ham, squid, chocolate, dried figs and bread, always bread. We talk and laugh. Inside, I still feel out of place. The fact that I am a priest and have not told my friends plagues me. Of course, I do not want to be a priest. I just want to be Jeffrey. The demon of self-doubt gnaws my gut.

I live with Msgr. Joseph Roth, pastor of the cathedral and a vicar general, in a two-bedroom apartment behind the Chancery. Msgr. Roth is renovating the Cathedral rectory for more than $500,000, and the plan is for me to move in when it is finished.

Short, obese, with a diet killing him, Roth has all the complications that come from obesity. I try to get him to eat better. He rebuffs my entreaties. I talk to several people about my efforts to help him, but we agree the effort is useless.

When the Cathedral rectory is completed, days before I am to move in, Msgr. Roth accuses me of betraying him. He says, "The bishop wants the Cathedral rectory to be a place of welcome for priests to visit. So, you can't move in."

"The Church has an obligation to house me. Where am I am supposed to live?"

"That's your problem."

Had I not had a farm an hour outside of Charleston, I would be sleeping in my car.

This occurs during the pedophilia crisis, when priests like me are beaten up verbally everywhere—walking down the street, sitting in a restaurant, in emails from strangers—even though we were led to believe that the problem was addressed years earlier and had no input on decisions that perpetuated the problem. Bishop Baker calls the priests to the Cathedral for Mass to speak a word of encouragement to us.

Before Mass, I remind Msgr. Roth, "I don't have any place to live."

"It's your own fault," he says.

In his homily, the bishop says, "Priests are our number one priority." He looks directly at me and pauses. Only weeks before, he made me homeless, and he knows I am not being paid. The movement inside my body is to stand up, rip off my chasuble and walk out. I remain where I sit and fume.

Several weeks later and in response to the condemnation that fell on priests because of the bishops' mishandling of the pedophilia problem, lay men and women invite the priests to a celebration at Bishop England High School to thank us for our work. I do not want to go but am expected to go. I end up sitting beside Msgr. Joseph Roth.

He leans over and asks, "Are you okay?"

His feigned concern after he was instrumental in my not being paid or housed constitutes the most heinous lie, an offspring of the lies of the father of all lies, the devil himself.

As people talk about how much they love their priests, the dichotomy between the abusive treatment I endured in the diocese and the lie of love expands into a void filled with agony and torment.

I leave early and walk out suppressing sobs. As I drive away, tears roll down my cheeks.

Months later, I ask Bishop Baker about my being made homeless.
He admits that he approved the decision. He also informs me that the
betrayal Roth accused me of was my criticism of his diet.

We take a photo of The Tribe inside the bar. Analisa comments, "We all look so happy." I feel happy and have a big, natural smile.

I debate walking thirteen kilometers to Villarente or twenty-six kilometers to León and taking a day off. I need a day off. I also want a place with solid internet connection so that I can email Anna. Not every café has Wi-Fi, and cafés with Wi-Fi have spotty connections. I say goodbye to everyone and tell them I will wait for them in León.

The Way courses through towns, villages and the countryside. Every step is painful. Despite all preventive efforts, I get new blisters each day. Blisters on top of blisters. Because of the pain in my feet when I bought these boots, I purchased boots one size too large.

I walk into the city León with three thoughts: *hotel, food, hospital,* in that order. I arrive in center as the gloaming falls. At *la oficina de turismo*, I get a map and directions to hotels. When I step out, the sun has set and the temperature has dropped.

A hotel has a room, but I will have to share it with a stranger. A second hotel has no room. The third has a room in the basement beside the bar. The fourth has no room. I wonder if I am encountering prejudice.

After a convoluted circumambulation in the dark cold, I find an *albergue* near where I entered the center. A Spanish woman standing in the gate to *Albergue del Monasterio de las Benedictinas* speaks English well, but I ask where I can find a hotel in Spanish and English. She explains that the *albergue* is here. Again, in

English and Spanish, I explain that I plan to take a day off, and on days off, I stay in hotels. She says she does not know where a hotel is. I walk up the street and find a hotel beside the *albergue* but no one at the desk. I wait, and the same woman walks in.

"Are you not the same woman I just spoke to?"

"Yes," she says reluctantly.

I smile and stare at her with seething contempt. The hospitaller at *Albergue Benedictinas* lied to me and treated me, a pilgrim, with prejudice. If I were more proficient in Spanish, I would ask if pilgrims were second-class citizens not permitted to stay in hotels in León. Instead, with a quiet, determined tone, I say, "I want a room for two nights. *Yo quiero una habitación por dos noches.*" I get a room.

I dine in the hotel's restaurant, and Mikai steps in. He has already eaten but invites me to join him for breakfast at a café by the cathedral.

In my room, I pop blisters and email Anna. In the subject line: "This is not junk mail." In the body: "I have emailed you but heard nothing back." I send this message five times.

Too tired, drunk and depressed to find a hospital, I go to bed.

Puente de Óbrigo

DAYS 52 - 56

Anna answers and says nothing about not responding to emails. Instead, she asks if I read her email about her brother having a brain aneurysm.

"My mom has breast cancer," Brandon says.

We are in my truck, and I am driving Brandon to drug court, a sentence given him in lieu of going to jail for burglary, crimes motivated by his addiction. I look over at him.

"When did she tell you that?" I ask. I have reason to be incredulous.

"When she picked me up to take me to drug court."

"She picked you up, and on the way to drug court, she just told you she had cancer?"

"We ran late."

"Why were you late? You've been good about being punctual. That can get you thrown into prison."

"I know. My mom picked me up late."

"So, she ran late and endangered your chance for a new life, then said she had cancer."

Brandon looks at me quizzically.

"Brandon, she does not have cancer. That's a lie she has told before to deflect attention from her irresponsible behavior."

No previous email mentioned the brain aneurysm. I email back and ask for details on her release. "Was it drug court?"

She answers: "There's so much to tell." Telling me nothing with vague comments about how much there is to tell was also something she did repeatedly. All in all, it sounds like the same Anna.

As I meander down to the cathedral, a man staggers and rants. Stone streets and stone buildings amplify his voice. People turn to look. I catch one word: *"puta,"* whore.

Mikai finds me, and we take coffee and eat pastries.

Friendly, talkative, completely different than when I first met him, Mikai's diametric change is scary. He keeps saying, "I want to change my life." He talks about moving to one of two ecovillages in Galicia. Pilgrims call them hippie villages. He warns me about *albergues* reputed to be infested with bedbugs but keeps coming back to changing his life. Mikai heads down the Way, and outside the café window, I see Stefan. To catch up, he caught a bus to León that morning.

Stefan and I tour the Cathedral's cloister and museum, then lunch in an Art Deco restaurant that serves *bocadillos*. Impressed with the thick, firm, big, substantial bread with big bubbles, we photograph the sandwiches, which screams tourist or, worse, pilgrim. The locals look at us with disdain. When we leave, Stefan characterizes the silent condemnation as "What are you people doing in our bar?" This is the second time I have experienced prejudice in León.

We almost literally walk into Joseph, who walks with downcast eyes. He tells us that everyone wants to stay at *Albergue San Francisco*. So, Stefan and Joseph go to the *albergue*. I return to my room and take a siesta.

I then visit La Catedral de la Santa María de Regala de León, best described with three words: tall, Gothic and stained-glass.

From the outside, the building evokes monumental, stately power. On the inside, arches soar to the heavens, and high walls allow the windows to filter sunlight in dramatic beauty, or so the woman on the audio guide says. The cloudy day mutes the windows' colors.

She also says that sunlight filtered through images of saints signifies how the myriad of saints are conduits for the light of the Son of God to come into the world through their unique personalities and work. I cry. I am no saint. I am a sinner. Whatever light in me was obscured by darkness long ago. More like a dirty, stained-glassed window in a lost, forgotten ruin than a well-kept work of architectural magnificence, if light shines through me, it is because my image is broken, and pieces are missing.

At the vigil Mass in the *chapella*, I sit, pray and cry.

The sun sets, and León grows cold. Magnified by humidity, the cold seeps into my bones. I buy a pair of Ecco boots in the desperate hope that new boots might help my feet.

At *Albergue San Francisco*, I find everyone except Analisa, who decided to sleep at *Albergue Benedictinas*. We walk there, and native Spaniards in our group send me up to find her. Stumbling through Spanish, I learn Analisa has not registered. We go back to *Albergue San Francisco* thinking she changed her mind. She is not here. We return to *Albergue Benedictinas*. Analisa is still not here. We finally realize she has skipped out on us again. We laugh, speculate, hypothesize and shake our heads. We are hurt but also realize that she, like us, walks her own Camino. "Where's Analisa?" has become a Camino refrain.

We squeeze into a crowded bar and order wine and various *tapas*, which includes *mochillo*. First described to me as blood sausage, I equated *mochillo* with Irish white and black blood sausage, which I detest and refused to eat it. Starving, I eat everything and love *mochillo*.

The moment I open my eyes, I know I am sick. I want to deny it, but I am exhausted and achy and have a sore throat.

As I walk to *Albergue San Francisco*, every step sucks out energy. I climb three flights of stairs to rejoin everyone in their room. The climb wastes my body. I have no energy in my legs and feel faint.

We head to the cathedral, and when alone with Mike, I show him an email Analisa sent. She is sorry she took off, hates that she has no money and feels like she mooches off us. She asks me to tell Mike that she loves him.

"Why didn't she email me?" he asks. He looks hurt.

"Mike, I can't explain how women's minds work."

I answer Analisa and acknowledge that her Camino is hers to make. I also tell her that I do not care about the money and that members of a Tribe have to look out for each other.

"The bishop can't understand what you need money for," observes Msgr. Roth. "Neither can I."

"To be paid. I am not being paid."

"When I worked at The Citadel, Mass was packed. I raised a lot of money and supported myself."

"Yes, but when Msgr. Sam Miglarese started that Mass, it was the only Sunday evening Mass in Charleston. When you inherited that Mass, it was still the only Sunday evening Mass in Charleston. When I got to The Citadel, three churches in Charleston had Sunday evening Masses, and only about twenty or thirty students attend Mass."

Despite this simple difference in circumstances, Roth tolerates no idea other than his own.

"I am working in five other diocesan and parochial positions, none of which support me," I continue.

"We're all busy."

"That is not the point."

"What is the point?"

I have this exasperating conversation with Roth dozens of times.

Before Bishop Baker became Bishop of Charleston, when he was a priest like me, he served as the campus minister at Florida State.

"It was hard work raising money to support the ministry, but I did it," he says.

"Yes, but there were about twenty-five thousand Catholic students at Florida State, from whose parents you could raise money. I have five hundred Catholic students at The Citadel."

The simple explanation of differing circumstances does not penetrate his mind. As we speak, his facial expression reminds me of stone statues. I have multiple conversations with him. No rational explanation matters. Diocesan staff discuss whether Baker is a sociopath.

Santiago and Joseph visit the cathedral, then walk down the Way. Mike and I eat at a café filled with locals and wait an excessively long time to get service and even then force the issue by insisting the waitress take our order. This is the third time I have experienced pilgrim prejudice in León.

As an offering for the healing of my feet, I leave my wasted boots between the cathedral's two massive doors at the base of a statue of Mary.

Mike, Santi, Mar, Stefan and I leave together. We find Joseph and Santiago at a café in the small town La Virgin del Camino. I can walk sick, but my body craves food. I eat a second breakfast.

West of town, we go cross-country and walk through villages, wide fields and undulating hills. Hawks hunt the empty land on streams of air. As they reel, the sun silvers their wings.

Wearing a bandana on his head, sunglasses over his eyes and his smart phone's earplugs in his ears, Mike looks intense, introverted, deep in thought. Analisa is on his mind.

Worsened by my sore throat, each weary step drains energy. Warm in the sun, cold in the shade: the sun shines, disappears, reappears. I walk with my jacket open, closed, take it off, put it back on. Heavy clouds blow in, the sun disappears and the temperature drops.

A rainbow blesses our arrival in the village Villar de Mazarife. Both ends touch the earth, and all seven colors shine brilliantly: red, orange, yellow, green, violet, indigo, blue. A second rainbow hangs above the first. Behind the rainbows, turbulent clouds float in shades of grey, from light to dark. We gaze at the magnificent meteorological drama.

We then register in an *albergue*. Mike, Joseph, Santiago and I take a room, which has no heat. The hospitallers say they will turn on the heat before lights out.

We contribute to a supper fund, and Mike cooks. At a large dining room table in the heated reception room and for three euros apiece, we dine on salad and pasta with a cream sauce flavored with bacon, onions, garlic and mushrooms. We drink four bottles of wine and one large bottle of beer. Some days, we eat damn well for pilgrims—or anybody else, for that matter.

I dress in all my warm clothes, crawl into bed and wrap myself in my woobie. The hospitallers turn on the heat. The radiator warms up enough to keep itself from freezing.

I move my kit into the hall, then step onto an interior balcony where I hung clothes out to dry the night before. I snap my frozen clothes to break ice crystals and lash them to my backpack.

In darkness, I navigate downstairs and through the courtyard, where Santiago smokes a joint in dark, freezing cold. He wears a deep, contemplative expression. All a sudden, he has an epiphany. He is adamant that non-native speakers understand languages better than native speakers.

"Santiago, I think the marijuana's doing the thinking."

The bar opens, and Santiago tells me that the temperature has dropped to "four grades." Sick and tired, I push aside icebergs to think through imperfect English and cognates to equate "grade" with "gradient" and decipher "four degrees." The temperature has dropped to minus 4 degrees Celsius. Joseph arrives, and these old Spaniards congratulate me on being in Spain in miserable cold.

I leave at dawn and keep warm by walking fast but that zaps energy. I slow, precariously balancing walking speed, body heat and energy.

After passing fields, pastures and scattered farms, I walk into the small town Hospital de Óbrigo and come to Puente de Óbrigo, a thirteenth century bridge, 204 meters long, with bends and undulations and supported by twenty arches.

In the fifteenth century, Don Suero de Quiñones, a knight of León, fell in love with Doña Leonor de Tovar, who spurned him. A prisoner of her love, Don Suero donned an iron collar. To free himself of this enslavement, he proposed to defend Puente de Óbrigo until three hundred lances were broken. King Juan II approved the joust, and Don Suero, along with nine fellow knights, defended the bridge against sixty-eight knights, broke two hundred lances and killed a knight. Ecclesial judges then decreed that he defended his honor and granted him leave to remove the iron collar. Freed from imprisonment, he pilgrimaged to Santiago.

Anna and I are in my truck driving on Remount Road. It is night, one of many when I came to her when she called, wanting money for heroin. Many times, we argued about money, and I ended up giving her money. Often, I was simply too worn down by her addict-fueled tantrums to fight her insanity when my own insanity placed me in the middle of the no-win heroin-versus-prostitution nightmare. This is one of those nights. I do not argue. I just give her money.

Brandon calls, wanting something. They argue, but Anna gives in to what he wants.

"I can't say no to my son. I am such a codependent," Anna says.

I jerk my head to look at her. I can never say no to her, and it clicks. I am a codependent. I have no idea what a codependent is.

For my fiftieth birthday, I bought myself *Co-dependent No More* by Melody Beattie and spent that evening reading it. I fit the profile. A codependent does not find a sense of self-worth in himself but in the other person and sacrifices himself, his well-being, to save the other person, while being destroyed by the person he seeks to save. Codependency develops in an abusive childhood home. A codependent often feels empty on the inside.

The longer I persevered in the Catholic Church, thinking justice and common sense would prevail and that I served Jesus Christ, the longer the abuse continued, the crazier I became. While not being paid, I learned that the Diocese of Charleston was financially supporting an accused ephebophile, a priest with a sexual attraction to adolescents who had accusations considered valid. The Catholic Church treated a priest accused of sexual abuse better than the Church treated me. I thought, *The Church values sex abusers more than me.* And since I knew the severe damage caused by sexual abuse, having been victimized myself, I felt crushed, devastated. After being made homeless and forced to commute from Round O to work in Charleston, I stared at concrete bridge supports and imagined driving into them. Nobody would know I committed suicide. Everyone would think I fell asleep at the wheel.

I bound myself to Anna, and her self-destructive tendencies drained my energy, time and finances. She was the addict, and I went insane. Days after my fiftieth birthday, I walked around my rectory in tears, wondering if it would be more effective to slash my wrists or put a gun under my chin. I googled "charleston, counselor, co-dependency." Melissa's name came up first. We met the following week.

Modern psychology has stripped away the Romantic notions of chivalry that cloaked Don Suero's codependence. With Anna, codependency chained me to the twin horrors of prostitution and heroin. I wanted to help her out of those hells and suffered terribly as I persevered. I wanted to defend Anna's honor and help her recover her identity, but I lost mine. In the Church, I justified myself with Jesus' admonition to carry the cross, but my interpretation of the faith anointed abuse.

As I cross the Bridge of Codependency physically ill, my singular thought is *I am sick and have to get better.* A kind, helpful pharmacist gives me antibiotics.

I pause beside *Albergue Verde* and wonder if Analisa left a note but keep walking.

The temperature climbs above freezing, and the sun comes out. On a hill in the countryside and in rock art, someone wrote "Anna" in stones and, under it, formed a heart with stones. A few rocks are kicked aside, and a line splits the heart top to bottom. I mostly saw Anna with the broken and kicked heart but rarely her true heart, which radiated compassion and beauty.

As Anna and I walk through Target, a young boy, maybe four years old, pushes himself along using a walker to support his disabled legs. Everyone ignores him, except Anna.

"You can really power along."

When she speaks to him, his face becomes determined, and he pushes himself with more energy.

I come up behind Daniel and Pepa. We climb onto a small plateau, where a tent stands before a ruined building. David, the hospitaller, invites us inside. We crowd in and sit on a mattress set on plywood. Heavy rugs hang from beams supported by posts. David adds wood to the stove and makes tea. I feel the warmest I have been in days. We converse in English and Spanish. David stopped doing drugs cold turkey and moved to this location to rebuild the ruined building and transform it into an *albergue*.

Mike comes down the Way. I yell to get his attention. He sticks his head inside and asks, "Jeffrey, are you making party?"

"Yes, come in and join us." Mike squeezes in.

David stamps our passports with the name of his *albergue: Casa de Los Dioses*. The monotheist in me smiles. The pilgrim in me reminds myself that I do not walk to argue with anyone about anything. I take photographs and drop a couple euros in a donation box. As Mike and I walk away, David rings a cow bell in thanksgiving.

Old blisters pain me, but a worse problem has arisen. When the toes of my new boots bend, the leather pushes down against my big toes, causing intense pain.

We descend from the plateau and make a flat, straight run toward Astorga, a town on a hill above a plain like Lauzerte in France. I stop to take a photo and discover that the camera battery has dropped out. In Reina de la Puente, someone borrowed my camera and dropped it. The camera worked, but the battery has fallen out repeatedly. Sometimes, I caught it in my hand. Sometimes, it clattered on the pathway. The last place I took a photo was David's tent, which had a thick rug. It fell out without a sound. I hope someone finds it and brings it along. That is the miracle scenario. Most likely, I will buy another.

In Astorga's *albergue municipal*, Mike and I end up in a room with Daniel, Pepa, Stefan and Mark from Germany. When Mike takes off his boots and socks, a cloud of putrescence billows into the room. The accumulation of sweat and grime on the stitching of socks not washed for a week rubbed his soles raw. Then, bloody fluids of popped blisters soaked into his socks. The noxious stench sickens us. We make him put his boots outside the room and wash his socks.

"Mikai's crazy," Daniel says. "I don't like him. He's too difficult to deal with."

I listen without comment. I found several people on the Camino difficult. I am sure some people found me difficult. I think it best to accept people for who they are without concern for whom I think they ought to be, with the critical proviso that they not trespass upon who I am.

Mike and I want to eat inexpensive local food. The recommended restaurant is closed. So, we go to an expensive hotel restaurant. I order a local specialty that tastes like grease, which I cannot eat.

"I want the kind of woman with whom you never know what to expect," Mike says.

"Analisa is your girl," I say. "More than anything, I want to love and to be loved. I want a woman with whom I can build something, a life, a relationship. I'd like to accomplish things and have adventures." In our relationship, I built a mountain of debt, Anna a mountain of lies.

As we walk into the *albergue*, Stefan and other pilgrims head out for hot chocolate. Chocolate came to Europe in Astorga, and hot chocolate has been drunk here for five hundred years. Sick or not, going out for hot chocolate is a moral imperative.

We crowd around two tables pushed together and drink fantastic hot chocolate, which redeems Astorga's gastronomical honor. Bruce from Matavenero invites me to visit the ecovillage. He claims to have found a piece of the Holy Grail, which intrigues me. In medieval Christian literature, the Holy Grail is an object with miraculous powers. Sometimes, it is even equated with the chalice Jesus used at the Last Supper. From a mythic, typologic perspective, the Holy Grail is an almost impossible to attain goal, the seeking of which transforms the seeker.

I tell everyone that I lost my camera battery at David's hut and ask if anyone found it, admitting it would be a miracle. Stefan walked into David's tent, looked down, saw the battery and picked it up. Everyone is dumbfounded.

Because my frozen clothes did not dry in the cold, I cannot wash the clothes I am wearing. I sleep in dirty clothes for the first time. I desperately need a good night's sleep. Daniel snores loudly.

Toward morning, I fall asleep but do not get to enjoy it. A male hospitaller opens the door, turns on harsh, overhead, fluorescent lights and yells *"Buenos días!"* Everyone wakes disgruntled.

My frozen clothes dried during the night. I put those on and throw dirty clothes into the washer in the basement laundry. I look askance at the dryer. After sorting my kit and getting my camera battery from Stefan, I go back down to the basement laundry. With nothing to lose but euros, I risk the dryer.

Pilgrims pile into a nearby bar. The woman working the bar does not bring me butter or jam or a knife when she brings me bread, although she brings those things to other people. When I ask for them, she looks miffed. *Strange how I have to fight for the smallest things in the most benign settings.*

As we mill about, we discuss our plans. Mike thinks he will go to the hippie village. Santiago and Joseph do not know their plans. I tell them that I intend to walk but will take it easy. I promise to catch up.

I pull warm, dry clothes out of the dryer and change clothes right in the laundry. Warm clothes feel transcendent. In Camino lore, the Miracle of the Dryer equals the Resurrection of the Rooster and the Hen.

Stefan and I attend Mass at the cathedral and leave Astorga late morning. The sun shines, but dark, broken clouds hurry across a sky painted with rainbows small, radiant and complete. Too sick to maintain my normal pace, I slow, and Stefan walks ahead.

The weather turns cold, the sun hides behind clouds and sprinkles fall off and on. I stop at several bars to eat and reenergize my body, but even so the last seven kilometers, a gentle climb, takes two and a half hours, much longer than usual.

In the small town Rabanal del Camino, I stop at *Albergue Nuestra Señora del Pilar* and say to the owner, *"Yo estoy infirmo. Yo necesito dormir bien."* In an act of profound hospitality and for fifteen euros, double the price of a dormitory bed, he gives me a room in his house.

"Muchas gracias," I say with hands folded in prayer.

He leads me up uneven stairs, through a living room and down a hall to a room smaller than a monk's cell but quiet and warm. I shower, then sleep for ninety minutes.

I feel better when I wake but do not have the energy to find a restaurant and wonder what I am going to do for food. In the common room, which is warmed by a fireplace, Nicola from Italy cooks rice and invites me to join him. His offer is a godsend.

I sleep eleven hours undisturbed except for another nightmare about Anna in which she sleeps with another man. The dream ends with the admonition, "Wake up."

I climb to the village Foncebedón as the weather alternates among sun, clouds and rain, with cold the only constant. At *Albergue Monte Irago*, the yoga *albergue*, I decide to go to the hippie village because of my interest in sustainability and because this is likely the only opportunity I will have in my life to visit an ecovillage. Also, I am curious about the Grail.

The road to Matavenero starts as a gravel utility road for an electrical waystation, then becomes a logging road in thick forests. After an hour and a half, mostly on a decline, I see a cluster of thirty buildings on the arm of a mountain. At this point, the road becomes rough, only navigable by feet and four-wheel-drive vehicles. I come to an autopark atop a crag, where vehicles deteriorate among trees and bushes. I loop right on a slick, rocky path that doubles as a creek, using my *batôn* for balance.

The village feels deserted, but I find a man in a wood shop. He looks apprehensively at me, a stranger. I tell him that Bruce invited me and ask for directions to his house.

Bruce makes tea, and I share almonds, dried figs and dark chocolate. After talking about many things, I ask about the Holy Grail.

Bruce worked as a carpenter in a commune in southern Spain. Over a sacred space, he built a double tetrahedron, a religious symbol important to him. At once, it resembles a multilayered Star of David and a Yantras, a symbolic form of a deity in India. One day, he found a small hidden cave. He crawled into it and heard a voice say, "Dig." He pulled rocks out, then found a rock that shone with light, which, he concluded somehow, was one piece of the Holy Grail. There are three pieces, and because the Matavenero valley was a last holdout of the Knights Templar, who had interests in relics, he thinks a piece might be hidden here. He shows me the Holy Grail. It looks like a nondescript rock. He admits that people think he is crazy.

I think him deceived—the connection between the Knights Templar and the Grail is pseudohistory—but say, "It's not uncommon for people to think spiritual people to be crazy."

After tea, he gives me a tour.

Natural springs fill the valley, but pumps and black rubber hoses, ugly and inartistic, snake everywhere and bring water to the houses. Sun-powered electrical systems atop houses power lights and computers. The residents separate themselves from the world but wire themselves to the world.

A long building houses the common room, which has a kitchen and long tables. Two men, high on marijuana and who arrived the week before, beat on tall drums with aboriginal designs. Anne from Australia, a pilgrim who arrived ten days earlier, makes a tasty vegetarian lunch, which she shares with me. She has no desire to leave. She has found her place.

I move my bowels in the communal outhouse, a two-story, two-room building. I sit in the top story, and my donation to the compost pile falls to the bottom story. I feel the sickness leave me. *There's a lot of shit I need to get out of my life.*

Anna looks twice her age, concentration-camp thin and gutted. She walks with short steps, as if each step hurts. She reeks with her own feces.

"I have to have money for heroin. I can't stand it anymore."

"You've already gone two days. Just a couple more days and you can be free of heroin forever."

"I can't do it." Her voice sounds pitiful, broken.

"Even now, I see your beauty. I know you don't feel beautiful now, but you are. Only a few more days, and you get your life back. You get yourself back."

"I can't do it. And if you do not give me money for heroin, I am going to shower, dress up and trick."

We talk for an hour, and I give her $200.

Bruce introduced me to kind, friendly people, but Matavenero is not for me. And I feel restless off the Way.

"I'm heading back to Foncebedón." Bruce looks hurt. "You've been a great host, and I enjoyed my visit, but I have to get back on the Way. God has something for me in Santiago."

"But it'll be dark soon, and you don't know the way."

"I walked down here. I can walk back, even in the dark." I put my headlamp around my neck. "I have my compass, my headlamp. I'm good." Not keen on walking in the dark, I am more resolute than good. I have to return to my quest for my Grail, not a fiction but Ultimate Reality, not a thing of creation touched by the Creator, but my quest for God himself.

I ask Bruce for a *sello*. He draws a tetrahedron on my passport.

With no energy in my legs and no food in my stomach, I climb out of Matavenero as the sun sets. When I reach the auto-park, my legs are blown, and darkness descends. My eyes adjust, and I see well enough to walk. I replay in my head and in reverse everything about the walk in. When I see the light at the electrical waystation, I feel jubilant.

I approach the village from a different direction than I departed. By instinct, dead-reckoning and intuition, I navigate to the village, then through the village and step onto the road across from the yoga *albergue*. Except for that one light, I navigated through darkness for more than two hours. A sense of accomplishment fills my heart, especially since, echoing my father, Bruce told me that I could not do what I just did.

I wrangle food as the kitchen shuts down. The simple fare tastes great. I sleep on a mattress on the floor in the second-floor dormitory. A storm blows in during the night. Winds and torrential rains beat the roof and windows.

Through the Valley

DAYS 57 – 58

I have no idea where the Tribe is or where I will walk. I simply start walking. Water drips from buildings and trees and runs through ditches. I walk through and around puddles on the flat sections of the trail, as I climb up to El Cruz de Ferro, the cross where pilgrims drop the rocks they carry.

I expected a gigantic pile of rocks. There are not many. I expected a tall, impressive cross. A small cross sits atop a wooden pole. A woman walks up, drops a rock, touches the log, says a prayer and keeps walking. Thinking it better not to dwell on disappointment but to imitate her, I walk up, drop my rock in the pile, touch the cross and pray, "Lord, please unburden me from the rocks I carry in my heart and in my mind."

The air is humid, and the day has already warmed up. At roof-covered benches opposite the cross, I strip naked, take off underlayers, then redress. Rain begins to fall in a light shower.

The hamlet Manjarín consists of a house and a bar: a canvas tent over long tables covered with trinkets and coffee pots. As I take coffee, the tent flaps part and in walks Laurence. Smiles radiant as the rising sun break across our faces. We give each other big hugs. She takes coffee, then we walk downtrail together.

Wrapped in clouds and mists, the Montes de León look mystical and dreamy. I think the Precious Frenchman, who told me what a terrible decision I made, to have a limited understanding of beauty, a prejudice for one kind of weather, a desire for a sanitized Way and lacking a true understanding of the Way. Rain falls on Laurence and me, and we laugh through the rain.

Ten-meter-long puddles block the trail. When the brush is thin, we walk around puddles and through mud. When the brush is impenetrable, we shuffle sideways along puddles' slippery edges, using *bâtons* to keep from falling into muddy water. Most of the time, we walk together, but our paces differ, especially downhill, when she walks fast.

I arrive at one end of a monstrous puddle, with no way around, just as Lucia de León arrives at the other end. She walked to Santiago and now walks home.

"Ladies first." She laughs. "I am a gentleman," I explain.

She negotiates the left side, then says, "Now it is your turn gen-tle-man." She emphasizes every syllable. I laugh and negotiate the right side. Again, at opposite ends, we wish each other *"buen Camino"* and go our Ways.

Laurence and I come back together on Collado de las Antenas and descend to Acebo, a village of grey stone and white plaster buildings with slate roofs, where we find a warm bar. We enjoy Calda Berçano, a lentil soup of Galicia and perfect for a rainy day.

The rain stops as we leave town.

"As a mother, I sense that you carry a lot on your heart, and I want to sing a prayer with you."

At the crest of a hill with a view of the valley below, we sing "Come Now Is the Time to Worship." She sings the stanzas in French. The English refrain we sing together. After we sing, I hug her.

We walk farther, then she realizes that she left her phone at the bar, after plugging it into the wall to charge, and goes back for it.

I descend to the bottom of a ravine, hear sheep bells, then see, on the opposite side of the creek, a herd of sheep. The noisy parade crosses the creek in front of me and trots down the path to a field, followed by a shepherd and his dogs.

For hours, the day dances on the edge of beauty. Then the sun comes out, and the birds sing.

In the village Molinaseca, I study my guide. Ponferrada, a small city, is only eight more kilometers. Though worn out, I can walk to the far side of Ponferrada and cut the distance between me and my Tribe by five kilometers and not relapse. Too tired to walk fast, I maintain a steady pace.

In Ponferrada, the Way passes a Templar castle pilgrims describe as a must-see. From the high walls, I look out across wide valleys to distant mountains, but with spent legs, I cannot climb the towers. I tour several museums, but exhaustion overwhelms appreciation of history.

I visit the church in Ponferrada's main square. Because of my condition, I say a brief prayer and leave.

In a maze of apartment blocks, I find no hotels, demi-pensions, pensions or *albergues*, no restaurants or cafés. I have walked into western Ponferrada's pilgrim desert.

At a school with an athletic field under construction, with a chain link fence to the left and thick bushes to the right, a thick-chested man with black hair and dressed in a black suit and white shirt blocks the path. I wonder if I am about to be mugged. *If I act like a mugging victim, I will be mugged.* I walk straight toward him. He tries to sell me religious pamphlets. Because of his ambush site, this Christian preys on pilgrims.

I walk into the sacristy, and Msgr. Charles Rowland is here, which surprises me. I am scheduled to say Mass.

"We have a problem," he says.

"Okay."

"The electricity in the school is not working."

"I guess someone has called SCE&G?"

"Yes, and you are going to call them again."

"But if they have already been informed, they are on the way. We don't need to call them twice."

He puts his finger in my face. "You are going to call them right now and tell them that our school has no electricity."

"Would it not be better to go over and chat with the kids and the teachers and make light of the situation for their sakes?"

"We have an entire school that is not open because we do not have electricity." He puts his face in my face. "You will call them and tell them to get someone over here right now to fix the electricity."

I call the power company and, in a nonplussed tone, inform them of the situation of which they are already informed.

Msgr. Rowland stomps out of the sacristy and over to the school. I pull out candles to light the altar for Mass. There is no light in the church either.

Msgr. Rowland comes back into the sacristy and again orders me to call SCE&G.

"They know about the problem. They are on the way, and we can't make them move any faster."

He grows enraged, puts his red face in my face and orders me to call SCE&G yet again.

So, I call and apologize for calling. The woman I speak with is frustrated. "We have crews on the way. Please stop calling us. We have other customers who need assistance and call this same line." I apologize again and thank her.

"Why are all these candles out?" Msgr. Rowland asks.

"I thought I'd say Mass by candlelight like the old days."

"There will be no Mass today."

"Why not? We say the first part of the Easter Vigil in the dark. A daily Mass will be easier to celebrate with little light than that liturgy."

"Father, there will be no Mass in the Church today, and you are going to call SCE&G again."

"They are getting upset with us and asked us to stop calling."

"You are disobedient."

"No, I am reasonable, sensible, and if you think it is such a good idea to call them yet again, why don't you call them?"

I go into the church, sit down and pray in the dark. Thirty or forty parishioners are also praying in the church. Msgr. Rowland walks down to me and yells, "You are disobedient and don't care that our children can't go to school." He stomps out the back of the church.

A man comes over and says, "Msgr. Rowland is having a bad day."

"No, he is like this every day."

With a firm "No" to the man peddling pamphlets, I keep walking.

I head uphill and pause on a ridge. The setting sun backlights dark clouds. One massive flame-shaped cloud cuts across the sky. Dark in its center, the cloud's edges burn orange and yellow, as if the sun's last word flames against darkness, before the sun sets, the light goes out and the gloaming darkens to night.

I pass through suburbs and small towns, sometimes separated by countryside but other times connected by narrow roadways with no place for pedestrians. When automobiles approach, I step aside and turn on my headlamp so that they can see me. This precaution slows my pace, and there are lots of cars.

In the village Camponaraya, I find an *albergue* closed for the season and ask about hotels. The nearest hotel is in Cacabelos, six kilometers distant.

I walk into the dark countryside on a long gravel road. Cold, hungry, alone, with no solution to my problems in sight, in the dark, on dangerous roads, worn out beyond exhaustion, with no energy in my legs, no food in my stomach or my backpack, only self-preservation holds enveloping depression at arm's length.

The path veers toward a road where I see headlights, which give me hope. I cross the road, and a car pulls over. Weakened by exhaustion, I lose my balance and fall in a ditch. The energy to stand up zaps what little is left in my legs. The driver offers me a ride. The temptation excites me, but I decline. My code forbids transportation other than by foot, and the man tells me Cacabelos is only two more kilometers. Even dead, I can walk two kilometers.

With a gas station on a corner and twentieth century, three-story buildings lining the streets, Cacabelos reminds me of towns in the States. When I step into a hotel, I have walked fourteen hours and forty-seven kilometers.

The hotel restaurant has no food more substantial than salad and tortillas, appetizers to the feast my body needs to recover its strength. Too exhausted to walk to another restaurant, I return to my room.

I check email. Anna has not emailed me since León. Neither has The Tribe. I am separated from my friends and have not heard from the people I love.

My physical exhaustion opens a void and eases the emotional slide into depression, and depression, held at bay in the darkness, overwhelms me and expands within. My demons grow to giant size and rise out of the void on wings that rend the air with sulphureous poison, and I breathe their foul air.

I doubt any of them love me: not my Tribe, not Anna, not God. I do not think I am worthy of being loved.

All the questions I wrestle with crash into my consciousness like train cars piling up on an engine that has come to a dead stop. I reel as I sit on my bed. If I was drunk, I would fall over and not move. I wish I were drunk. I wish I were dead. Thoughts about suicide flicker through my head. The windows of my third-floor room open a few inches. I wonder if I can squeeze through. I look down to the parking lot below and wonder if the fall will kill me or just injure me.

I email Melissa, my counselor, and dump on her. She responds immediately and quotes Proverbs: "It is the glory of God to conceal a matter, to search out a matter is the glory of kings."[11]

With that Word, I sober up. *I have to find what God has always concealed from me, and I will not search out the hidden matters of God tonight.*

For most of the morning, I traipse through foothills under a cool, blue sky, but as I walk into the village Villafranca del Bierzo and the Ancares Mountains, clouds roll in, and temperatures drop.

I reprovision at a grocery store and snack at *Albergue de la Piedra*, a modern building built against natural rock walls. Conan the Barbarian, a large dog with a thick yellow coat, visits with me. I bury my cold hands in his warm fur.

I walk out into a light sprinkle that becomes a light shower and grows into a heavy downpour. The Way follows a mountain pass where the Camino merges with the highway, with every step on concrete or asphalt. The road tilts, and as I take off-kilter

---

11 NIV, Proverbs 25:2

steps, sharp pains shoot through my ankles and knees. I try to take solace in the beauty of the mountains, but pain surpasses beauty. My head hangs down.

"This is fucking horrible," I blurt out. I look up and see, scrawled on the back of a sign: "No pain, no glory."

The rain stops, and after several painful hours, I escape the highway and walk on hilly, country roads.

In the late afternoon, I walk into the village Vega de Valcarce with Pepa. We find an *albergue* rumored to be run by Buddhist monks, and here find Daniel. He has seen The Tribe, and they asked about me. They climbed to O Cebreiro that afternoon. Daniel also says the two men who run the *albergue* practice Buddhism but are not monks.

I sit down in a quandary. To reach The Tribe, I will have to climb a mountain in the dark cold, with spent legs, possibly in the rain. When Daniel explains my quandary to the Buddhist who registers us, he waves goodbye to me and says, *"Buen Camino,"* which does not seem very Buddhist. I walk out.

Half a minute later, someone calls my name. Patrick and Elisabetta step out of a café. They have registered at the Buddhist *albergue* because the food is reputed to be great. I like their company. Again, I fall into a quandary: stay or walk. I vacillate and chat as the day grows colder and darker. Elisabetta hugs herself to stay warm. I say goodbye and keep walking.

Two kilometers later, I pass a hotel in the hamlet Ruitelán. People eating and drinking by a fireplace tempt me to stop. The owner comes out.

"Es tarde," he says, then adds, *"Yo tengo las mejores habitaciónes en Espania."*

I laugh. *"Yo credo. Lo credo."* I mix Latin and Spanish.

"Mis amigos están en O Cebriero." All in Spanish, we talk about food, whether it would snow and the danger of a night march up the mountain.

"Es peligroso."

"Es verdad," I say.

I walk to where the climb begins and stop, turn back, stop, restart, stop, and turn back again. With no hamlets or *albergues* identified on the climb in my guide, this is my last opportunity to change my mind.

Thinking a backtrack a failure and cowardly and desiring to find my people, I make one last turn and walk into the darkness of the woods that shields the Camino from the last vestiges of ambient light. Rocks embedded in mud and decaying leaves form a dark path. Rain falls. Water drips from trees. I emerge onto a high meadow as the rain stops, but the air feels so humid that I expect water to gush forth. Perspiration from within and rain from without saturate my clothes. The wind blows, and the breeze chills me. Only body heat created by the effort to climb holds off hypothermia.

Against black hills and a dark grey sky, white clouds float like specters above and below me. One cloud, buoyed by a zephyr, ghosts up a small valley with mocking ease as I trudge over ridges with heavy legs.

In the hamlet La Laguna, I pass a home. Farm animals live downstairs, the family upstairs. Dim lights in the barn illuminate a farmer performing evening's last chores. I pass an *albergue* with a brightly lighted common room, where pilgrims laugh and talk. They see me walk past, their faces expressing surprise, incredulity and horror.

At the edge of La Laguna, the Camino turns into the woods. A road heads the same direction. Exhaustion, the possibility of a twisted ankle, the fact that I am alone and the threat of hypothermia recommend that I stick to the road. By light shining out a house window, I check my map. My map does not show the road, but it leaves the village in the same direction as the Camino. I reason that the road and the Camino must follow the same pass.

The road switchbacks as it climbs. I top a high ridge line, where the land falls to either side. To the west and east and far below shine lights. I have reached the top of the mountain. The wind blows strongly.

I come upon crossroads with no waymarker. The wrong decision will lead me on a longer walk, made dangerous by accelerating threats of exhaustion and hypothermia. I shiver and layer up, enduring the same double-chill cycle I suffered when I crossed the Pyrenees. With my headlamp, I check my compass and my map, discern the subtleties of the terrain in the dark and turn left. Half a kilometer later, light glows in fog above a black tree line. My spirit lightens, and I walk into the small village O Cebreiro.

In two days, I walked eighty-five kilometers with 1,887 meters of elevation change, not counting undulations and detours. Both days, I walked from 7 a.m. to 9 p.m. Since 7 a.m. yesterday, I walked twenty-eight out of thirty-eight hours. The journey was as epic as it was inane.

I step into the first bar I find and take a room at a hotel. I drop everything on the floor and shower in a bathroom with a motion-activated light. As hot water cascades over my head and down my body, the light clicks off. The dark discomfits me. My soul needs light. Several times, I move to turn the light back on.

I find the *albergue municipal* and, in the common room, The Tribe, including Analisa.

"And you children thought you could outwalk an old man like me?"

After hugs, laughter and loud "hellos," we sit around a table and talk like we have never been separated.

The *albergue* has a kitchen but no dishes, so we go to a restaurant. Here Stefan and Mark sit with a young, sweet, genuine, friendly, happy, innocent South Korean woman named Kim. I catch up with them, then catch up with my Tribe.

Analisa worked at a bar to make money. Part of her pay included a *navaja*, a knife, the basis for the name of her Navajo Tribe. So, the multitool I dropped off was not needed in God's plan. God solved the problem without my intervention. *I could use more of that kind of help.* Analisa then waited in Foncebedón. They stayed at a different *albergue* than the yoga *albergue*. Their hospitaller read their Camino cards, a kind of Tarot card for the Camino. He also got them drunk off their asses.

From Foncebedón, they went to Ponferrada, where Mar cooked dinner to celebrate her last night. "The dinner was delicious," they say. Mar also had sex with someone. The words used to describe this are a little obscure, and when I do not get it, Santi makes the sound of a woman having an orgasm.

"I do not want to know any more about it," I say. I still regret not taking up her invitation to walk together, even though it would have derailed my Camino.

The next night they stayed at the *albergue municipal* in Villifranca del Bierzo, then came to O Cebriero.

Analisa left us notes at *Albergue Verde* in Hospital de Óbrigo, where my intuition prompted me to check for a note and I had not listened. I shake my head.

I recap my journey: eleven hours of sleep in Rabanal, my impressions of Matanevero, and my walk from Foncebedón to O Cebreiro.

"I saw Laurence."

"Oh, how is she?" Analisa asks.

"She is about a day behind and looks good," I answer.

"She is so beautiful."

"She is also spiritual," I point out, thinking Analisa only thought about Laurence's physical appearance, something I have been guilty of at times.

"Spiritual women are beautiful," Analisa answers, summing up in a single sentence my master's thesis on Mary. Although physically the most beautiful woman to ever live because of her Immaculate Conception, Mary's spiritual beauty, also the greatest of any woman because of her unity with the Holy Spirit, exceeds her physical beauty just as the beauty of God transcends the beauty of creation, and that true beauty is spiritual.

Back in my hotel, neither my room nor I warm up. Wearing two pairs of wool socks, my feet freeze all night long.

Storm on the Mountain

DAYS 59 – 60

I loathe wearing the same clothes I have worn four days straight even as I dress in them but want to keep my one set of sorta clean clothes sorta clean, and I have every reason to wear dirty clothes. Heavy rain falls.

In the dark, before dawn, The Tribe and a dozen other pilgrims mill about the bar. I do not want to walk in the rain. No one does, but no one talks about not walking. Every day we get up and walk, regardless of weather, spirits, physical condition, where we are or whom we are with. There is comfort in habit, safety in routine, a sense that the walk is our work, and we need to work. We join acceptance of fate to an attitude of perseverance. We also possess a faint hope, if not belief, that God has something for us on the Way, an explanation of the sufferings of our lives, maybe even me*tanoia:* transformation, reworking and reordering of our inner selves. We walk as individuals, with jumbled motivations and unique personalities, but also as part of a community with a goal, a purpose, an overarching hope, and we do what our people do. My people walk. I walk.

The sun rises, and we depart in ones and twos. I leave last.

When I step out, I see O Cebreiro in daylight. A small, grey stone church with a bell tower stands at the highest point. I go inside and thank God for my friends. I do not know what to say about Anna. A Benedictine monk sits quietly behind a desk. He wears a brown habit, has a long, grey beard and looks wan, as if he mortified his body through years of fasting. His kind, loving smile exudes peace. A sense of peace fills the church. Then I walk out into the storm.

In pine woods, I come up behind a female pilgrim. Too tired for Spanish, I introduce myself in English, which is Lucia from South Africa's native language.

"What possessed you to walk in a storm on the side of a mountain? I have a good excuse. I'm crazy."

"My son died two months ago."

Her openness and honesty shock and touch me.

"I am so very sorry."

Jamie was seventeen years old. The pain is raw. Two weeks after his death, she made plans to walk the Camino.

"There're lots of stupid ways to respond to pain that would hurt you and not help you heal. You didn't choose those. You chose something good. You chose life." I want to be positive and come back to the present. "Are you at least having an adventure?"

"I'm just trying to breathe."

Half an hour later, she tells me, "Jamie committed suicide." He attempted suicide before and was in a home for troubled teenagers. He made new, good, supportive friends, was intelligent, creative, talented and good-looking. She wonders if she missed a sign.

"What about you?" she asks. "Why are you here?"

I chuckle. "I have walked for two months and fourteen hundred kilometers and not told a soul. All I've said is 'God and I have a lot to talk about.'" I look at her, smile, and tears seep out of the corners of my eyes. Even in the heavy downpour with rain on my face, she sees my tears.

"I'm sorry for what you are going through."

I smile and laugh. "Well, it's my own damn fault, I guess." We walk silently for a minute. "You have been so honest and open, I really ought to tell you."

"No, no. I respect your privacy. Don't tell me if you don't want to."

She knew little about the Camino when she decided to walk. A travel agent made reservations and arranged to have her suitcase transported. She carries a daypack.

I tell her that several of us have bonded into a group called The Tribe.

"I'll introduce you to my friends."

We walk into the hamlet Linares and are soaked. We duck under a portico of a church bell tower. Lucia pulls a rain poncho over a rain jacket and rain pants. After she sorts everything, she looks at me and opens her hands. "Well?"

I look at her blonde hair, angular face and cute lips, and answer: "Beautiful. Absolutely beautiful."

We step back out into a heavy shower, the day grows colder and rain deteriorates into a mix of freezing rain, sleet and snow. We slog along a ridge line, then climb to the hamlet Alto do Poio, the day's high point. The wet cold sucks energy out of my legs, and with waterlogged boots, drenched pants and saturated under-layers, my legs and feet feel three times as heavy.

Pilgrims overcrowd the one bar in the hamlet. A few pilgrims even stand in the kitchen. Backpacks lay heaped in piles. We slide past each other to get to the bar and the bathroom.

Lucia and I join Mike, Santiago and Joseph, who sit by the fire-place. Joseph introduces himself to Lucia and starts to introduce me. I interrupt, "Joseph, Lucia and I are old friends." And I introduce her to everyone. No one has seen Analisa or Santi since O Cebreiro.

Santiago dries his shoes by the fire and holds them too close to the flames. One shoe smolders, and the industrial stink of burnt rubber fills the bar.

"I hate this fucking weather. I'm not going back out in that fucking shit," Mike says.

"We're walking down this mountain today," I answer for myself and Lucia. "We're not staying here. We're walking out of it. It is solved by walking." He does not know Lucia's suitcase heads to Triacastela, and she has no choice but to walk. We have mocked suitcase pilgrims, and I do not want Lucia to hear that from my friends.

When Lucia and I step outside, nothing falls. We think we have made a good decision. But after its rest, the storm returns with fury. Howling winds blow freezing rain, sleet and snow horizontally across our path or directly into our faces. Sleet stings my skin and shoots into my eyes. I hang my head to protect my eyes, and unable to see more than half a step ahead, I splash into one icy puddle after another. Ice and snow accumulate on my hat's brow and freeze my brain. To ease the pain, I pull the hat off my brow with one hand. Ice melts into my full-finger cycling gloves. When that hand freezes, I switch to the other hand, until it freezes, then switch again.

Lucia and I have a few, brief respites, when the trail descends onto sunken farm roads and the wind blows over our heads. Once, with wind howling up a sunken road and whipping our clothes, I stop and look at Lucia. Standing in icy puddles, plastered with layers of ice and snow, I holler, "Today, you're having an adventure whether you like it or not."

The trail meanders between farm roads and a two-lane asphalt road. Some pilgrims stay entirely on the road, always at the mercy of the wind. Some walk. Others run.

Mikai runs down the road and, on the treeless side of a mountain, catches Lucia and me. He points to a break in the clouds and a patch of sunlight on the valley floor.

"I want to get down there where it is safer."

"Mikai, let's stop talking about it and do it."

He runs ahead, while Lucia and I walk as fast as we can.

We pass onto a road, and a bicycle bell rings behind us. I turn, raise my arms and yell, "Mike, I knew you'd come down." He rings the bell again and passes us as if we stroll. Once out of the worst of it, Mike slows down. Lucia and I catch him, and we walk into Triacastela. The town is quiet, no wind blows, the sun shines, the streets glisten. It feels surreal.

Mike wants to see what the others want to do before registering at the *albergue*. Lucia finds her hotel, and I take a room there. After showers and laundry, we meet in the hotel's bar. Mikai walks in, plunks half a dozen foods on the table and explains why each one is good. I talk him out of giving me all of them. Lucia looks at me perplexed. Propelled by nervous energy, he shoulders his backpack and heads to the Benedictine monastery in Samos.

"The first time I met Mikai, he looked like he wanted to fight me, and all I did was say hello. Now he gives me things."

We find a restaurant for lunch. Lucia, a wine connoisseur, orders our wine. We drink two delicious bottles. We talk about South Africa, horses, her real estate work, the Camino, South Carolina. Twice, Lucia moves the conversation toward why I walk, and I guide the conversation a different direction, still not sure if I ought or want to tell her. The third time, I say, "You made yourself so vulnerable to me when you told me why you walked. I owe you the same trust."

I take a breath. Lucia looks intently at me.

"I am a priest."

She gasps, leans closer and says, "A priest."

"Yes, a Catholic priest."

I fold my hands in prayer and place them between Bishop Thompson's hands. He asks, "Do you promise respect and obedience to me and my successors?" I smell gin on his breath.

"I do," I answer.

The bishop lays hands on my head. He hands me the book of the gospels. At the end of the rite, he embraces me as a sign of fraternal love. At each ritual sign, I smell gin on his breath.

The Mass for my deaconate ordination started at 10 a.m. After Mass, at the reception in the hall at Nativity Church in Charleston, Father Paul McDuffie comes up to me.

"Now that you are in holy orders, you are invited to join a group of us who are praying that Bishop Thompson be taken to purgatory soon."

"I don't think I can pray for the bishop who just ordained me to die," I say.

"Getting into purgatory is a guarantee that he will reach Heaven. We are praying for him to go to Heaven."

"Yes, I know the theology," I say, and I look at him. "I just promised to respect the bishop. I don't think I can pray for his death."

Father McDuffie walks away.

I think, I have just been ordained into dysfunction.

A year later, I am ordained a priest.

I tell Lucia about the abusive experiences and that I do not want to be a priest. I do not tell her about Anna.

"You're having an existential crisis," she concludes.

"You are more right than you know. The priesthood is a character sacrament. When a man is ordained, God places an indelible mark on his soul. *'Tu es sacerdotes in aeternum secundum ordinem Melchisedech.'* 'You are a priest forever in the line of Melchizedek.'"[12]

"So ..."

"Once a priest, always a priest," I explain.

She asks about confessions. To someone who does not make confessions, the confessional is mysterious.

"Priests do not have a prurient interest in people's sins," I assure her.

"What about penances?"

"I try to be creative," I say. "Sometimes, people confess things that are not sins. Sometimes the biggest problem is people do not forgive themselves. Sometimes, people are so upset that their tears are their penance."

After a couple hours, the waiter acts like he wants us to leave the dining room. So, we move into the bar, order another bottle of wine and talk until dinner.

Mark, Stefan and Kim sit beside us, and we push tables together. Marco from Italy joins us and articulates the proverbial witticism, "No Vino, No Camino" as we drink more wine.

Mike, Santi and Santiago arrive. They tell me that Joseph, exhausted, went straight to bed when he got down, and Analisa ran down. The Tribe is safe. I am relieved.

After dinner and another bottle of wine, Lucia and I say goodnight. I have encountered so many prejudicial misconceptions in South Carolina I am more worried than relieved that I have told someone I am a priest. I asked her to keep it a secret and am confident she will. But I wonder if she will want to walk with me in the sobriety of morning.

---

12 Vulgate, Psalm 109:4, NAB, Psalm 110:4

I do not wake up hungover, a bad sign I dismiss with rationalizations that I paced myself as I drank and that a long day on my feet negated the effects of alcohol.

Lucia and I meet in our hotel's bar and breakfast on bread and coffee. We talk quietly and act subdued, feeling out how to interact in the sobriety of morning.

"How did you sleep?"

"Terribly, and I even took pills the doctor prescribed to help me sleep. How did you sleep?"

"Well enough. Except I think I drank too much wine."

"We did drink too much. That was my fault."

She took the initiative to order the wines, but I kept drinking. "I think it was both of us."

We all head to Sarria, Lucia to her hotel, The Tribe to Santi's parents' apartment. I invite her to join us for dinner. Two routes lead out of Triacastela, one via Samos along a twisty asphalt road, one through hills along dirt paths. We want to go through the countryside.

Waymarkers start us down the road, and we stop. Above us, on the back of a road sign, someone has scrawled, *"El Fin del Camino es el Cielo."* I agree. I think the Way a metaphor for our journey to Heaven and the recording of our names in the Book of Pilgrims symbolic of the recording of our names in the Book of Life.

Rain falls hard. We huddle under her poncho, guides in hand. She sees my handwriting and asks, "Can you read your handwriting?"

"Is that important?"

She pouts with her beautiful lips. I want to kiss them.

We backtrack, find the rural path and go into the hills. Lucia becomes sick to her stomach and bends over. I offer to wait. She insists I go on. I have no idea what is going on: emotional trauma, hangover, a desire to be alone or not to be with me. I remind her of the invitation and trudge uphill.

Remembering that it is Sunday, I turn my focus to Mass and Sarria, seventeen kilometers and eight hundred meters of elevation change away. If I hustle, I can arrive between noon and 1 p.m.

After soaking my clothes and boots, the heavy rain changes into light rain and heavy mists. On dirt roads in wooded hills broken up by pastures and farms, I ascend Alto do Riocabo, then descend into valleys and hills with lush green pastures and streams gushing with rainwater.

With no place to get food in the hills, I eat what Mikai gave me and marvel at the providential need for his unexpected gifts.

With modern, dirty buildings, the town Sarria feels cold and impersonal. I cross a river, enter the old section, built on the face of a hill that rises from the river to a ridge, and ascend a long series of stairs. I arrive a few minutes late for 1 p.m. Mass at El Monasterio de La Magdalena.

At a tapas restaurant, I email Santiago, Joseph, Mike, Santi and Analisa asking for the apartment address. Analisa emails me with the location. I backtrack down the hill of Sarria, turn down several streets, find the apartment and camp out in a bakery.

The Tribe soon appears. They took the Somos route. All asphalt and longer, they hated it. Analisa says that she heard I have a "lady friend." I downplay "it" because I do not know what "it" is.

"I have to meet her. She can't be with you unless she meets my approval."

I am happy to have Analisa in my life, someone protective of me in my relationships with the opposite sex. I feel sure Lucia will meet her approval.

Mike, Santiago, Santi and Analisa find one open grocery store, a hole in the wall with less variety than *mercados* in villages. It has makings for a salad and pasta, but no cheese, no meat, no spices. The store has plenty of wine. We drink three bottles.

The long, narrow apartment runs from the front of the street to the back of the building, with three bedrooms, two bathrooms, a kitchen and a living room. Joseph and I share a room with two single beds. Santiago gets a room to himself. At his insistence, Santi sleeps on the couch. Mike and Analisa share a room with a queen bed.

"Are you sure about the arrangements?" I whisper to Analisa.

"It's okay," she says.

"We can rearrange where we sleep." Mike is drunk, and I feel angst in him. And something inside says something is wrong.

She insists, "It's fine."

The Fey Pilgrim

DAYS 61 – 63

As Analisa and I sort laundry and pack bags, she puts her bag in the hall "to make space" in the narrow apartment. I think that strange but accept her explanation.

I buy pastries at the bakery, and Santi makes coffee. He, Analisa and I eat together. Santiago and Joseph join us. And we are all eating pastries and getting up for coffee and the bathroom. Then Mike comes in.

"Where's Analisa?"

"She's around here somewhere," I say.

"I looked," he says. "She's not here."

"She's probably in the bathroom."

"She's not in the bathroom."

"Oh, she put her bag in the hall to make space. She's probably messing with her kit."

Mike looks in the hallway.

"Her bag's not there."

"What?" I jump up and look outside. Her bag is gone.

A round of "Where's Analisa?" circles the table as we laugh with dumbfounded disbelief.

"She's a very emotional girl, this Analisa," says Joseph.

"The problem begins when we try to understand a woman," I say.

"It takes one man ten lifetimes to understand one woman," Santiago adds.

"We know where she is going," Joseph says. That elicits a spate of laughter.

Mike is quiet. I wonder if my intuition about sleeping arrangements was foresighted. Mike finds notes Analisa wrote to each of us. Analisa signed each note with a heart and her name, except for Mike's which she signed, "Camino Lust, Analisa."

"What is lust?" Mike asks.

"Lust is when one person uses another person to satisfy sexual desire. It's the opposite of love," I explain.

As a teenager, with an emotionally abusive father, I like the attention I get from Leo Snow, a teacher at Freedom High school. He asks me to join the debate team and makes me feel like I can do something well, the opposite of what my father tells me: "I can't." He also likes what I have to say and what I think, which makes me feel valuable, since my father rejects all my thoughts and ideas.

Leo Snow drinks George Dickel whiskey mixed with Coca-Cola. When I visit his house, he gives me alcohol, and I like it. I spend many evenings there. He begins to play wrestle with me, which I do not like. I resist, and he makes the resistance a kind of game. I tolerate the physical attention because of the intellectual affirmations.

On a debate trip, when he and I share a bed, he kisses me while I slept. I confront him about what happened, and he explains it away saying, "Sharing a bed with my wife, things sometimes happen in the middle of the night. It doesn't mean anything."

We planned a debate practice on a Saturday morning at his house, and I spend Friday night there. After we prepare for the mock tournament and drink alcohol, he makes me share a bed with him. I feel uncomfortable and curl up on the side of the bed in a fetal position. I wake up as he is masturbating me. I start hitting his hand and yell, "Stop, Stop," and he stops. I curl back into a fetal position. In the morning, he dismisses what he did with the same excuse he used before.

Mike looks introspective. I remember the word the man by the nut orchard wrote to Mike—"Do not do to others what you do not want done to yourself"—and wonder if something Mike is supposed to learn on the Way has been revealed.

I ask Santi for a *sello.* He draws a Triskelion on our *passportos.* Galatians brought the Triskelion, a three-legged sign in which each leg forms a spiral, to Western Europe between the sixth and third centuries BC, when they migrated from present day Turkey to present day Spain. The province of Galicia, where we are, is named for this ancient people. The Triskelion is interpreted by different cultures according to their beliefs. The spectrum ranges from Christian (Father, Son, Spirit) to pagan (Creation, Preservation, Destruction). Discarding interpretations, the sign flows as if in constant motion and embodies a deep truth about pilgrims in their spiritual and physical journeys. Whoever we are and wherever we are, we journey.

We climb the stairs of Sarria and pass into the countryside. Waysigns change to short concrete obelisks with yellow *conchas,* a yellow arrow underneath and the number of kilometers left to walk.

At a church in the village Barbadelo, a man stamps our passport, then motions to the donation box. I chuckle and donate happily, especially since I got a cool *sello:* Saint James on a leaping horse, cross in his left hand, upraised sword in his right.

Thinking only about Santiago, I miss the one-hundred-kilometer marker but stop in a bar in Morgado, a one building hamlet, half a kilometer after the famous marker. The bar's *sello* has "99.5" along the bottom. Mike walks in, then Stefan. When Stefan photographed the one-hundred-kilometer marker, a German shepherd dog walked up, lifted his leg and pissed on the marker.

We all laugh, and I say, "And who says God doesn't have a sense of humor?"

"*Ya,*" Stefan says.

Walking among many pilgrims we have never seen before, Mike looks around and asks, "Where did all these people come from?" We know most pilgrims a day behind or ahead but see lots of new faces. And a few familiar faces.

I catch up with Patrick and Elisabetta. They loved the food at the Buddhist *albergue* but thought their hosts strange. They made pilgrims sit at one end of the dining room table until they prepared everything, then allowed them to move to where the food was. Other similar, strange requirements made them uneasy. They climbed to O Cebreiro in the storm, walked to Hospital de la Condesa and rode out the storm in an *albergue* with a roaring fireplace. They saw Analisa that morning. Elisabetta says, "She ran past us and looked angry."

Mike and Santiago are somewhere ahead, Santi and Joseph somewhere behind. I walk alone, with too much to think about. The priesthood, Anna, Lucia, Mike, Analisa, God. The closer I get to Santiago, the more lost and confused I am becoming, the more I know God has an answer for me in Santiago.

I come to the Río Miño and stand atop a cliff, where the river has cut a deep valley. Down below, an old bridge leads to the ruins of stone buildings overgrown with grass. I cross a new, high bridge, climb a long, steep set of stairs into the small town Portomarín and find Mike and Santiago in a modern, attractive bar. I drink two beers and eat a plate of *pulpo,* grilled octopus, which tastes wonderful.

Santiago waits for Joseph, who walks in pain. Mike wants to keep walking. Analisa is on his mind. I decide to let Analisa go. If she needs to separate from us, I am not going to stop her. Lucia plans to stop in Portomarín. I am undecided about what to do: stay and find Lucia, stay with Santiago or walk with Mike, with questions about what transpired in the back of my head. Mike waits for me to finish eating, but if we are to go, we must go soon. The sun will set in an hour. We shoulder our backpacks and walk out.

"Lucia is messing with my head."

"Why don't you get a room and fuck her?" Mike says.

"I am looking for love, not sex."

I follow a woman up a set of stairs. Thin, medium height, black hair, in her thirties, not weatherworn, she looks good. The house has three stories.

"This is a big house. Is it yours?"

"No, a friend lets me stay here to keep an eye on the place. And I'm doing some renovations."

Paint on plaster walls is peeled. The finish on hardwood floors is worn. Vinyl floors curl up.

We lay on a four-post bed and talk. I want to kiss. Some prostitutes will kiss. Some will not.

She refuses. "It's an old song, but you're singing it. You're looking for love in all the wrong places."

Well, the Catholic Church is the wrong place too, I think.

The waitress told us rain is predicted the following day. Putting women out of my head, I decide to walk another stint to shorten the next day's walk in the rain.

Within an hour, Mike and I cover five kilometers and climb Monte de Torrós. The sun sets, and where sky and earth meet, a swath of molten gold fades into clouds shaded red, pink and purple.

In the dark, we slow and reach *Albergue de Gonzar* at 6:30 p.m., walking 7.7 kilometers with a two-hundred-meter climb in 1.5 hours. Emboldened with the pace and since the only thing on my mind is Santiago, I want to keep walking. Mike wants to stop. It is a prudent stop. We register and walk down a short hall that opens into a small kitchen, and here sits Analisa.

"You found me. If anyone found me, I knew it would be the two of you." She hugs Mike, then me.

Analisa eats out of her backpack as does everyone else. There is no food in the village Gonzar: no restaurant, no café, no bar, no grocery, no nothing.

After showers, we gather in the kitchen to see what we have to eat. I have almonds, and Mike has a cucumber left over from the night before. He sautés almonds and sliced cucumber together. The combination tastes terrible, but we eat it. Analisa gives us each half a banana. Someone cooks rice that sat in a cardboard box long enough to absorb the taste of the box. I get a couple spoonfuls of cardboard rice.

Analisa asks if I have heard from Lucia.

"No, nothing. That's alright." I shrug and wonder if telling her I am a priest scared her off. I have not heard from Anna either. She has stopped talking to me. That leaves God.

A smartphone alarm sounds, a single note introducing a symphony. Other alarms join the music, then the full orchestra rises in crescendo. A few harsh tones clash with gentle tones, but soft tones predominate and overwhelm the harsh ones. Then the music falls away in a diminuendo of a few sweet alarms, then one, then none.

Pilgrims pack in the dark by flashlights and headlamps, then someone turns on the overhead lights. Pilgrims abed pull sleeping bags over their heads.

Downstairs in the kitchen, Mikey from Israel gives me two hard boiled eggs. He boils half a dozen every morning: two he eats, two he saves for lunch, two he gives away. I am so very thankful but still starve.

When I leave, several pilgrims express surprise that I head out in the dark.

"The sunrise will look more beautiful on the Way than in the *albergue.*"

A ball of molten gold rises in the twilight and flings yellow and orange across the horizon. Cold, with light cloud cover and no rain, I walk in great weather.

I also walk through four villages and find neither a café nor a *mercado*. After ten kilometers and three hours, in the hamlet Airexe, I step into a café desperate for food. Pastries sealed in plastic sit on the counter, but someone works in the kitchen. Twice I ask, *"No tiene otra comida? No tortillas?"* I get no food out of the kitchen and eat two stale pastries and drink bad coffee.

With too little food and too many questions, I feel heavy and drag myself forward. I cannot reconcile God's call to the priest-hood with the abuse I suffered in the Catholic Church, and after the abuse, I do not want to be a priest, but if God wants me to keep serving as a priest, I have to hear his voice again.

Twenty-five years old and at a loss as to what to do with my life, I make my first Catholic retreat at Holy Spirit Monastery in Conyers, Georgia. In the chapel, lancet arches rise high above the floor and frame the sanctuary. Long rows of choir stalls run most of the length of the chapel and face each other. An altar rail separates the monks' seats from everyone else, who sit in the back.

At Communion, I make the long walk to the sanctuary, receive the Host, walk back, sit in my pew and say to God, "Tell me what to do, and I'll do it."

A tiny bubble rises from my stomach. It grows so that the bubble is bigger than me, and I feel its arc rise through me. I look down in wonderment and confusion. When the arc reaches my head, there are three words.

"Be a priest."

The voice is the most amazing I ever heard. Powerful, authoritative, compassionate, gentle, loving, merciful, kind and more all at once and in fullness, so that each virtue is perfect in its completeness but with a totality that does not diminish any virtue, and yet the sum is greater than the parts and beyond all imagination.

The voice was so magnificent that it is hard to remember its tenor, as if it were a dream. Yet it was not a dream, and I can never forget.

With minimal food in my body and too much spiritual weight on my heart, the relatively flat eight-kilometer stroll from Airexe to the small town Palas de Rei takes three hours.

I find a new, stylish Art Deco café, keep a lookout for Mike and Analisa, and wave them down. We take a long rest and leave together. Mike stops at a bar for beer, but I keep walking, impelled by the desire to get to Santiago. As I grind out kilometers in the countryside on hard packed trails under the hot afternoon sun, I fling myself headlong toward Sanitago where I hope, expect, know that I will hear a word from God that will reorder the insanity of my life into something that makes sense. I cannot stop until I walk into exhaustion.

Several hours later, I pass through an industrial park with old, abandoned buildings and new occupied buildings, then though a section with three- and four-story twentieth century buildings and finally into Melide's inner city with twisting, medieval streets. I find the *albergue municipal* on the western side of the old section. I have achieved my goal. I have walked into an exhaustion in which I cannot think.

Because we walk off-season, we all go into a first-floor dormitory that is a quarter full. A double row of bunk beds line one wall, so that we sleep head to toe. I take a bed that puts my head against a wall. I do not want to smell anyone's feet.

I go to a *pulporía* with Stefan, Mark, Kim and Daniel a middle-aged pilgrim from South Korea.[13] On the way, we meet Mike and Analisa, who have found a private *albergue* that costs the same as the *albergue municipal*. After eating a big plate of *pulpo*, I drop by Mike and Analisa's *albergue*. Mike is cooking chicken with potatoes, mushrooms and a cream sauce. Cooking for friends brings him a sense of peace. Mikai is here.

"I saw your lady friend," Mikai says.

"Have you heard from her?" Analisa asks.

"I have not. I'm not sure if she is my lady friend," I answer, then ask Mikai, "What was the Benedictine Monastery in Samos like?"

"I'll tell you, Jeff. It was awful. There was no heat. I was wet. I was cold. I hated it. That's it. I'm leaving the Catholic Church. I'm changing my life. I'm becoming Christian."

"The Catholic Church is Christian," Analisa and I say simultaneously.

"I know. But I'm changing my life. I'm changing everything. I tell you, Jeff. I'm changing my life. I'm changing everything."

13 Every reference to Daniel from this point on refers to Daniel from South Korea, not Daniel from Germany.

Back in my *albergue,* as I lie in bed, I realize that this is the first day in many that I have not cried.

Obnoxious snores reverberate off the walls, but a worse affliction befalls. The Demon Bowel Prophecy comes to fulfillment. Someone's bowels pump the noxious stench of the sewers into the room. The fetid malodor asphyxiates me.

I take my sleeping pad and woobie to the second floor. Motion-sensitive lights flick on. Dormitories are locked. So, I find a sitting area and lie in a corner. Every time I roll over, the lights turn on. I rearrange chairs to block the sensor, sleep a couple hours, then return to the now quiet dormitory, where the intimation of feces hangs in the air. I wake exhausted.

I take a coffee at a bar and buy pastries, then at Mike and Analisa's *albergue*, take more coffee and share pastries with everyone. Mike had a terrible night's sleep also. The hospitaller slept in his room, got up every hour to go to the bathroom and slammed the door to the room each time. He looks as bad as I feel.

Mike, Analisa and I go to the bar where I drank my first cup of coffee. Mark, Stefan, Kim and Daniel sit at table. A passel of locals fills the bar. Determined not to let a bad night of sleep slow me when I am so close to Santiago, I drink more coffee. Mike orders a beer.

Mark, Stefan, Kim and Daniel leave, then Mike, Analisa and me. We intermingle as we cross streams and walk though woods in cool, sunny weather. But, yet again, I surge ahead. Impelled and more than impelled, I am fey and rush to the doom that awaits me in Santiago. Cursed by God when he created me in the womb, cursed again when he recreated me as a priest: there is no escape from my destiny, no escape from the curses that lay upon me, no escape from the quest to reach Santiago, no escape from the word God will speak at the end of my pilgrimage, no escape from God.

I walk into the town Arzúa at a frenetic pace, barely moderated by exhaustion and hunger. I eat an inexpensive American breakfast of bacon and eggs but am hungry enough to eat twice as much food. Mike and Analisa arrive, and we run errands: groceries, cigarettes, prayer at a church, more beer, more coffee.

Sometimes I walk alone, sometimes with Mike, sometimes with Analisa. Sometimes we walk together.

Analisa tells me, "Mike asked why I did not draw a heart on the note I left for him and that he looked hurt."

"I had to explain what lust meant," I say.

"How did you explain it?"

"Lust is when one person uses another person to satisfy sexual desire."

"Mike will certainly understand that."

Mike insists that we stop at a bar in the village Calzada. He looks worn out. I am not sure if it was because he had not slept or because he needs another beer. I am worn out myself, in body and spirit, and over-caffeinated. Analisa looks great.

Mike orders a beer and says, "The Camino is making me an alcoholic."

Analisa asks me, "Are you afraid of the answer that you might get in Santiago?"

"Yes," I say. My voice wavers, and as I look at her, tears well in my eyes.

"What sign are you?"

"Virgo."

"So, you are always starting over." That is one of the truest insights I have ever heard. I have restarted my life over and over again. I am tired of it.

Painfully insightful, she says, "You have not been happy during your Camino, have you?"

"No, I have not."

"Is it because of the decision you have to make?"

"The decision is probably more symptom than cause. It's complicated."

I want to walk twelve more kilometers to the village O Pedrouzo, because that puts us twenty kilometers from Santiago. At that distance, we can reach Santiago the next day in time for the Noon Pilgrims Mass. So, we head there.

The wear and tear on my body and soul frazzle me. It is all I can do to put one foot in front of the other. I walk without energy to move my legs. I walk by rote, by habit. I walk like a man walking to his death. I cannot think. I cannot talk. Analisa talks incessantly about what she is going to do when she gets home. Home is the last thing I want to think about. I have the same unresolved problems, the same unanswered questions, the same irreconcilable conflicts. The insanity that enveloped my life awaits my return. The more Analisa talks about going home, the more I dread going home, the more I know I must have an answer from God in Santiago.

When we arrive in the village Santa Irene, I think that we have reached O Pedrouzo. The realization that we have another hour to walk after I thought we arrived makes this last effort psychologically torturous. My boots hammering my big toes and pain in my back from my childhood golf injury constitutes physical torture. Analisa's back begins to hurt. All three of us are exhausted. Rain begins to fall. The sun sets. The temperature drops. We walk into O Pedrouzo in a cold, dark downpour and misery.

We find a private *albergue* with lots of beds, an arboretum and one other person. We practically have the place to ourselves. I wash my clothes, and the dryers suffer the curse. The Miracle of the Dryer was a one-off. The curse is not lifted.

As I lie in bed, I think about the curse God laid upon me. How can man lift a curse inflicted by God unless the God-man, Jesus Christ, lift it? God has to lift the curse. I have to hear his voice. Nothing else will suffice.

Santiago

DAYS 64 - 66

When I shoulder my rucksack, Mike and Analisa stir and wake. I smile and say, "See you in Santiago."

I step onto streets that glisten in the dark under streetlights and pass out of town and into dark woods. I walk through the woods and a subdivision and under a bridge. The sun rises as I climb Alto de Barreira, then light rain falls as I descend. The rain saddens me. I want God to bless the culmination of my pilgrimage with beauty of the sky and glory of the sun.

I blow through villages and walk on long, straight gravel roads where I see no one ahead or behind. Neither do I see waymarkers. I worry that I have walked off the Way, wonder if I am lost so close to Santiago.

"Who am I?" I ask myself.

"I am a priest," I answer.

I come to the hamlet San Marcos, which confirms that I have held the right course, then to Monte de Gozo, so named because from its heights, pilgrims first looked upon the cathedral's high towers, which elicited cries of joy. I only see trees, which over the centuries have grown tall and blocked the view.

I descend from the height and walk into a city that looks like every modern city: tall buildings and roads crowded with cars.

After a couple kilometers of traffic and noise, I walk through Porta do Camino, the place where pilgrims enter the old city. I follow waymarkers embedded in the streets at regular intervals, until Plaza de Cervantes where the spacing inexplicably widens, and I lose them. *So close, and I'm still wandering in circles.*

After several minutes, I pick up waymakers and continue. A couple blocks later, I walk into Praza da Inmaculada and stop. To my left stands a building that looks like a church. For all the effort I put into reaching the cathedral, I have not once looked at a photograph. I have no idea what La Catedral de Santiago de Compostela looks like. Two narrow, scaffold towers draped in blue plastic rise high on the west side of the building. I surmise that they hide spires. The façade of the north transept looks ecclesial. The beggar at the door confirms that I have reached the end of my pilgrimage as much as anything else. I too beg at the door.

I walk to the doors slowly, not fully aware, not believing I have reached the cathedral.

In my imaginations, I would walk up to the altar and lay my hand on it and break down in tears. In sober moments, I expected the sanctuary to be roped off. I remind myself that anticipating my entrance into Saint-Jean-Pied-de-Port, no possibility I imagined was fulfilled.

At Rankin Memorial Methodist Church, which I attend with Nana, my maternal grandmother, at a time when everyone greets each other during the service, I have a moment to reflect and think, This room is no different than any other room I have ever been in.

A week later, I go to Saint Benedict's Catholic Church. I know the priest here, Father Conrad Kimbrough, through a mutual friend. I almost attended Mass here once. I put my hand on the brass door pull on the church's front door but turned and walked away because, not being Catholic, I was not allowed to receive Communion.

Again at the church entrance, I put my hand on the same brass door pull I touched years earlier, open the door and step inside. Something feels different. The outside felt cold and harsh. But the inside does not feel warm and soft. Instead, I feel something powerful. I have walked in on Mass, the Real Presence of Jesus Christ in the Eucharist, the reality of Communion, for the first time in my life.

I sit down and think, This is where I always was supposed to be.

A well opens inside of me, and I fall into it. As I fall, the well widens and becomes so great that I feel tiny by comparison. I swoon and descend onto a plateau, invisible in the darkness but real. My fall stops. I think the experience cannot become worse. The plateau dematerializes, and I fall deeper into the well that grows into an abyss as I become even tinier. The fall-plateau cycle repeats again and again. Each time I think it cannot get worse, I fall deeper. When Father Kimbrough says, "The Mass is ended. Go in peace," the immensity leaves me.

I walk inside the cathedral. Ropes block off the sanctuary. Organ pipes protrude from walls and over the nave in an obnoxious, vulgar gesture. The altar piece looks grotesquely ornamental. I do not see the great thurible. I am not sure I am in the right place.

I walk around as if in a dream. I look at everything and take nothing in. Confused, lost, I circle the interior again. I sit in a pew in the back. I have no thoughts. I am dumb. I want to weep, but no tears come. Cold, hungry and tired, I feel numb.

God, I want you to speak to me.

A security guard taps me on the shoulder and says, "You must leave." Backpacks are forbidden in the church, he explains. I shake my head, then nod.

I find the pilgrims' office and hear Mike and Analisa's voices. They sound upset. They walked in heavy rain. When Analisa learned that she had to pay two euros to store her bag, she blew up. A thousand kilometers with little money wore on her, and this small charge zapped her last nerve. Mike rebukes her.

"Analisa, you've walked one thousand kilometers and still do not understand the Way?" That profound question resonates with me more than any other wisdom I have heard on the Camino. Pilgrims do not change the Way. The Way changes pilgrims.

At Mass, I sit with Mike and Analisa and watch the priests on the altar. I say to myself, "I am not a priest anymore."

When I receive Communion, I wait to hear the voice of God as I had years before. God is silent.

We go back to the pilgrims' office. The man Analisa lambasted gives us our *compostelas*, and not wanting to make trouble, he does not check our stamps. We receive *compostelas* with our first names written in Latin. My Latin name is Godefridus.

"Maybe the answer to your question is in your Latin name," Analisa says.

Of Teutonic origin, Jeffrey is derived from one of three Old German names that mean district, traveler or peaceful pledge. The common understanding of the meaning is God's peace or divine peace, the very thing I have never known. When I look at my name in German, "Gottfried," I always make the connection between "frie" and "free" and think, "Freed by God" or sometimes jokingly "Free of God." Neither have I experienced in my life.

We find a place to eat, and Analisa runs an errand. Half an hour later, she has not returned. After an hour, we decide that she has ditched us again.

Mike is upset and says that he does not like a woman who "makes a story." I interpret his words to mean that he thinks

Analisa lied about everything. After my experience with Anna who lied again and again, I wonder if I have been duped for the last seven hundred kilometers. That would be a fitting end to my Way, and an answer to many, many questions and, in a way, an answer from God. My sullenness disappears, and I laugh heartily. After more conversation, I gather that Mike meant to say that he does not like women who make scenes, like the one Analisa made when she blew up at the guy at the pilgrim office.

"Lack of money has worn on her nerves," I proffer.

"If Analisa has run off again," Mike says, "I'll never talk to her again. I will burn her letter and make the ashes in the ocean."

Analisa runs up out of breath. She was at the police station. Someone charged purchases in Paris on her credit card. She tells us to meet her at Los Angeles, a bar across from the police station.

Mike and I finish lunch, retrieve our bags, then get passports for the Santiago-Fisterra section at the information center, where we learn that we can get *compostelas* at Muxia and Fisterra.

Next, we go over to the Praza da Inmaculada, where *El Monasterio de San Martiño Pinario*, a monastery now divided into a seminary and a hotel-like *albergue,* has inexpensive, private rooms. As we discuss where to stay, Santiago calls out. He got up at 5 a.m. and walked forty kilometers to reach Santiago. Joseph and Santi will arrive the next day. We take rooms at the monastery.

When I drop my kit on the floor of my room, I break down. I walked sixty-four days. I suffered, prayed, persevered, starved, froze in the cold, roasted under the sun, got drenched in rain and frozen in a blizzard. I walked in pain step after step, avoided sex, struggled to slay the demons that haunt me. I talked to God and begged him to speak to me. He knew I needed to hear his voice again. He was silent, hidden, invisible, indifferent. He did not rescue me. He did not help me. He did not save me. He did not lift the curse. Every sacrifice is unrequited. When Jacob wrestled with God through a dark night, contending with "divine and human beings," Jacob "prevailed."[14] But God "prevailed" over Jeremiah.[15] And God has prevailed over me. Anger rises in my heart like bile boiling up from my gut. I weep bitter tears. My volcanic anger erupts.

God, I am not going to let you destroy me. If you do not want to talk with me, to hell with you.

I wash my face to mask my emotions and drive thoughts about God from my mind.

Mike, Santiago and I walk to the plaza in front of the cathedral where dozens of pilgrims gather. With everyone in a celebratory mood, I decide I am not going to let God ruin this moment. The more we talk, laugh and smile, the easier it is not to think about God.

Stefan and I have our photographs taken together. He is keen to have a photograph with me, the first pilgrim he met. I am happy to have my photograph taken with him.

I think I see Bini, whom I have not spoken with since we walked out of Roncevalles, seven hundred and fifty kilometers back. I lean around someone as she leans around someone. We hug and have our photo taken together. Standing with arms around waists, she leans her head on my shoulder, which surprises me. I lean my head toward her.

She smiles, until I ask if her questions have been answered.

"It's confusing."

"I understand," I say, then add, "It will work itself out," which I say to reassure myself as much as her.

When she leaves, Daniel, who looks twice her age, leads her away by the hand. Bini looks at me with a worried expression. I watch her go. I am out of the rescue business.

14 NAB, Genesis 32:29
15 NAB, Jeremiah 20:7

When the Franciscan Church opens, we walk over *en masse*, but I lead us into the church. About three hundred years old, with a neoclassical façade, a spacious, well-lighted interior, and tall, thick columns, the church exudes drama and power. I get my Franciscan Compostela, then Mike, then everyone else.

Mike and I find Analisa, and we retrieve her bag from the pilgrim office. They take a room at the monastery. I go to my room and crawl in bed. Alone, thoughts about God flood my mind, and I weep.

I breakfast at the hotel in a converted chapel that retains the peaceful spirit of a chapel, then attend Mass in the Cathedral. After Mass, Laurence walks up, and we hug. She wants to see Analisa, and we agree to meet for lunch.

Confessions are scheduled to start at 10 a.m. I step outside, and here stands Pierre. He bussed back from Fisterra that morning. I watch his rucksack while he goes into the cathedral to offer his last prayer of his Camino. We hug goodbye.

"I am now going to walk another Way," he says and is gone. Even though, since Le Puy, we walked together once and saw each only four other times, I feel a loss when he leaves the Way.

I go to the cathedral office, talk to the sacristan and show him my *celebret* and a letter from Bishop Guglielmone, both of which identify me as a priest in good standing. I tell them I need to make a confession and need a priest who speaks English. They think I want to hear confessions.

"No. Yo necesito hacer una confessión. Yo tengo grande pecados."

The wonderful, competent nun, who runs the desk and keeps information moving, mocks my claim that my sins are great with exaggerated gestures and exaggerated words. She telephones the priest, and I wait.

When Father Juan Carlos arrives, I tell him that I am a priest and that I need an hour and a private room. He sees that I am on the verge of tears. He speaks with the nun and the sacristan, who send us up a narrow flight of stairs to a room above the sacristy's high ceiling. This storage room also has a high ceiling and is filled with things no longer used but not yet discarded, like a man-sized cross, an empty manger and tall candle sticks without candles.

I unburden myself of everything. I talk about the years of abusive treatment in the Diocese of Charleston, how I descended into a venal life with many women, how I met Anna, that she is a heroin addict and a prostitute, that I wrecked my life and myself to help her out of that nightmare. I weep and talk nonstop for thirty minutes and only brush the highlights of the hell I endured. I show him photographs of Anna and George.

"I have lost my faith. I do not trust God. I do not want to be a priest."

"God wants to kiss you, to hug you," he says. "Step one, clean heart. Step two, will of God." He pauses between each thought, translating Spanish into English. "Discern without dog, without she."

He thinks a full minute before giving me penance and says, "To forget sins."

He then adds what sounds like a well-practiced but nonetheless sincere sentence: "At the end of confession, when I give you absolution, you will be filled with the Holy Spirit."

When we finish, he hugs me. In Le Puy, the day before I started, I asked a priest to hear my confession. He refused, saying in perfect English that he did not speak English well enough to hear a confession. So, I walked nine hundred miles to find a priest to hear my confession and found the perfect priest. I am sure the confession was hard on him, but he was saintly. He had to be a saint to hear my confession.

I go down to the tomb of Saint James, a crypt under the altar, accessed by narrow stairs. From the anteroom, a central hall and two smaller side halls lead to the tomb. Iron gates block the halls. I am alone, and I pray. Several tourists come down, then more. Then a revolving turnover of tourists chatting and talking on cell phones parade through. A nun sprays the side halls with Febreeze. More tourists come. The peace disturbed, I walk out.

Joseph and Santi walk into Santiago around noon and get *compostelas* and rooms at the monastery. Mike and Analisa move from the monastery to the Last Stamp *albergue*. Lucia and I email each other and plan to meet for lunch after the Saturday noon Mass.

At outdoor tables in Praza de Quintana and in the warm sun, The Tribe lunches with Laurence and two of her friends: Randolphe and Florence, a couple who rode horses on the Camino for their honeymoon. We tell stories and reminisce about friends we met: Mar, Nara, Janey, Patrick and Elisabetta and many others.

We then take The Tribe photo. Santiago, Joseph, Mike, Santi, Analisa and I sit on a concrete bench with the cathedral's north façade in the background. Locals take photographs with our cameras.

Later, Mike, Analisa and I attend the Friday evening pilgrims Mass, which ends with the swinging of the great thurible. Six *tiraboleiros*, dressed in heavy red robes, carry the censor into the sanctuary and attach it to a rope that hangs down from the tower above the sanctuary. Priests scoop incense into the *botafumiero* with a large spoon. One *tiraboleiro* pushes the *botafumiero*. All six pull the rope in a jerky sequence to start the *botafumiero* moving, then pull with a deep rhythm. The *botafumiero* swings from transept to transept and higher and higher. Mike, Analisa and I sit in the north transept by the center aisle. As the *botafumiero* swings above our heads near the ceiling, we bend our heads back to watch it fly above us. It comes down with accelerating velocity, swings past the front of the altar and up to the ceiling in the opposite transept. After a few minutes, the *tiraboleiros* hold their position, and the great thurible swings back and forth until it stops in front of the altar.

After Mass, we say goodbye to Santiago. We try to talk him into walking to Fisterra.

"If I walk to Fisterra, I'll never walk the Camino again. I need to walk it again." He looks west toward Fisterra as he speaks. We hug goodbye, and he catches a bus home.

I join everyone for supper, but sullenness pervades my heart. I leave early, go back to the hotel, crawl in bed and weep.

I breakfast with Joseph. He advises me to carry an umbrella. "Do what the locals do. They carry umbrellas. That should tell you something." He carries an umbrella. We hug goodbye, and he leaves.

I then go to the Last Stamp *albergue* and get the Last Stamp *sello* on the last square of my pilgrim passport. Mike, Analisa and I take coffee, then I run errands. Umbrellas fill stores, and I buy one.

After the noon Mass, I find Lucia at the corner of Praza de Quintana and Plaza de Paterías.

"I wanted to tell you why I was sick the day we parted. It was the two-month anniversary of Jamie's death."

"Are you feeling better now?"

"I am."

"Good," I say. "Analisa wants to meet you."

At the monastery dining room, we lunch with Analisa. Lucia asks about Analisa's Navajo background, and they talk about the practices and beliefs of her people. In their spiritualities, they have a lot in common.

"I had to meet you to make sure you were acceptable for my Jeffrey, and you are." Analisa takes off her necklace and gives it to Lucia. Lucia takes off one of her necklaces and gives it to Analisa. Being the object of their charity and love stuns me.

I planned to eat lunch with Lucia and Analisa, say goodbye, then meet Mike and Santi in Negreira, twenty-one kilometers away. At 2 p.m., I step into the hall to gauge the weather. A large inner courtyard with trees and bushes sits within the monastery walls. Rain pours in a heavy shower.

I go back to the table. Lucia has ordered a bottle of wine.

"You must stay and help us drink it," she says.

I decide I can wait one more hour, leave at 3 p.m. and, at an easy pace, reach Negreira by 8 p.m. At 3 p.m., I check the weather—steady rain—and walk back to the table. Lucia has ordered another bottle of wine.

"You must stay and help us drink it."

We stay another hour, then I insist we leave and stop drinking. We end up at a *tapas* bar, where we eat great *tapas* and drink more fantastic wine, chosen by Lucia.

Analisa has a 6 p.m. train to Madrid. We hug goodbye. I will miss her but know our promises to keep in touch are not Camino smoke like it is with so many others.

Lucia and I shop for gifts for friends at home and, at her insistence, go to another bar and drink more wine, then go back to her hotel.

She changes clothes, and we lay on the bed. We kiss and dry hump. I take off her clothes, kiss her face, breasts, stomach and legs. With her body desensitized by heroin, Anna often treated making love like work, even with me. Lucia is eager, aggressive, hungry, desirous, alive. I take off my clothes and get on top of her. Tired, drunk and out of practice, I soon have an orgasm. I roll on my back. She crawls on top of me and plays with me until I am hard, then rides me until her body heaves in ecstasy.

"I'm satisfied," she says, then rolls off me.

I think about the possibility of her becoming pregnant. If she becomes pregnant, I will lose my priesthood, a thought that surprisingly makes me feel distraught. I do not want to lose my priesthood because of a drunken romp in Santiago. I fall asleep tortured by guilt, fear and worry.

Finis Terrae

DAYS 67 - 70

Lucia sleeps quietly as a steady rain falls. I gather my clothes, which were flung off the bed along with hers. She wakes hungover and asks, "Are you hungover?"

"No, but I've drunk way too much alcohol on the Camino," I say.

"I've only gotten drunk with you," she says, which makes me feel terrible. I have not encouraged her to drink—she propelled our drinking more than me—but I had enough of that with Anna.

"Did you make a confession?" she asks.

"Yes."

"What penance did the priest give you?"

"To forget my sins."

"That's the type of penance you would have given."

I think for a second and say, "That does sound like me."

"Are you going to have to go to confession again, after what we did?"

"Yes," I concede.

She laughs and says, "I don't think we committed a sin. What we did was natural."

"It was natural, but I still think the Catholic Church will call this a sin."

"So, what are you going to say in confession?" she asks.

I want to say, *That I made love to a beautiful woman whom I love.* But I don't say it. Love scares me. It's gotten me in trouble before. And after just going to confession, I don't want to dwell on it. Instead, I say, "Let's talk about something different."

Since she stayed in hotels her whole pilgrimage, I tell her about the demonic snoring in Grañon, the alarm symphony in Gonzar and the "grocery store with no groceries" meal in Sarria.

"Next time, I walk the Camino, I want to do it the right way. You met so many interesting people from different walks of life. All I did was chase my luggage."

"The Camino has been one hell of an adventure. But I'm not sure if I did it the 'right' way. There are lots of ways to walk the Way. I made lots of mistakes. You had the Camino that you needed. That's what's important." I feel too confounded to make the same assertion about my Camino.

We are quiet for a few minutes. "Next time, I might start farther back than Le Puy-en-Velay."

"Farther back?" She sounds surprised.

"Yes. Farther back, like Rome or Jerusalem. And I think I'll take less money."

"Less money?"

"Yes. Less money. I'll try to trust God more, give God more space for providence."

Again, we are quiet.

"I'm going to go," I say. She gasps. "I promised to catch Mike and Santi. I have a long way to walk to catch them." I sit on the bed beside her and look into her beautiful eyes. "I hope that the wound in your heart will heal."

"That will never happen." Her face becomes stern.

"Then, I hope that even with the wound in your heart, that you can be happy and know love."

Her expression softens, and she says, "Thank you." She has a tender face.

I kiss her. It is hard to say goodbye, but I have to walk to the end of the earth. I step out of her hotel into dark, cold rain.

I go to Sunday Mass but do not receive Communion. After sex the night before, I do not want to receive Communion with grave sin on my conscious.

"I don't believe it is only a symbol," I say.

"The Methodist Church teaches that Communion symbolizes Jesus Christ," says Mr. Sossman in the confirmation class at First United Methodist Church in Morganton, North Carolina.

"But I think it is the real thing."

Because of parental expectations, I have no choice but to be confirmed but begin to fall away from the Methodist Church even as I am confirmed.

I gather my kit and walk out of the hotel with my umbrella partially shielding me from the deluge. Because of the thick, black clouds, dawn breaks late. The Way plunges into a river valley, then crawls up to a height, and the rising sun transforms the sky to light grey. I look back on Santiago. The cathedral looks silent and indifferent to the broken hearts who walk in and out on bent backs carrying weights greater than backpacks. I wonder what Lucia is doing and thinking. Part of me regrets leaving, not being with her. I consider walking back into Santiago to find her. I bow my head and turn toward Fisterra.

I walk through hills, valleys and occasional villages. After several hours, the heavy rain stops, but sprinkles fall off and on.

In the town Negreira, I have to decide: stop here, skip Muxia and meet Mike and Santi in Fisterra or keep walking and catch them on the way to Muxia. Vilaserio lays thirteen kilometers ahead and has an *albergue* open year around. A woman at a café where I order food acts none too friendly. I head to Vilaserio.

I stroll through more valleys, over more hills and walk into the village Vilaserio minutes before sunset. So accustomed to the Way, I time my walk perfectly. The *albergue* is closed, and to reach Santa Mariña, I have to walk eight kilometers. Bad sleep the night before, worn down by too much alcohol, too little food, too much weight on my back and on my heart and another night march ahead of me, a shroud of depression cloaks me as dusk blackens into pitch-dark night.

On country roads, I hunt for waymarkers with my headlamp, expecting to find them at regular intervals and especially at intersections where wrong turns are likely but find none. The dearth of signs slows me. My map, inadequate for night navigation, helps only a little. At crossroads and side roads, I look down different paths to judge the direction based on experience, instinct and intuition. I choose correctly each time, but exhausted and in the dark, the ordeal wracks my nerves.

I reach the hamlet Santa Mariña and, with stone exterior walls and a modern wooden interior, the wonderful *Albergue Casa Pepa*. A kind man runs the *albergue*, and his wife cooks good but salty food. Local men drink at the bar.

Too tired to converse in Spanish, I sit apart from two middle-aged Spanish pilgrims, whose large bellies push them away from their table. They initiate a conversation in Spanish, bragging that they are part of an official Camino organization. Not impressed, I only want to eat and sleep.

I skip a shower, crawl in bed, fall right asleep but do not sleep. The snores of these men do not reverberate off the bottom of the inferno as had Rupert's but erupt out of the gluttons' circle of Hell.

Most snorers quieten by early morning. These men snore all night long. I leave early and skip breakfast.

Knowing Mike and Santi and reading the map, I guess that they slept in Olveiroa, fourteen kilometers away. Because they are inclined to late starts, I might catch them before they leave. I feel lost and cling to one thought: find my friends.

The sun rises, and fog rises with it, but the sun burns away the fog, and the day becomes sunny with a few clouds.

After walking through hills and valleys, past farms and through woods, I walk into the village Olveiroa and, outside a café, find Santi. He greets me with "Where's Jeffrey?" We hug and go inside. Mike sits at the bar. I pat him on the back. We smile.

Without detailing my delay, I explain, "I was waylaid by wine and Lucia." It occurs to me that nonnative English speakers might interpret "waylaid" as "laid." I elaborate on "out-of-control drinking."

Mike, Santi and I walk alone and together but never far apart. We come to the fork where the left trail leads to Fisterra and the right to Muxia. Half-tempted to make for Fisterra and end my Way, I turn right with them.

By noon, the sun warms the day, but in the afternoon, clouds blow in and block the sun. The weather turns cool. After we top one of many small hills, we see a grey something. Mike stops and says, "The ocean." I think we see hills. The sight disappears and reappears as the trail undulates, but the farther we walk, the more I realize we have reached the Atlantic Ocean.

We turn west and walk up hills and down ravines. Finally, we descend to the small town Muxia. I have walked eighty-four kilometers in two days in variable weather across highly undulating terrain. I am done for, again.

At a small beach, Mike strips to his skivvies, jumps in the ocean and splashes around. He invites me and Santi to jump in.

"Fisterra is the end of my pilgrimage," Santi says.

"Mine too," I say.

As the sun rises over Muxia, I wonder if the answer that I did not get in Santiago waits at the end of the earth. I leave on a coastal road and walk through forests, pastures, hamlets and into a village. In the courtyard of an *albergue*, I find an umbrella-covered table with a *sello* and stamp my passport. The stamp has two musical notes and says "Lires." I have reached the village that marks the day's midpoint and stand fourteen kilometers from Fisterra.

My boots are still causing toe pain. *If this is not a metaphor: boots that don't fit and pained feet from beginning to end.*

The afternoon turns warm and sunny. I descend one of many hills and hear Mike's voice boom from the top: *"Ultreia!"*

I have not heard that word since France. I certainly have gone "beyond" and "farther" in the realm of the geospatial, but in the realm of the spiritual, I do not know where I am. I return his cheer nevertheless.

"Ultreia!" I yell back.

Mike catches me, and as we walk the last kilometers, I want the walk to end and think it will never end. As we enter the small town Fisterra, we meet a drug dealer. Mike and the dealer arrange to meet later. Finally, we reach the *albergue municipal*. A woman verifies the *sellos* on our *passportos*. A man fills out *compostelas* and enters our names in a book.

"Donde esté?" he asks.

"Estados Unidos."

"Que trabajo haces?"

"That question is up in the air." The idiom confuses him. I do not want to say that I work as a priest.

"Escribiendo," I answer and gesture as if writing with a pen.

"Ah! *Un escritor."* He writes *"escritor"* by my name.

Mike and I cross the square and sit in an outdoor section of a café. Santi and Stefan walk in, and we toast our accomplishment with beer and wine and feast on grilled peppers, *pulpo* and calamari.

Mike waits on the drug dealer to show up, and I keep him company. That my time is highjacked by a drug deal feels more disconcerting than laughable. I lost a year of my life enduring that stupid thing, and now it haunts me to the end of the earth. In this case, at least, I am indifferent and uninvolved. I feel so relieved that I thank God.

When we register at the *albergue municipal,* Lucas from Czechoslovakia stands in front of us. I have not seen Lucas since Puente la Reina, seven hundred and fifty kilometers back, when he played his didgeridoo. He and a cute, young woman cling to each other. Their hands slip down to the back pockets of each other's pants. I think about Anna. In France, I thought I would walk to Santiago and return home to find her with another man. When I decided to walk to Fisterra, I thought I would walk to the end of the earth and return to find her with another man. I wonder if Lucas and this woman are a sign.

On a harbor jetty, I watch the sun rise over the hills on the far side of Cape Finisterre. I stand mesmerized by the minute, infinite, subtle transitions of the land, sea and sky as the sun rises and the wind blows, in which every moment is filled with a beauty greater than itself, as if the glory of God breaks into creation, as if God screams in silence, "I am here." *God, I am also here, broken, wounded, hurt, lost.*

Back at the *albergue*, I change into clean clothes. I have worn the same clothes for five days and want to wear clean clothes on my last day.

Stefan is taking the early bus, and I see him off.

"I thought you might like to know that the first pilgrim you met is a priest."

"You are a priest!?"

"Yes, and I have not had a happy priesthood and am discerning whether or not to stay a priest, but I think you owe it to yourself to test your vocation."

"Maybe it is a sign," he says.

Mike, Santi and I spend the morning at a café with Lucas and his Camino girlfriend while they wait for a later bus.

Standing with Lucas, I ask about his Camino girlfriend.

"When I saw her, I thought, I've got to get to know this woman," he says.

Lucas is walking because he has two women at home he cannot choose between. His Camino girlfriend has a boyfriend at home.

"One of the reasons I am walking is because of a woman at home," I say.

"There's always a woman," he says.

I have seen his Camino girlfriend several times, but because she looks about twenty years old, I never spoke with her. I introduce myself.

"My name is Jeffrey."

"I'm Anna."

With depleted emotional reserves, I have not one ounce of emotional energy left in my body. I simply nod and say, "Of course, you are."

Lucas asks everyone, "Is the Camino real life or is life at home the real life?" and launches a discussion. I stay out of it.

The answer is not "either-or" but "both-and." The difference is intensity. Pilgrims say, "A day on the Camino is like a week in real life." The concentration of experiences and revelations might be more like a month to a day, even a year to a day. The intensity overwhelmed me again and again, but Santiago and now Fisterra have saturated me. I can hardly take the emotional upheaval anymore. To me, the Camino has compressed a lifetime into days.

Lucas and Anna leave on the bus. Mike, Santi and I search for an *albergue*.

As we search, Mike says, "My goal is to get laid in Fisterre."

"That's my goal too," Santi says.

"It's not my goal," I say.

"Why not?" Mike asks.

I shrug and say, "The answer to that question is a long story. You would have to walk a long way to hear all of it."

I offer no input on the choice of *albergue*. They choose an *albergue* named Peace, an *albergue* with my name, the one thing I desperately want and have never found. Maybe it is a sign. Maybe I will find peace at the end of the earth.

I go to the beach north of town. The sun radiates brilliance in an azure sky. God blesses the true end of my pilgrimage with unseasonably perfect weather.

I lay out my blanket, take off my clothes, run into the water naked and play in the ocean like a child. Waves crash over me, and I sink under the water. I taste salt and gritty sand churned up by turbulence. Waves push me toward shore. Undercurrents pull me into deeper water. I float on the surface as the ocean lifts me on crests and drops me into troughs. I splash about and ride the waves into shore.

I dress and sit on my towel. Sunlight sparkles like diamonds on the water. The face of the sun shines on my face. The breath of the wind brushes my body. The ocean heaves. Waves crash. Shore birds dance on the airs. I listen to the ancient, eternal, mystical voice of the ocean and wonder why God did not speak to me.

With his silence, God left me to sort it out on my own. Maybe that is the message. Maybe God is not in the rescue business. Jesus redeemed us on the Cross, but our salvation is worked out in our lives, when his transformative grace remakes us. Maybe God is in the "I will give you the grace to rescue yourself" business. After all, Jesus rose from the dead under his own power. Despite all my efforts, I did not rescue Anna. In my life as a priest, despite all my efforts to effect change in the culture of cruelty of Diocese of Charleston, I never rescued myself.

I spent my entire life searching for something outside of me just as I spent my Camino looking for signs outside of me. Signs abounded, but none were sufficient.

I decide, *I am the sign.* I do not need anyone, not Anna, not the abusive Catholic Church, to justify me, and God must honor whatever decision I make. After all, God created me to be free.

This is my seventieth day on the Way. In ancient Hebrew, to make a covenant is literally "to seven oneself." When God and Abraham made the bilateral covenant, they agreed to a relationship with blessings for fidelity and a curse for infidelity. God promised Abraham the blessing of homeland and progeny. Animals were split in two, God cast Abraham into a sleep, and the flame of God passed between the animals: infidelity would bring upon the unfaithful the judgement inflicted on the animals. God and Israel remade the Covenant time and again. The definitive re-making was when God became man, and when Jesus Christ, who without sin, took the curse upon himself when he was crucified and transformed the curse into the blessing of the resurrection.

From the day I joined the Diocese of Charleston as a seminar-ian, I experienced the curse, not the blessing. The cross, never the resurrection. Death, not life. Hate, never love. The culture of cruelty in the Catholic Church imperiled my salvation.

God, I am free to remake the covenant. For the sake of my salva-tion, here is my part of a renewed bilateral covenant: I will not dwell in an abusive Church. What are you going to do for your part?

The sun falls down the sky, and I head to Faro de Finisterre, the lighthouse at the end of the earth.

As I pass through town, I buy a bottle of red wine, but the store does not have a corkscrew. The multitool with a corkscrew that I picked up and then dropped off had a purpose and, out of all places, at the end of the earth. *God, I have to trust that you will open the bottle of wine.*

After several kilometers, I reach the Faro and see the Waymarker of Waymarkers: "0.0 Kilometers." According to guidebooks, I walked about 1,650 kilometers or 1,000 miles. Counting the Matavenero jaunt, the times I got lost, countless undulations and wanderings around cities, I probably walked closer to 1,750 kilo-meters or about 1,100 miles.

The lighthouse sits on a promontory formed by volcanic rock with natural benches and steep drops. I sit with a view of the sun-set. Above and below, to my right and my left, twenty pilgrims sit scattered about. The ocean heaves and crashes against rock far below. Above the horizon in a sky with few clouds hangs the sun.

I crumble Analisa's sage into my *concha* and light it. The leaves glow, then smolder. The gentle ocean breeze keeps the sage smoking. I face the wind, and the smoke wafts around my face. As the sage burns, I pray for the people who hurt me. Like a thousand dead spirits freed from their graves, anger spirals up and out of me like the smoke rising from the incense and carried away by the wind. I close my eyes and let the smoke blow over my face until it burns out.

The time to celebrate has come. I stand up, bottle in hand, and ask, "Does anyone have a corkscrew?" Borja from Spain has one. So, God opens the bottle of red wine. I share the wine with everyone who wants some.

Celia from France walks by singing:

> *Oh pilgrims, let's go down,*
> *Let's go down, come on down,*
> *Oh pilgrims, let's go down,*
> *Down to the Faro to pray.*

I sing with her, then we photograph each other.

I stand on a rock ledge with my feet lost in darkness. Behind me and to my right, the golden sun brushes the horizon. Its upper half hidden by a thin cloud, the sun's rays pierce the top of the cloud and, passing above, reach into eternity. On the horizon, orange, red and purple light bend across earth's arc. The sunlight paints the sky in shades of blue and illuminates the ocean with motes of dancing lights. Silhouetted against the glory, a dark shadow against the light of the setting sun, I hold my arms above my head in victory.

When Celia sees my photo, she recounts lore a Spanish woman shared with her: "At the end of our pilgrimages, we leave our shadow selves at the Faro and start a new life."

Celia goes down below and kneels.

A few minutes later, I hear, "Jeffrey!"

Mike stands atop a rock. He has a big smile, holds his staff in his left hand and makes a peace sign with his right hand. He sits beside me, and as the gloaming darkens, I point to the horizon on a west-southwest azimuth. "My home is right there. The only thing that separates me from home is the ocean. I can't walk home from here."

And the sun sets on my Way.

Afterword

I am not a fan of the photo on the front cover. When I took the photo, I did not know that a photo from that spot would form the front cover of a book. Had I known that, I would have taken dozens of photographs until I got that perfect photo. Nevertheless, I decided to use the photo I took there because that decision is consistent with the code I followed as I walked: to accept what the Camino gave me. The photo of me on the back cover, along with spectacular weather, was as unexpected and unplanned as a photo can be, yet it is a great photo. So, the Camino gave me an average front cover photo and a fantastic back cover photo. But I like the bookends, and I like my code, and in a book filled with prophetic revelations of all kinds, even these circumstances are thematically consistent with the progression of events in the story of my walk. I have published the way I walked.

Also of note, the writing and the publication of this book form a giant step forward in my journey toward healing, not the last step, but perhaps the most important step on a journey much longer than the Way.

About the Author

Jeffrey Kendall thinks vintage Peugeot bicycles are first among equals, the equals being Bianchi, Colnago, Panasonic, Raleigh, Schwinn and Zeus.

The flight of arrows enraptures his imagination.

He loves to hike, sees the handiwork of God in the beauty of creation and is an amateur naturalist.

He loves art and has created his own signature style of mandalas.

History is his favorite form of literature to read, but his favorite book is The Silmarillion.

He is steadfast in his denial about his coffee and chocolate addictions.

He enjoys many different forms of exercise and sports, but the older he gets, the more he dreams about becoming a Tai Chi master.

He is dyslexic, which makes the arduous task of writing twice as arduous, but he loves to write.

At least half a dozen unwritten books are jumbled in his head.

He would love to master a foreign language.

He has ambitions of completing a PhD.

He believes the most important prayer he offers is the petition for wisdom.

More about the author, including possible future books and photos of his Camino and of his art, can be found at:

JEFFREYALEXANDERKENDALL.COM